KINGS OF THE HELLENES

The Greek Kings 1863–1974

Also by John Van der Kiste

all published by Alan Sutton Publishing unless stated otherwise

Frederick III, German Emperor 1888 (1981)

Queen Victoria's family: a select bibliography (Clover, 1982)

Dearest Affie: Alfred, Duke of Edinburgh, Queen Victoria's second son, 1844–1900 [with Bee Jordaan] (1984)

Queen Victoria's children (1986; large print edition, ISIS, 1987)

Windsor and Habsburg: the British and Austrian reigning houses 1848–1922 (1987)

Edward VII's children (1989)

Princess Victoria Melita, Grand Duchess Cyril of Russia, 1876–1936 (1991)

George V's children (1991)

George III's children (1992)

Crowns in a changing world: the British and European monarchies 1901–36 (1993)

KINGS OF THE HELLENES

HELLENES

The Greek Kings
1863–1974

John Van der Kiste

ALAN SUTTON PUBLISHING

First published in the United Kingdom in 1994
Alan Sutton Publishing Ltd · Phoenix Mill · Far Thrupp · Stroud
Gloucestershire

First published in the United States of America in 1994
Alan Sutton Publishing Inc. · 83 Washington Street · Dover · NH 03820

British Library Cataloguing-in-Publication Data

A catalogue record for this book is available from the British Library.

ISBN 0-7509-0525-5

Library of Congress Cataloging-in-Publication Data applied for.

Jacket illustration: left, Constantine I by de Laszlo; right, George I by an unknown
artist. Both reproduced by kind permission of HM King Constantine of the
Hellenes (photograph: Tim Hawkins)

Typeset in 10/13 pt New Baskerville
Typesetting and origination by
Alan Sutton Publishing Limited.
Printed and bound in Great Britain by
Butler & Tanner Ltd, Frome and London

Contents

Illustrations

Thanks are due to the following for kind permission to reproduce photographs: Commemorative Collectors' Society, 25 Farndale Close, Long Eaton, Nottingham (4,6,7,16); Theo Aronson Collection (2, 5); Hulton Deutsch Collection (27,28). The others are from private collections.

Foreword

The Kings of the Hellenes – in other words, the six monarchs who reigned in Greece between 1863 and the declaration of a republic just over a century later, who were officially recognized Kings of all the Hellenic nation, whether living in Greece or not – have so far been the subject of curiously little attention from British biographers. In some ways this is hardly surprising. The monarchy in Greece was abolished, for the second time this century, as recently as 1974, and it is still much too early for a definitive assessment.

On the other hand, by any standards the story of the six Kings in modern Greece, and the rapidly changing fortunes of their family, is a remarkable one. The Prince from Denmark who was chosen to wear the crown in 1863, and the Russian Grand Duchess whom he married four years later, went on to found a dynasty whose princes and princesses would marry into several other European royal houses. None did so more notably than the Prince who was born at the nadir of his parents' and his family's fortunes, and at the time of his birth was regarded as having few prospects. That he married the heir apparent to the throne of the United Kingdom, and thus became the consort of Her Majesty Queen Elizabeth II of Great Britain, was in retrospect some consolation for his parents' troubles.

Some of the Greek royal family have written and published their own, inevitably (and justifiably) somewhat partisan, memoirs. Among them were three of King George I's sons. We can readily share the dismay they evidently felt when he told them that he had destroyed the diary which he kept faithfully for many years.*

Two books entitled *The royal house of Greece* have since appeared, some forty years apart. The first, by Air Vice-Marshal Arthur S. Gould Lee, was written with the benefit of close acquaintance of, and assistance from, several of his illustrious subjects. As he readily admitted, under the circumstances 'subjective analysis of character was neither possible nor desirable'. More recently, Alan Palmer's account, with a foreword by HRH Prince Michael of

* See p. 53.

vii

Greece, has provided us with a well-illustrated and valuable, albeit brief, history of the family almost to the present day. E.E.P. Tisdall's *Royal destiny: the royal Hellenic cousins*, has some value, though like so many of the author's books it reads more like a novel with dates than a biography.

King George I was the subject of a biography by Walter Christmas, published one year after his assassination. The few monographs in existence on King Constantine I, shamefully vilified during the First World War, were generally written with an axe to grind. Such titles as *Constantine: King and traitor*, by Demetra Vaka, published in 1918, are at least honest as regards their point of view, if nothing else. *No Ordinary Crown*, by Stelio Hourmouzios, a biography of King Paul, the last of his three sons to reign, was published in 1972.

Throughout, I have kept the emphasis firmly on biography and family relationships, rather than a history of Greece, although naturally it is never possible to separate the two entirely. Readers will appreciate that it is too early to attempt an objective or analytical study of the last years of the Greek monarchy. For now, a basic if perhaps somewhat bland statement of events must suffice; and I make no apologies for condensing the last two reigns into a single chapter. To coin a phrase, history requires distance. The myth of King Constantine I's pro-German leanings during the First World War has long since been exploded, but it may be many years before the full facts of the 'Colonels' coup' of 1967 and the subsequent events which culminated in the abolition of the Greek monarchy are known.

I wish to acknowledge the gracious permission of Her Majesty The Queen to publish certain material of which she owns the copyright. In the extracts from King George I's correspondence, published here for the first time, I have taken the liberty of correcting his invariably shaky spelling.

I am also greatly indebted to Theo Aronson; Paul Minet, of Royalty Digest; Robin Piguet; Steven Jackson, of the Commemorative Collectors Society; and Charlotte Zeepvat, for their advice, assistance and loan of certain materials; and the staff of Kensington and Chelsea Public Libraries, for the run of their magnificent biography collection. As ever, particular thanks are due to my parents, Wing Commander Guy and Nancy Van der Kiste, for their encouragement and many hours spent in reading through the draft manuscript; and to my editors, Jaqueline Mitchell and Rosemary Prudden, for their work in seeing the book into print.

John Van der Kiste

Prologue

OTHO, KING OF GREECE

Modern Greece came into being in 1829, at the end of a long, bitter struggle for independence and freedom from Turkish occupation. Her independence was recognized at the London Protocol of 1830 by the Great Powers, namely France, Great Britain and Russia. It was on their understanding that a 'hereditary Sovereign Prince of Greece' should be chosen from outside their own ruling houses. In post-Napoleonic Europe, the monarchical system of government, be it absolute or constitutional, was generally accepted. The Greeks' innate sense of equality, and rivalry among the leading families, made the idea of one of themselves becoming head of state quite inconceivable. No self-respecting Greek would accept another fellow-countryman as his or her sovereign.

In the meantime Count Ioannis Capodistrias, who had been elected President by the Greek National Assembly in 1827, would remain in office until a sovereign prince could be found to assume the throne. The Assembly's first choice was Prince Leopold of Saxe-Coburg, uncle of the future Queen Victoria, who declined the offer. His prudence was rewarded, for a year later he accepted the crown of another new and rather more stable European kingdom, that of the Belgians.

The assassination of Capodistrias in 1831 made the quest more urgent, and the following year seventeen-year-old Otto, son of King Ludwig I of Bavaria, was chosen. He arrived in Greece on board a British frigate in January 1833, accompanied by a Council of Regency consisting of three of his own countrymen and 3,500 Bavarian troops. He inaugurated his reign by taking the Hellenic version of his name, Otho, and adopting Greek national dress.

In 1832 the population of Greece was less than 800,000, and covered less than half of present-day Greece. About three million Greeks lived in what remained Turkish territory, and another 200,000 in the British-controlled Ionian Islands. The expansion of Greece to include all these territories, in effect reconstructing the Byzantine Empire with a capital at

Constantinople, became known as the *Megali Idea* (Great Idea), and the supreme goal of the nation.

The prince who was prepared to assume the throne of this emergent nation would need extraordinary skill and good fortune to maintain his throne. King Otho had neither. The country had no constitution and the King, assisted by a circle of Bavarian advisers, had unlimited power. When he came of age, he insisted on presiding at all Cabinet meetings in person, so that criticism, which would normally have been directed at his ministers, was levelled at him instead.

Neither the people nor individual Greek leaders had any real influence at government level, and the country also had serious economic problems. The population of Greece fell in the early years of independence, mainly through migration to Turkey, and very little new industry was established. In 1843 a peaceful revolution expelled the Bavarian advisers from Greece and forced Otho to accept a constitution that established Greece as a constitutional monarchy in 1844.

When war broke out between Turkey and Russia in 1853, King Otho supported Greek demands to side against Turkey in order to help free the Greeks under Turkish rule. However, Britain and France, who had pledged to support Turkey against Russia, compelled the King to renounce his alliance with Russia.

According to visitors' reports, King Otho and Queen Amalia combined a considerable love of Greece itself with a tactless inability to please its people.[1] His lack of leadership qualities, a disastrous inability to accept candid criticism of his faults, and a fatal belief in monarchical infallibility, that administration of Greece depended on the manipulation of elderly, inept politicians, ultimately proved his undoing.

He might have saved himself had he and Queen Amalia, born a Protestant Princess of Oldenburg, whom he married in 1857, had children. So long as they remained childless, the succession was in doubt, and none of the King's brothers was prepared to accept the constitutional condition that the successor to the throne must be a member of an Orthodox Church. Though the question of the succession was much debated in Athens, the King and Queen chose to ignore its significance.

Anxious at rumours of his growing unpopularity, the British government sent an envoy, Sir Henry Elliot, to Greece in April 1862 to warn King Otho of the increasing discontent among his people. An experienced diplomat, Elliot had already served as British Ambassador in

Naples, and was subsequently to make his mark in Turkey. He arrived in Athens in May and stayed until the end of June. En route he had discovered, to his surprise, a widespread belief in Corfu that 'a British prince' was likely to succeed to the throne before long. The people of the Ionian Islands assumed that King Otho's hold on the throne was so insecure that to replace him with Queen Victoria's second son, seventeen-year-old Prince Alfred, was quite practicable. This would have the further probable effect of reuniting the Ionian Islands, a British protectorate since 1815, with Greece. Arriving in Athens, Elliot concluded that there was a considerable feeling in favour of Prince Alfred, but the overwhelming preoccupation of the Greeks was to depose King Otho.

The Bavarian government looked to the Great Powers to maintain the King, come what may, but the other ambassadors felt that only the lack of an alternative kept King Otho on the throne at all.

Elliot had three separate audiences with King Otho. In his letters he complained that he had to shout because the King (still only in his late forties) was so deaf, and this reduced his meetings to the status of a harangue. He found the King appeared to pay little heed to the British government's warnings.

Four months later King Otho was deposed, with scarcely a voice raised in his favour. Having been assured by obsequious ministers that he faced no revolutionary threat in Athens, he had gone visiting the more remote islands of his kingdom. He tried to return to his capital, but was debarred from landing at the Piraeus. The Great Powers refused to intervene, and he had no choice but to leave Greece, which he did, as he had arrived, on a British warship.

According to Elliot, the King had 'done absolutely nothing for the development of his country or to improve its position'.[2] He had brought about his own downfall by gravely underrating the forces at work in his adopted country, in particular the emergence of a new generation of leaders, the revival of British ascendancy in Greek affairs, and the discontent caused by a monarchy which professed an alien religion and held no prospect of an heir.

The Bavarian government hoped that King Otho's reinstatement would be the Powers' overriding aim, but they were more concerned with choosing his successor. Otho had nominated his younger brother Leopold, but the revolutionary leaders and provisional government of Greece rejected him, while making clear their intentions of 'adhering to the monarchical form of rule'. The Powers were asked to nominate another king. Under the terms of the 1830 Protocol, members of the ruling powers' families were ineligible, though this did not prevent the Greeks from continuing to clamour for Prince Alfred.

On 18 November *The Times'* Trieste correspondent noted that 'the choice of Prince Alfred for the Greek throne is regarded as certain'. Though Prince Alfred was virtually unknown in Greece, the advantages of choosing a son of Queen Victoria were inestimable. Much capital and prestige, it was assumed, would follow him into his new kingdom. The Prime Minister, Lord Palmerston, recognized that the Greeks were 'panting for increase of territory'. Great Britain, they assumed, would make King Alfred a coronation gift of the Ionian Islands, and perhaps persuade the Turks to relinquish the coveted territories of Epirus and Thessaly to Greece.

Portraits of the Prince were carried through the streets of Athens, accompanied by cheers from those who expected him to arrive among them as their sovereign almost immediately. Peaceful demonstrations outside the British Legation in Athens repeatedly called his name, and the crowds would not leave until the Ambassador came out to address them personally. In Liverpool a meeting of the Greek community unanimously supported a motion nominating him as the next King of Greece.

Queen Victoria was adamant that Prince Alfred should not accept the throne. He was personally committed to a career in the Royal Navy, and in addition was being groomed as successor to his childless uncle Ernest, Duke of Saxe-Coburg Gotha. The British government also pointed out that no member of the reigning house of any of the protecting Powers could become King. The Duke of Leuchtenburg, a nephew of Tsar Alexander II, Russia's preferred candidate, was similarly debarred. Among the next alternatives suggested were Ferdinand, titular King of Portugal, Prince Waldemar of Holstein, and Archduke Maximilian of Austria, brother of Emperor Francis Joseph and shortly to become the ill-fated Emperor of Mexico. Also nominated was Ernest, Duke of Saxe-Coburg Gotha.

To Queen Victoria's anger, the Duke declared that he would be pleased to accept the crown if nominated, and go to Athens, while retaining his ducal title and its attendant privileges; Prince Alfred, he said, could go to Coburg forthwith and act as his Regent. In January 1863 *The Times* published a letter, signed by one M.E. Mavrogordato, writing on behalf of the Greek mercantile community in England. He hoped that Duke

Ernest would accept the crown as it would bring the advantages of British friendship to Greece, as well as a close alliance with the royal family. Moreover the Duke, he continued with more flattery than accuracy, was cherished by England as the champion of constitutional liberty in Europe, and chief of that powerful dynastic connection which stood at the head of continental free governments; 'in fine, we discern in Duke Ernest the same noble character for which England honours the memory of his lamented brother, the Prince Consort, and we discover in him the personal qualities . . . which, in our opinion, the King of Greece ought to possess.'[3]

Elliot arrived back in Athens to supervise matters, still emphasizing that Prince Alfred was ineligible for the vacant crown. Even a near-unanimous vote by the Chamber of Deputies in Athens, and continued pro-Alfred demonstrations outside his windows, continued to make their choice clear. Some of the possible contenders, few of whom showed any great enthusiasm for following in ex-King Otho's footsteps, were ruled out in Athens for various reasons. King Ferdinand, a Roman Catholic childless widower, was not taken seriously. When Elliot asked whether it was not rather humiliating to suggest that Greece could not support her own King, the Greek Minister for Foreign Affairs replied that they would naturally vote him an allowance, 'but we think it would be well that he should decline to receive it!'

When Britain was thought to favour the Duke of Saxe-Coburg, it was suggested that the British government should award him an allowance of £80,000 per annum, this being half of what Britain would save by ceding the Ionian Islands to Greece. The French ambassador favoured the choice of the Duc d'Aumale, one of the sons of the late King Louis-Philippe, until Emperor Napoleon heard about it and vetoed any preference for a prince from the house of Orleans.

Despite Elliot's objections, the Chamber of Deputies insisted on holding a plebiscite to nominate their next King. Out of 241,202 votes cast, 230,016 (over 95 per cent) were for Prince Alfred. The second choice – though far behind – was the Duke of Leuchtenberg, who received 2,400 votes. Ninety-three electors declared for a republic and precisely one for ex-King Otho.

Much to the delight of the French Ambassador, and of Queen Victoria, the Duke of Saxe-Coburg formally refused the throne in February. His decision was followed by demands for a member of the English aristocracy to the throne – almost any would do, as long as he was wealthy. At the beginning of March, a member of the Assembly proposed the election of 'a private Englishman, even if he should not belong to one of the "Princely Families"'. This was thought to refer to Gladstone, who had supported Greece over the Ionian Islands, or the Earl of Derby, Leader of the Conservative Opposition at Westminster.

However, by this time a new, younger, and altogether more eligible candidate was being considered – seventeen-year-old Prince William of Denmark. This representative of the modest Glucksburg family was as yet little known throughout Europe, but he was extremely well-connected by marriage. His eldest sister, Princess Alexandra, had just married Albert Edward, Prince of Wales.

PRINCE WILLIAM OF DENMARK

Prince Christian William Ferdinand Adolphus George was born on 24 December 1845, the second son and third child of Prince and Princess Christian. The family lived at the Yellow Palace, Copenhagen, a less palatial residence than its name would suggest. Although adjacent to Amalienborg Palace, the King of Denmark's official residence, it was a pleasant, unpretentious house in a side street. Homely it may have been, but hardly private; the front door opened directly onto the pavement, and passers-by could glance in at the ground floor windows.

There were six children of the marriage. Prince Frederick, born in 1843, was destined to succeed his father on the throne of Denmark. Princess Alexandra, born in 1844, would become Princess of Wales and Queen Consort of King Edward VII. Prince William was followed by Princess Dagmar, or 'Minny', the future Tsarina of Russia, born in 1847. After a six-year gap came Princess Thyra, born in 1853, and to complete the family in 1858, Prince Waldemar.

Little is known of the childhood of this closely-knit but, by royal standards, impecunious family. Photography was still in its early stages, and Prince and Princess Christian could scarcely afford portraits or miniatures of their growing brood. Princess Christian's artistic skills were limited to portraying her children from behind. Moreover no lesson books, letters, diaries of parents, children or governesses have survived to help future generations reconstruct daily life in the nurseries of the Yellow Palace or summers spent at Bernstorff, an eighteenth-century hunting lodge a few miles from Copenhagen, which King Frederick VII had put at the disposal of Prince Christian and his family.

The twice-married, twice-divorced King Frederick VII now lived with a mistress, whom he created Countess Danner and married morganatically, but he had failed to provide his country with an heir. Next in succession was Princess Christian's brother, Prince Frederick of Hesse-Cassel, but he was debarred from the succession, largely on account of his German sympathies which had led him to take the side of Holstein during the inconclusive war of 1848 between Denmark and the duchy of Holstein. The duchies of Schleswig and Holstein were technically Danish territory, although the dispute was destined to be a perpetual bone of contention throughout the nineteenth century. Princess Christian was officially the next in line to the Danish throne, but she was debarred because the Salic Law ran in the Duchies, though not in Denmark itself. On 8 May 1852 the London Protocol, a settlement guaranteed by Russia, France, England, Prussia, Austria and Sweden, affirmed the indivisibility of Danish territory and designated Prince Christian as heir to the Danish throne.

This honour brought no corresponding increase of income to the family. Even education was a luxury that Prince and Princess Christian could hardly afford for their children. The Prince supervised their physical education, while the Princess taught her daughters music, dancing and riding.

The children had English nurses, and English was their second language. The princesses became fairly fluent in French and German, and received careful religious instruction. Otherwise, their educational attainments, and those of their brothers, were meagre. However, neither of the parents was particularly scholarly-minded. The children had a happy childhood and were well known for their rough-and-tumble behaviour, as well as a fondness for practical jokes.

Prince William was a handsome, tall, cheerful, unaffected youngster, with his full share of the family high spirits. At an early age he joined the Danish Naval Academy. He was among the party who travelled from Copenhagen to England with his elder sister in March 1863 for her wedding. As they landed at Margate, the Lord Mayor ceremoniously presented her with an address of welcome on a scroll of parchment. She accepted it with due solemnity, but moments later she was seen hitting her brother on the head with it as he ran away, trying to dodge the blows, both helpless with laughter.

By March 1863 the number of potential candidates for the vacant throne of Greece was narrowing. Princes and Royal Grand Dukes from the Protecting Powers were ineligible; princes from the house of Orleans were ruled as ineligible at the behest of the Emperor of the French; and the Greeks were not permitted to indulge their preference for wealthy British noblemen. Prince William of Denmark was one of the few not thus debarred, and an offer was accordingly made to him through King Frederick VII as head of his family.

Three stories, all doubtless highly fanciful, have been told as to how he was chosen. The first was that the young Prince had 'taken the fancy' of a Parisian hostess, Esther Guimon. She recommended him to the Duc de Persigny, who accordingly passed the recommendation on to Emperor Napoleon.

Another was related many years later by Princess Alexandra to Randall Davidson, afterwards Archbishop of Canterbury. One night in March 1863 Prince William, who had stayed on in London after his sister's marriage, was asked by Lord Palmerston, Prime Minister, and Lord John Russell, Foreign Secretary, if he would like to be King of Greece. Realizing that to accept such a position would surely mean an end to any naval examinations, the Prince replied laughingly that he would like nothing better. Having thus 'accepted', the Foreign Office consulted privately with the King of Denmark, and before anything official was said to him or his parents, he was formally nominated King and his consent made known throughout Europe.[4]

Doubtless with tongue firmly in cheek, he later told one of his sons that one morning when he was a naval cadet, he left the Yellow Palace as usual with a packet of sandwiches for his lunch. One of them contained sardines, and was wrapped in an extra piece of newspaper to prevent the oil from leaking out. 'I glanced at the paper and read to my delighted amazement that I was King of the Hellenes. No one had told me a word about it. I had just been hoping, though, that something exciting would happen.'[5]

If Prince William was excited, his parents were extremely reluctant. Before his son could be considered, Prince Christian stipulated that King Otho must first issue a formal abdication of the Greek throne, and the house of Bavaria must renounce all rights and claims. Until the King had voluntarily or formally abdicated, he was the only legitimate King. Moreover, the Great Powers should offer Prince William some financial guarantees.

On Augustus Paget, British minister in Copenhagen, devolved the task of persuading Prince Christian to give his consent. He assured the concerned father that King Otho had forfeited his throne by his own misdeeds, and was merely suffering the just deserts of his conduct over thirty years. The Greeks were greatly to be admired for desiring to find a better king for their country, and driving out the unsatisfactory one without bloodshed. Moreover, the financial benefits for the incoming sovereign were obvious. As King of Greece, Prince William would enjoy an income a thousand times larger than he could ever hope to have as a young naval officer in Denmark.

To this, Prince Christian protested that at least he would be living quietly among his own family and not exposed to the vicissitudes and dangers he would have to encounter in Greece. He himself had a very low opinion of the country and its inhabitants, and his cousins by marriage, the Landgrave and Landgravine of Hesse, were particularly hostile to Prince William's candidature. Moreover, in thirty years, King Otho had lost everything, including his own private fortune. 'But why did he calmly look on at the scandalous waste of public money?' was Paget's retort.

At their next meeting Paget remarked that he hoped Prince Christian had changed his mind. On being told that he had not, Paget suggested that Prince William was 'of an age to have an opinion for himself regarding his future life. He is very quick and intelligent and from what I have always heard of him I believe him to possess many great qualities. How will you be able to endure the just reproaches which Prince William will have the right to address to you if you deprive him of the brilliant career which has opened to him?'[6] The Greeks would surely find themselves some other Prince, whose success would some day be gall and wormwood to Prince William.

King Frederick VII regarded it as a great honour for Denmark that his heir's son should be chosen for the vacant throne, and was irritated at Prince Christian's hesitation. Having thus gained the sovereign's assent, Paget spoke to Princess Christian. He found her at one with her husband's misgivings, but she was prepared to admit that their son was very anxious to accept the throne, appealing to them not to reject it, 'saying that if it could only be kept an undecided question till he was of age, he would himself take all the responsibility and go to Greece without any condition whatever.'[7]

By this time, King Frederick VII had telegraphed his consent, and on 30 March Prince William of Denmark was proclaimed King George I of the Hellenes 'by the unanimous election of the Assembly'. There were two significant differences from the proclamation of King Otho. Firstly, King William was elected by the Greeks, not imposed upon them; and, secondly, he was to be King of the Hellenes, not simply of Greece. These factors underlined the constitutional and democratic character of the new monarchy; and his proclamation as King of the Hellenes inferred that he was sovereign of all the Hellenes, whether living in Greece or not.

Even so, Prince Christian still seemed determined to prevent his son from accepting the throne. A meeting was arranged between a delegation from Greece and their chosen King. The delegation, wrote one observer, Dotezac, 'appears to be greatly enamoured of their young King. Prince Christian, on the other hand, makes no attempt to conceal his hope that the scheme will fall through. It is a sad position for the young Prince. You cannot imagine with what impatience Prince William is waiting for the difficulties that stand in the way of his departure to be cleared up.'[8]

The Prince could not see why he must make his First Communion according to the Lutheran rites, as once he reached Athens he intended to be received into the Greek Church. 'I am going to do the exact opposite of everything King Otho did', he insisted. 'I am going to become wholly Greek!'

At length, Prince Christian recognized that it was difficult to withhold his consent, particularly as his son was so eager. However, he still clutched at straws. A few days later, Dotezac noted that Prince and Princess Christian had appealed to Queen Victoria, 'begging her not to ask their son to accept a throne from which her motherly solicitude has saved Prince Alfred of England. They have also charged the Princess of Wales to use all her influence with Palmerston and Russell against the plan. The Prince and Princess of Denmark see in the Greek crown nothing but a crown of thorns.'[9] Yet he gradually realized that it was impossible to swim against the current. At the end of April a Council of State was held at Skodzborg, in which Prince Christian declared that he wanted to guarantee his son against accidents by an apanage for which the Three Powers would be responsible; it was 'the only satisfactory security and my consent depends on it'.

King Frederick was irritated at Prince Christian's demand for conditions, but still he could not persuade him to give his unequivocal consent. The French minister, alluding to Prince Christian's scruples about King Otho's abdication, pointed out that the Duc d'Aumale and Prince William of Baden, who had both been candidates for the throne, 'demanded no renunciation of rights from Bavaria; and the house of

Hanover ascended the British throne without bothering whether the Stuarts had abdicated or not.'[10] Just as the impatient Greek delegation was about to leave Copenhagen, a telegram was delivered in which the Powers declared themselves prepared to convert a debt of £12,000 sterling, jointly owing to them, into an annuity for the King of the Hellenes.

At last, Prince Christian gave his consent. He stipulated that as long as Prince William remained in Denmark he should be given neither the title nor the honours of a King, except at a royal audience when King Frederick would announce the Prince's acceptance of the throne, and at the actual departure of the new King for Athens.

King Frederick was reported to be 'radiant because he has got his way', while Prince and Princess Christian were resigned to the inevitable. As for the young King himself, he was apparently delighted. The endless delays had plunged him into deep gloom, and he had sent a message to the Greek delegation 'to say that he is no way to blame for the delays and difficulties that have arisen, and that with his whole heart he belongs to Greece!'[11]

If an account written by his youngest son Prince Christopher, some seven decades later, is to be believed, the Prince was not quite so full of youthful naïveté as was supposed. When Prince Christian, the King of Denmark and others sent for him, he listened quietly to all they had to say, then asked to 'think it over' for an hour. He 'went into the garden and there fought out his battle all alone, gave up for ever the peace and security of Denmark, his cherished dream of the sea'.[12]

Prince William's 'state of joyful intoxication' contrasted sorely with the depression of his parents. When the Court Marshal came to ascertain Prince Christian's wishes for the conduct of the acceptance ceremony, he was told, 'Do whatever you like. It's all one to me. My sole duty is to obey.' Dotezac thought that 'King George' should proceed to Athens at once. If King Frederick – whose complaints about his sufferings were so frequent that the family scoffed at his hypochondria, declaring that he would outlive the lot of them – was to die suddenly, the government would fall, and King Christian might be unwilling to let his son go to Greece after all.

On 3 June Prince William was raised to the rank of Captain in the Danish Navy. Three days later, the long-delayed ceremony took place. It was attended by the King of Denmark and most of the Prince's family, members of the Privy Council, the ministers of England, France and

Russia; and the Greek deputation, all summoned to the Appartementsaal of the Castle of Christiansborg, where the throne stood under a canopy of crimson velvet.

At midday King Frederick VII entered the hall, leading Prince William by the hand. He was preceded by the dignitaries of state and followed by the royal princes. The King took his seat on the throne and on his left stood Prince Christian and Prince William. First Admiral Kanaris, the veteran Greek naval hero, read the appeal from the Hellenes to the King of Denmark. The King then officially announced that it had been made a condition of the acceptance of the crown that the Ionian Islands would be ceded to Greece by Britain, so that the young King would be 'greeted as the harbinger of the fulfilment of this well-founded and long-cherished wish'. The strategic value of the islands, particularly Corfu, had become unimportant to Britain since they last played a part in the operations leading up to the battle of Navarino in 1827.

Next, he invited Prince William to ascend to the second step of the throne, and delivered him an address, advising him, 'let it always be your endeavour to win and to retain the love of your people', and 'abide firmly by the Constitution of your Country. Strive constantly to make it recognised and see that it is adhered to. If you make this your rule, it will go down well with you and your country.'[13]

In his reply the young Prince assured everyone solemnly that

I feel deeply the responsibility of the vocation that has fallen to my lot; I will devote to it the best powers of my life, and I rely upon the loyal support of the Greek nation in order that we may attain our common object, the happiness of Greece. I have grown up in a country where lawful order goes hand in hand with constitutional liberty, and which has thereby attained a great and beneficent development. The lessons I have learnt here will go with me and guide me in my new country, and I shall always keep before me the motto, which is that of the King of Denmark. The people's love is my strength![14]

After the speeches, a banquet was held for two hundred and fifty guests in the Hall of the Knights. The Greeks were in high spirits, and King Frederick was so delighted that he poured out generous amounts of champagne for the newly elevated young King, who had the good sense to keep a clear head as he proposed the health of King Frederick. Prince

Christian was still in sombre mood, and when Paget congratulated him, he answered coldly, 'Congratulate yourself, not me. It is a disgrace to me and to my son that the throne has been accepted without King Otho's having abdicated.'

The election of King George I was ratified on 13 July by a treaty between the Protecting Powers and Denmark. Among its terms were that his successor should belong to the Greek Orthodox Church, although King George was not obliged to change his Protestant faith; and it was established that the crowns of Greece and Denmark should never be united under one sovereign, although all members of the royal house of Greece would automatically be Princes or Princesses of Greece and Denmark. Financial provision was made for the new King, namely a sum of £12,000 per annum, relinquished in his favour by the Three Powers from Greece's annual loan repayments, and an additional £10,000 from the revenues of the Ionian Islands.

CHAPTER ONE

'God give him strength and patience'

Attired in the uniform of a Danish Admiral, King George left Copenhagen on 17 September 1863. With him went Count Sponneck, a former Danish Minister of Finance and Director General of Customs, who had been appointed his political mentor, two naval officers who were to act as his aides-de-camp, Baron Guldencrone and Lieutenant Funch, and a small suite. It had been arranged that the entourage would travel to Greece via some of the European courts with which the King needed to become briefly acquainted first, particularly those of the Protecting Powers whom he could thank in person for the support they had accorded him in his election to the throne.

On 20 September they reached St Petersburg, where the King was entertained by the Tsar and his family for six days. Next he went to take his leave of the family at Rumpenheim, before proceeding to Brussels, where King Leopold of the Belgians – who might so easily have been celebrating over thirty years as King of Greece himself – threw a grand banquet at Laeken Palace in his honour. Other guests included the Duke and Duchess of Brabant and the Count of Flanders.

Next he went to Calais and sailed for England, arriving at Victoria Station, London, on 5 October. The Greek community of London turned out in force to welcome him. So did the Prince of Wales, who escorted him back to Marlborough House. The physical contrast between the brothers-in-law was noticed: King George, who was recovering from a rough crossing, 'looked somewhat pale, and far from so robust [*sic*] as the Prince of Wales'.[1]

Though the Princess of Wales feigned delight at her brother's future and was delighted to have him staying with them, she was still deeply concerned at what lay in store for him. A few days after the ceremony in June, she had written in apprehension to the Dowager Queen of Denmark: 'God give him strength and patience, to stand up to what the future may bring.'[2]

In Britain he attended a *Te Deum* at the Greek Church, London Wall, where he declined the offer of a throne to sit in, expressing a preference to stand in accordance with the Orthodox practice of the Church in Greece. Hymns were chanted, unaccompanied by instrumental music, and prayers were offered by the chief ministers of the Greek Church in England, Liverpool and Manchester: one for His Majesty, one for 'all the faithful', and one for those who had died in the cause of Greek independence. Going north, he paid a traditional duty visit to Queen Victoria at Balmoral, and in London *Punch* observed drily that 'Before leaving town, KING GEORGE AGAMEMNON received an address from the Statue of Achilles in Hyde Park, and promised to write to him from Greece.'[3]

After stopping at Paris for a final courtesy call on Emperor Napoleon, the party proceeded to Athens, landing at the Piraeus at 9.00 a.m. on 30 October 1863. *The Times* correspondent suggested that his welcome was muted at first: 'Athens is reported to be quiet, and the people well disposed.' This restraint only lasted a few hours, for the real celebrations took place that night. It was reported, by the same correspondent, that:

From 6 o'clock in the evening all the houses were dazzling with light; the most beautiful illuminations were those of the English Legation, the Kapnicarean Church, the Italian and Prussian Legations, and the French Art School. The King drove through the principal streets in an open carriage, receiving everywhere the acclamations of an enthusiastic crowd; and, I will add, that what must have touched the heart of the young Sovereign was those miserable hovels illuminated by one or two lampions only and the enthusiastic cries of the real people.[4]

King George's first official duty after arriving in his kingdom was to take the oath of fidelity to the constitution of Greece at the National Assembly, which he did on 31 October. After receiving addresses from the Metropolitan Bishop and the President of the Assembly, he declared solemnly and firmly that 'in the name of the consubstantial and indivisible Trinity', he swore to protect 'the dominant religion of the Greeks, to maintain and to defend the independence, the autonomy, and the integrity of the Greek State, and to observe its laws.'[5]

Horace Rumbold, at that time British Ambassador to Athens, was greatly moved at 'the sight of this slight, delicate stripling, standing alone amongst a crowd of callous, unscrupulous politicians, many of whom had been steeped to the lips in treason.'[6]

In the evening a dinner in his honour was given at the palace, followed by firework displays throughout the city. The festivities lasted for three days, 'without the slightest sign of disturbance of public order'. King George, it was noticed approvingly, visited various parts of Athens in an open carriage and on foot, accompanied only by two officers in attendance, to loud cheers wherever he went.

For the next few days he continued with his excursions on foot, horseback and in a phaeton. It was evident that the enthusiastic young man could not see enough of his capital. Sometimes he walked through the streets alone, stopping to talk to people, visiting the vegetable market and inquiring the price of goods for sale. As he was not yet fully conversant with the Greek language, it must be assumed that he took an interpreter in discreet attendance. Nevertheless, the contrast with his predecessor was acute. King Otho, people recalled, 'never went out at all but with the greatest solemnity'. The sight of this affable, accessible young sovereign made a favourable and lasting impression on the Athenians.

His 'modesty of character and simplicity of habits' gained immediate approval. He went to divine service on foot, and at the Cathedral in Athens he ordered a sumptuous dais erected for his benefit to be removed, saying to the Minister of Public Worship that 'in the temple of the Lord all men were equal, and a simple stall would suffice for him in future'.

In 1863 Athens was not a city, more a conglomerate of villages, with a population of some 45,000. (By comparison, the Copenhagen population was 158,000.) Though there was no sense of metropolitan community in the capital, the people were welcoming enough. The same could not be said for the palace, which had been built by King Otho. When King George arrived, it was in a sorry state. The building, a simple, stuccoed, pillared and pedimented block, 'like a huge cardboard-box', was barely inhabitable. It had 365 rooms, but only one bathroom, 'and no one had ever been known to take a bath in it for the simple reason that the taps would scarcely ever run and, on the rare occasions when they could be coaxed into doing so, emitted a thin trickle of water in which the corpses of defunct roaches and other strange animals floated dismally.'[7]

In winter the wind whistled down the palace corridors and the cold was unbearable. Some rooms had fireplaces, others had porcelain stoves, 'which gave out a fierce but concentrated heat so that you roasted the side that happened to be your nearest to them and shivered from the draught on your other side'.[8] Lighting was provided by oil lamps suspended from the ceiling or set on the tables, which gave off a strong odour and a thin blue smoke causing everyone's eyes to water. Some of the reception rooms had a certain grandeur, but the private apartments, decorated in what the previous Bavarian occupants had fondly imagined to be the ancient Greek style, were hideous.

In addition to all these shortcomings, the entire palace had been ransacked since Otho's departure. Doors had been smashed, fittings torn out and furniture stolen. While only to be expected, the evidence of such vandalism could hardly have been a welcoming or reassuring sight for the young King. Otho's possessions, such as had not been removed, lay scattered around on the floors, and one of King George's first orders was that the goods should be collected and despatched at his own expense to their rightful owner.*

Until he was married, King George occupied only a small part of the palace and many of his belongings remained in their crates. On more than one occasion, he lightheartedly teased intransigent or procrastinating politicians by reminding them that his bags were still packed and he could leave at any moment. He would not 'be caught napping' like his predecessor.

Another of King George's immediate tasks was to organize his own staff. From the motley group of unpolished functionaries assigned to him, he had to select aides-de-camp and court officials, to train his own butlers, footmen and grooms. Still not yet aged eighteen, he was expected to set the tone of his court. Yet he was 'still boyish in many ways and with a flow of animal spirits that sometimes made it difficult for his daily companions to maintain the respectful reserve and gravity due to his royal station.'[9]

One thing which his naval training had imbued in him was a respect for being turned out smartly. He set great store by having members of his household properly dressed. His Greek aides tended to wear only military

---

* King Otho had returned to his native Bavaria, where he died in 1867 of measles, aged fifty-two. At his request he was buried at Munich, wearing Greek national dress. Queen Amalia, who had become very fat in later life, died in 1875. Her demise was apparently hastened by a heart attack brought on by shock at being refused burial alongside her husband because, the ungallant King Ludwig II told her, the tomb was too small.

uniform, which he personally disliked, and he insisted that they should wear evening attire at court. None of them liked wearing tails and starched shirts, but he insisted. On one occasion at dinner he made them all rather uncomfortable by administering a sharp rebuke across the table to one of his suite for his untidy appearance.

At the same time King George was tactful enough to identify himself with his new country as much as possible. He soon mastered the language, though he always spoke it with a slightly guttural accent, and later he cultivated a drooping, typically Greek, moustache. Although he remained a Protestant, he paid full respect to the Greek Orthodox Church and agreed that his children would belong to the native faith; he worshipped privately in the chapel adjoining his department at the Palace.

No man, his youngest son would write one day, ever worked harder than King George; 'His day was never shorter than ten hours and more likely to run into twelve or even twenty-four when there was any crisis to be faced.'[10] Rising at 7.30 each morning, he worked on correspondence until breakfast two hours later. Next came conferences with domestic staff, looking at accounts and giving directions for the entertainment of guests. Then he went to his study, where he spent the rest of the morning receiving his ministers and giving audiences. It was not unusual for fifty to sixty people to be shown into the royal presence before luncheon, as anyone who wanted to see him had only to write his name in the audience-book and the appointment would be made.

King George was anxious to avoid the accusation of being unduly influenced by the advisers he had brought with him. Still technically a minor at the time of his accession, he was intelligent enough to realize that the less scrupulous of those around him would not stoop to cloak their own personal ambition behind an ostensible desire to assist him on account of his youth.

In February 1865 he was forced to order his paternal uncle, Prince Julius of Glucksburg, to leave the country by the end of the week. Prince Julius had been working hand in glove with several former ministers who had held office under King Otho, with a view to ejecting Count Sponneck from his position and supplanting himself as the King's chief adviser. Declaring that he would allow nobody, whether a member of his house or a stranger, to interfere in the affairs of the country, King George angrily sent his uncle away. Nevertheless, the self-confident Count Sponneck soon made his position untenable by his persistent tactless remarks, and also returned to Denmark in due course.

Rumbold soon became aware of the young King's growing confidence. At an open-air fête, he observed His Majesty deep in conversation with Monsieur Lombardos, a radical leader known to be connected with some of the most active members of the revolutionary party in Italy and Austria. Noticing Rumbold's discomfort, he later asked if the diplomat was ill. Rumbold explained that it made him uneasy to see his sovereign talking to a man against whose intriguing nature he could not warn him strongly enough. Flaring up, the King said he knew what was best for his interests, and turning on his heel left Rumbold abruptly.

At dinner that evening relations between King and diplomat still appeared distant. Half-way through the meal King George sent for a pencil, scribbled something on his menu card and whispered instructions as he handed it to a footman. The man came and presented the message to the unhappy Rumbold. Written in German, it 'said in the kindest terms, that he wished what had passed between us to be forgotten'.[11] Deeply touched, and immensely relieved, Rumbold bowed across the table. Later he had the menu framed, with a portrait of the King on either side.

This affable, personable approach won him ready popularity from the nation. So had Britain's gift of the Ionian Islands. In Greek eyes, this was the first tangible step towards the Greater Greece, and it was fondly assumed that the Powers would give the nation further support towards her territorial ambitions in years to come. When he was deposed King Otho had taken the crown and other regalia which he had brought from Bavaria back with him. King George, when asked where his crown was, replied proudly that the Ionian Islands were the only jewels he had brought with him.

King George intended to go in state to take over the Ionians from the British, including a tour of the islands at the same time. Sir Horace Rumbold and the ambassadors of Russia and France were invited to accompany him. The ceremony took place on 1 June 1864, when HMS *Revenge* bearing Rumbold joined the royal yacht *Hellas* in Navarino Bay. A Russian ship, *Oleg*, and a French ship, *Magicien*, had already arrived. The cortège steamed out into Katacolo Bay, *Hellas* leading with the King, and the others following. A 130-gun vessel, HMS *Duke of Marlborough*, her decks alive with redcoats and guns crashing in salute, carried Sir Henry Storks, Lord High Commissioner of the Ionian Islands, with the last battalion of the British garrison. A state barge, flying the Ionian standard, came plunging across from *Marlborough* with Sir Henry and his staff. They struck their colours alongside *Hellas* and Sir Henry carried the folded standard on to the royal yacht. He reverently advanced to the King and laid the Ionian standard at his feet. Now the islands were officially Greek property, though the sharp-eyed Sir Henry thought that the King's staff were celebrating the surrender behind his back with a rather insulting display of triumph.

One of King George's first political initiatives was to insist that the protracted proceedings of the National Assembly, which had been engaged in preparing a new constitution since before his arrival in Greece, should be completed as soon as possible. The debate appeared to be never-ending and prevented the passage of urgent measures to improve the national economy. Frustrated by the politicians' prevarication, he boldly asserted the royal prerogative by demanding that the draft constitution should be put to the vote, or else he would return to Denmark forthwith. His word was obeyed, and on 28 November 1864 he was able to take the oath in the Assembly.

From that date Greece became in fact as well as in name a 'democracy under a King' (*vasilevomeni dimokratia*). The rights and liberties of the people were now enshrined in law, and the irresponsibility of parliament was curtailed. The King's powers were considerable, but strictly defined. They went far beyond those implied in the phrase that 'the sovereign reigns but does not rule', but he could not act without the advice and signature of his ministers.

It was a state of affairs which suited him perfectly. Throughout his reign he was prepared to put complete faith in his ministers, keeping himself fully informed on government measures and never interfering with their administrative work. When documents were brought to him for approval, he signed them first and read them afterwards. To some of his European contemporaries, such reliance on his politicians might have seemed foolhardy, but this strict adherence to constitutional principles encouraged native political talent, and helped to ensure the gradual development of a political world in an emergent nation which had been independent for a mere thirty years or so. Parliament was limited to one house, and the senate (*gerousia*) was abolished. It was replaced by a Council of State nominated by the Crown, abolished in turn in 1865. The single house of parliament (*vouli*) was to be elected by direct, secret and universal male suffrage. Deputies were to represent the nation and not individual constituencies, and provision was made for local government which had been hitherto neglected.

Despite his faith in the ministers, King George harboured no illusions over the unsettled state of Greece. While his people may have been proud of their democracy, they showed little skill at operating it. Elections were frequently corrupt, with a largely illiterate electorate often at the mercy of brigands; governments seldom lasted long, and the fate of both was often threatened by violence and bloodshed. Between 1864 and 1880 there were nine general elections and thirty-one different administrations. The arguments of political parties over the King's rights and revenue, combined with the spread of brigandage and other disturbances throughout the country, made King George feel ever insecure.

All the same he adhered to constitutional and democratic niceties to an extent which surprised his less scrupulous politicians. Early in his reign, when discussing the possible outcome of imminent elections with Bulgaris, his Prime Minister, and the likely success of his rival Coletti, Bulgaris insisted that they must prevent him coming to power. 'That depends entirely on the elections', the King replied. 'If the people want him they will vote for him, that is all.' 'Oh! I don't mean that at all, we must do away with him!' was his minister's answer.[12]

For the first four years of his reign King George never left his kingdom, apart from voyages along the coast. By ship, carriage, mule and even on foot, he visited every area of the country, and all the Hellenic islands. A correspondent from *The Times*, commenting on an excursion to the Peleponnesus early in 1869, noted that 'the time he selected for the journey was not very agreeable to his courtiers, but it was well chosen for affording His Majesty an opportunity of observing the backward condition of his kingdom, and ascertaining, by slow travelling, and personal inconvenience, what are the first wants of his subjects in the most fruitful and best cultivated province in Greece.'[13]

From the beginning of his reign the King regarded the Prince of Wales as one of his most trusted friends and allies, though he was inclined to overestimate the (very limited) influence that 'Bertie' could have on British foreign policy where the cause of Greece was concerned. King George kept him in touch regularly with home affairs, reporting on such matters as elections (17 February 1865):

You know perhaps that the elections went with great liberty and tranquillity in nearly all Greece, only in 2 Provinces there was some trouble for a short time; in Athens it went all with great order, and Mr Erskine and the French and Russian ministers made their compliment to me in cause of the order which had reigned in the town for those four days.[14]

In the same letter he discussed the delicate issue of a forthcoming visit by Prince Alfred. While assuring the Prince of Wales that he would 'always be very happy and flattered to receive one of your brothers or somebody of your family here in Greece', the plan was far from straightforward:

> Your government wrote to me that he should perhaps visit the Greek ports, but the Queen did not like that one should give him any official reception (that I got when I was at Athens). I asked Mr Erskine when do you think that Pr. Alfred comes. Well sir he said, I don't know, because the cholera is there, and he should be obliged to have quarantine, and therefore perhaps he don't comes. . . .

Another official suggested that it was better if Prince Alfred did not come, wrote the King, 'because he had been elected before I had been elected and therefore, that those men who were displeased would make some demonstrations to his advantage and that could be disagreeable – for me and the government.'[15]

The Prince and Princess of Wales were much concerned with the internal state of the country. 'You can well imagine how happy the Princess is to hear better news,' the Prince wrote to Lord Russell (22 March 1865), 'as all the last accounts have caused her great anxiety about her brother, who she was so anxious should never have accepted his present position. I am very glad to hear that you will keep two English ships at the Piraeus at present – it will at any rate have a good effect.'[16]

The efforts of the people of Crete to throw off the yoke of Turkey and unite the island with the kingdom of Greece soon afterwards involved the Prince of Wales in a new and protracted ordeal. Greek politicians tolerated if not actively encouraged Cretan agitation, which Turkey and the treaty Powers treated as unwarranted rebellion. In order to try and defuse the situation in a fashion acceptable to all parties, King George sought intervention from the Prince, begging his support for a compromise whereby the island might be placed under the protection of England or another of the interested Powers. He wrote to the Prince of Wales (4 October 1866):

The Powers are obliged to interfere now, you can't do otherwise if you won't that there shall break a revolution out in Thessaly and Cyprus, and Serbia and Montenegro; I think the governments cannot see quietly that other Christians are murdered not only the men, but the women and the children, of the Turks; if you won't give Candia [Crete] to Greece, take it, under your own protection, but you cannot continue abominable indifference against these good Christians; can you let them continue, now impossible, can you force them to go under the yoke again no certainly not, if you send troops there to, to finish the war you are obliged, to take that island under your special protection, or something other. I can't know what you decide in your country, but you are obliged to do something. How would not your name dearest Bertie be blessed when they [the Cretans] knew that you had some interest to their destiny.[17]

The Prince consulted Lord Stanley, Foreign Secretary, who was equally sympathetic and agreed that King George's proposal was worthy of consideration. But in the face of indecision from the rest of his cabinet colleagues nothing was done, and an insurrection against the Turkish government, which broke out in Crete, was encouraged and supported by Greece. An ultimatum to put down the rebellion, which Turkey delivered to the Greek government, was rejected.

To Queen Victoria's consternation, the Prince doggedly defended his brother-in-law's policy. A conference of the Powers was summoned to Paris to bring Greece to a more reasonable frame of mind. Lord Clarendon, who succeeded Lord Stanley at the Foreign Office in 1868, urged King George to be more conciliatory and accept the *status quo*, and the Queen drew the Prince's attention to Lord Clarendon's 'excellent' advice. She pointed out to him (28 December 1868) that 'all governments except that of Russia agree that there is nothing but what the Porte had the right to ask, and have urged the Greek government to comply'.[18]

Embarrassed by the Prince of Wales's partisanship of his brother-in-law, Queen Victoria was further discomforted by his proposal to pay a visit to Athens. Though it would be a purely family visit, she deemed it 'singularly ill-timed'. Even if hostilities between Turkey and Greece were averted, General Grey advised Lord Clarendon (21 December 1868), 'the occurrence of which would make it impossible to take the Princess there, it would hardly be right, Her Majesty thinks, considering what the conduct of Greece has been, that such an apparent encouragement should be given to its Government, as would be implied in a visit from the Heir Apparent of the English Crown.'[19] After persuasion by Lord Clarendon, the Prince postponed his visit.

By this time King George had taken the first steps towards establishing a dynasty, another area in which King Otho and Queen Amalia had been found wanting. The ministers frequently reminded him that it was essential to establish the succession. Shortly after his acceptance of the crown in 1863, there had been some talk of proposing Princess Helena, one of the Prince of Wales's younger sisters, as a suitable bride. This never came to anything, but within a few years he was anxious to find a wife. Rumbold recalled that he appeared to have 'a holy horror of all vice, and I remember being both touched and amused one evening by his confiding in me his determination to marry as early as possible in order to be placed at once out of the reach of the many risks and temptations to which he knew he was certain to be exposed.'[20]

The British Foreign Office was uneasy when informed early in 1867 that Tsar Alexander II had invited the King to spend several months in Russia, partly to find himself a Russian wife and partly to learn about the way in which the Empire was governed. Even the Prince of Wales had been concerned when King George had mentioned the scheme to him the previous autumn. 'Why are you always so afraid of the idea, that it would be so terrible if I married a Russian?' the King had asked (8 October 1866):

If I do it, it is only for the country, because she has got the same religion, which would be an immense pleasure for the whole country, but be sure dearest Bertie of one thing, when I shall marry a Russian, that, that cannot change my [word illegible] or anything, and what has in our days such a relation with one house and another to say, the best proof, was, when the Danish war* took place, in the moment I marry my wife cannot be other thing or belong to another nation than I do.[21]

---

* The war between Denmark and the combined forces of Prussia and Austria over the duchies of Schleswig and Holstein in 1864.

Leaving his paternal uncle, Prince Hans of Glucksburg (who could be trusted, unlike his brother Julius), to act as his Regent, King George departed for St Petersburg, to be welcomed by a deputation of the Tsar and his brothers.

On the night of his arrival he sat down to an imperial banquet given in his honour in the magnificent blue and silver hall of the Winter Palace. Three thousand guests sat down to a meal, illuminated by ten thousand candles, with decorations provided by exotic out-of-season blooms and fully-grown palm trees stretching towards a ceiling lit like a night sky. Accustomed to the spartan surroundings of his palace at Athens, King George was astonished at the Romanov splendour and delighted to see his sister Dagmar again, recently married to the Tsarevich, another Alexander.

King George visited the family of Grand Duke Constantine, eldest brother of the Tsar, at the Marble Palace and Pavlovsk Palace. Here he met for the second time their fair-haired daughter, Grand Duchess Olga, whom he had seen briefly while visiting the court on his way to Athens for the first time in 1863, and who at fifteen years of age was still officially in the schoolroom. The Grand Duke and Duchess were astonished that the young girl should have attracted the attention of their distinguished guest, yet within a few weeks they were betrothed and it was announced that the marriage would take place soon after her sixteenth birthday. When some of the family dared to suggest that she was too young, the Grand Duchess retorted briskly that 'Olga would not stay sixteen all her life.'

They were married in a magnificent five-day ceremony at the Chapel of the Winter Palace in October 1867. The young Queen of the Hellenes had pursued her studies in the schoolroom to the very end, insisting that a queen should complete her education and that she would take her governess with her to continue her education in Athens. She was the youngest bride yet to wear the traditional Romanov Grand Duchess's bridal array: the cloth of silver gown, cut in the fashion set by Catherine the Great, and the huge chains of diamonds of that Empress, the ermine and red velvet mantle, the flashing diamond *Kokoschik* with a miniature imperial crown set above it and the three traditional ringlets of hair falling to the shoulders at each side.

They enjoyed a brief honeymoon at Ropsha, one of the imperial palaces near St Petersburg, before setting out to take up their duties in Greece. With them went a trunkload of the Queen's favourite dolls.

When they arrived in Athens, Queen Olga, wearing a dress in the Greek colours of blue and white, found the reception overwhelming. As the crowds lining the streets shouted themselves hoarse in welcome, she was frightened and almost in tears. Before one reception she disappeared and was found in the palace, 'hiding in a dark recess under the staircase, hugging her favourite Russian stuffed bear, and weeping bitterly'.[22]

Yet without ever losing her love for Russia, she soon settled down to the country of her adoption. She had been right not to neglect her education, for when she arrived in Greece she spoke neither Greek nor English. Within a year, she had mastered both.

Queen Olga's first child, a boy, was born on 2 August 1868. National sentiment required him to bear the name of Constantine, the last Emperor of Byzantine Greece, as a symbol of the links with the splendid past as well as of the hopes for the future. The news that a Prince Constantine had been born on the sacred soil of Greece reached the most remote Greek communities, and was received with mystic belief as a sign that the unity and destiny of their race was at last to be achieved.

CHAPTER TWO

'He cannot depend on his ministers'

By the beginning of 1869 matters appeared peaceful in Greece. Most importantly of all, Crete was calm again, relations with Turkey were more amicable, and Queen Victoria gave her approval for the Prince and Princess of Wales to pay King George and Queen Olga a visit, stopping at Athens on their way back from Russia. King George 'received them at the Piraeus with youthful buoyancy', meeting them with a rather dilapidated carriage. As they drove to Athens, the visitors almost choked with dust on the primitive roads.

At Athens the King proudly conducted them over the Acropolis and other historic monuments of the city. Then they all went to Corfu, where Queen Olga and two infant sons, Constantine and George, the latter only a few weeks old, were in rural retreat. They spent a pleasant week together, marked by a refreshing absence of formality, mainly enjoying country excursions, including a boar hunt.

The Princess of Wales was delighted to see her favourite brother again. She had met her youthful Russian-born sister-in-law with a slight feeling of jealousy, and felt she was much too young to help her brother in the trials of his difficult life in Greece. A week of her company soon convinced her she had been mistaken, for Queen Olga was practical, methodical and had a tenacity which belied her tender years. A friendship sprang up between the women so concerned with the King's fortunes, which lasted until their deaths.

One day a British equerry was astonished by the approaching sound of tripping feet, male laughter and female cries of dismay. It heralded the appearance of King George, gleefully kicking the remains of a hat. Behind him, protesting, came the Princess of Wales. The King explained that she had been wearing an ugly hat which he did not like, so he took it off and kicked it. 'It was my hat and it was so rude of him,' the Princess complained, 'and now I can never wear it any more.'[1] A few days later, in the privacy of the garden on Corfu, the King and the Prince of Wales 'fought' a duel with over-ripe oranges.

King George's peace of mind was to be shattered the following year. On 11 April 1870 a party of tourists, mainly English, set out for Athens from Marathon, on the assurance of the Greek government that Attica was safe. That same afternoon, they were captured by a group of brigands and held to ransom. As most of the British party were aristocrats, the brigands believed that one at least was related to Queen Victoria and therefore expected a vast sum. One of the captives, Lord Muncaster, was allowed to go to Athens to make the necessary arrangements and to take the ladies of the party with him. The money demanded, £25,000, was promised and on its way.

Once the news broke in Britain, there was considerable anxiety and few were more alarmed than the Prince of Wales. Frederick Vyner, brother-in-law of the Prince's friend, and Lord President of the Council in Gladstone's ministry, Lord de Grey (afterwards Marquis of Ripon), was among the captives. To Grey, the Prince wrote from Sandringham (22 April 1870) of his anxiety, and that 'the demands of the Brigands are quite outrageous, but I trust that Vyner will shortly be liberated'.[2]

Unhappily, events had forestalled them. Disregarding a pledge not to take action against the brigands while negotiations were in progress, the Greek troops drew a cordon round them and on 21 April fired on them. In retaliation the brigands murdered Vyner and three other hostages, Mr E.H.C. Herbert, Secretary to the British Legation in Athens, first cousin of the 4th Earl of Caernarvon, former Colonial Secretary; Mr Lloyd, an engineer; and the Count de Boyl, Secretary of the Italian Legation at Athens.

Almost beside himself, King George poured his heart out in a letter to the Prince of Wales:

> I really don't know how I dare write to you after the terrible and horrible tragedy which happened the day before yesterday. You will excuse me if I do so, but I feel so dreadfully wretched and unhappy that it is impossible for me to do otherwise. I am sure you know now what has occurred, that these rascals here killed three English gentlemen and one Italian. I was at the time of their capture in the islands with Olga, and learnt this nearly a week after, on our return from this trip to the Archipelago. I can scarcely tell you how indignant

I was to hear of their capture, and now they are murdered. I feel as if I was going mad, I am so unhappy, and that is useless now, as these poor fellows are dead . . . I assure you, my dear brother, I am the most unhappy man in the world. I shall never get over this all my life. . . .[3]

It made matters little better that the troops killed twenty-nine of the brigands, leaving only nine survivors. King George was bitterly upset, if hardly surprised, at the violent denunciations of Greece in the British press. From Germany Queen Victoria's eldest daughter, the Crown Princess of Prussia, wrote (2 May 1870):

I do not wonder at everybody thinking and talking of little else than this appalling tragedy in Greece. It is really dreadful but I cannot help pitying Alix's brother, who has a pleasant position of being responsible for mischief he is too weak to prevent, as he cannot depend on his ministers or his army. The thrones of Greece and Rumania seem to me the most wretched and unenviable of positions.[4]

The Prince of Wales forwarded King George's letter to the Prime Minister, William Gladstone, with a covering note of his own (5 May 1870):

He is quite prostrated with grief at what has occurred, and what he feels still more keenly is – that he was utterly powerless to prevent the catastrophe. His position in his adopted country is also such a painful and difficult one, as he does his utmost to ameliorate the country, and is thwarted on all sides either by the opposition, or by the constitution which keeps his hands tied. Unless he has some absolute power given him, I feel convinced that his life is wasted in Greece.[5]

Mr Gladstone replied sympathetically, albeit vaguely, that 'the lapse of a short time will restore the balance of the public mind, and the cause of Greece and its Government will be appreciated with equity.'[6]

By 1875 feelings again ran high in the Near East. Greece was demanding Crete, Thessaly and Epirus from the Turks. These claims were by no means unreasonable, since Thessaly and Epirus offered natural frontiers for a modern state, but were impracticable – and troublesome – coming from a state in the peculiar circumstances of Greece. Benjamin Disraeli, now Prime Minister, was far more sympathetic to Turkey than Gladstone, his predecessor. Such a marked change of emphasis at the head of the government would make the Prince of Wales's task as a pro-Greek more contentious, not to say embarrassing, during the next few years.

In July 1876 King George visited his relations in England. With him came Queen Olga, their three elder sons and their daughter Alexandra (a second daughter, Marie, born only that year, stayed at home). At first, the King plaintively poured out his troubles to his sister and brother-in-law at Marlborough House, pleased to have sympathetic attention at last. However, his spirits rose when he was taken to such diversions as Sandown Park Races, the Royal Italian Opera, and to Crystal Palace to see Brock's Fireworks Display. A huge set-piece in coloured fire of the Parthenon with the words, 'Long life to King George of Greece', raised resounding cheers from the crowd. Perhaps, in his overwrought state, he interpreted this rather too literally as a British gesture of sympathy with Greek aspirations, for he was moved almost to tears. Indeed, it may have steeled his confidence for the important interviews to follow with the Queen, the Prime Minister and the Foreign Secretary.

At his meeting with the Queen at Windsor, she listened to him attentively, though she was very laconic when describing the event. 'Bertie and Alix brought Willy down with them here yesterday,' she wrote to the German Crown Princess (13 July 1876), 'and I gave him the Garter here in the house! He looks very well and unaltered.'[7]

On a less portentous note, he also met the ill-fated Prince Imperial at Marlborough House. After the overthrow of the French Empire, the dethroned Emperor Napoleon III, Empress Eugenie and their only son had settled at Chislehurst, a move which the ailing Emperor did not long survive. The widowed Empress and Prince remained lifelong friends of Queen Victoria and her family, though barely three years were to elapse between a meeting of the King of the Hellenes and the man who would have been French Emperor, before the latter was killed on active service in the Zulu war.

Family connections made the international European situation ever more complicated. King George's sister Dagmar, the Tsarevich's wife, saw mutual benefit for Greece and Russia in the 'Eastern question', and the Russo-Turkish War of 1877–8. In the enmity between Greeks and Turks, never far below the surface, she hoped that war between Russia and Turkey might benefit her brother's kingdom.

King George saw an opportunity to put his close family ties with Russia to good use. If Greece would come to Russia's aid in her fight against the Turks in Bulgaria, perhaps she might win for herself some Turkish-held territory, namely Epirus, Thessaly, maybe even Macedonia. That Russia had her eye on Constantinople as well, and distrusted Greek initiatives in the same direction, was conveniently overlooked.

For a while it seemed as if King George's hopes would be realized. Tsar Alexander II asked Greece to join Russia in the war against Turkey. King George and the Tsarevna were delighted, but not for long, for the alliance was not allowed to materialize. Britain and France, two of the Protecting Powers (Russia being the third), refused to countenance such a move, thus Greece was obliged to remain neutral. Though Britain and France were suspicious of Russia's territorial designs on Turkey, they had no wish to see Greece disturbing the delicate balance. Not for the last time in his life was King George forced to appreciate that, in some cases, family relationships counted for very little.

At the Congress of Berlin, held in 1878 to decide the peace terms after Turkey had sued for peace, Greece made some minor territorial gains, with rectifications of the frontier in Thessaly and Epirus granted in her favour. Disraeli had represented Britain at the Congress and he explained elegantly to the Prince of Wales (6 July 1878) that 'I did yesterday something for Greece. It was very difficult, but is by no means to be despised. It was all done for Her Royal Highness's sake. I thought of Marlborough House all the time, and it was not decided, after many efforts, until the last moment.'[8]

He knew how passionately the Princess of Wales was concerned with the cause of Greece and her favourite brother. While staying with him in Athens in the spring of 1877, she had had a long talk with the King about the problems of Greece and the difficulties of his own position.

Predictably, Turkey was reluctant to acknowledge or co-operate with such territorial changes. The Prince of Wales made every effort to reconcile his brother-in-law to the problem and wrote to assure him that England was putting every pressure possible on the Turks. King George replied tactfully yet firmly (30 August 1878):

I should be sorry if you thought I had been complaining against England for its attitude in the Congress. I have never said anything like it – I am on the contrary very much satisfied with what has been done for Greece, and thankful to England for having accepted and agreed to the proposition made by the French Minister for Foreign Affairs in favour of Greece . . . I understand the delicate position in which England was in at the time *vis-à-vis* of Turkey, and that he preferred therefore to let Mr Waddington propose the rectification of our frontier to those two rivers, instead of doing it himself. I have been reading all the different speeches which Lord Beaconsfield and the other English Ministers made in both Houses concerning this question, and I was very glad to see that they all looked upon this question as a settled one; saying that Greece ought to be satisfied with what had been given her – I can assure you that I am very glad and thankful for what has been done for Greece, and I suppose that the country is satisfied too – I only hope now that the Powers will press upon Turkey the execution of this European decision, the principle of which the Sultan himself has recognized by signing and ratifying the Treaty of Berlin without making any reserve or difficulty. I cannot have the slightest doubt that the Powers, and more especially England perhaps, will insist upon Turkey fulfilling her engagements, and so show her respect for what England has decided upon . . . One cannot doubt for a moment the impression it would make in England should Turkey disregard the wishes of a conclave to whom she is indebted for her very existence. I think that all the Powers have got an interest in seeing this question settled as quickly as possible, because of course the Greeks will be in a ferment as long as Turkey refuses to sanction claims which have received the sanction of Europe.[9]

The Prince of Wales begged Disraeli to send the King some 'encouraging lines', but the Prime Minister could recommend only patience and the need to restrain Greece from 'rash adventures'. To this the Prince felt morally obliged to warn him that 'some allowances must be made for the difficulties the King has in keeping his inflammatory subjects quiet.'[10]

As Greece's northern frontiers remained an intractable problem, Britain and France took the lead in trying to bring about a settlement. They arranged a meeting of a Graeco-Turkish frontier commission at Preveza in March 1879 and again at Constantinople that August, but without success. The Prince and Princess of Wales's fervent partisanship of King George irked their pro-Turkish Prime Minister, Disraeli, who dreaded his invitations to their London home, Marlborough House, particularly after the Congress of Berlin. 'The Greek question is becoming a serious and painful question under that roof,' he wrote to Queen Victoria (4 April 1879), '. . . and its [the Greek] Govt evidently count on the support of influences which in their nature are not responsible.'[11]

Angry at the way in which the British government was failing to secure the delineation of the frontier in accordance with the Congress, the King continued to press his case to the Prince of Wales (19 April 1879):

I read with great attention and some astonishment the letters and the memoire you enclosed in yours; I must confess that I never expected to see such a change in the ideas of an English government, which regards Hellenic interests. Of course one could not foresee this. I was very glad to see in your letter, my dearest Bertie, that you wish me accept the territory which the Berlin Congress recommended; Greece never asked for more, nor can it be permitted to her to ask for a smaller territory, or accept from Turkey something less than what was decided in Congress. This served as a basis for the Greek Commissioners in their negotiations at Preveza. As the Turks did not recognize this, negotiations could not go on any longer, and the Gr[eek] government was obliged to ask the powers for their mediation in this affair in conformity with the 24th article of the Berlin treaty.[12]

In turn the Prince of Wales maintained pressure on Disraeli, who was so exasperated that he contemplated withholding the towns of Janina and Larissa from Greece, which the Congress had specifically promised to surrender.

When a Liberal government, under the more pro-Greek Gladstone, took office in April 1880, both King and Prince hoped for more favourable results. That summer King George and Queen Olga were invited to stay with the Prince of Wales. Included on their busy social calendar were visits to the races at Ascot, to the Duke of Sutherland's seat at Trentham in Staffordshire, to the Duke and Duchess of Bedford at Woburn Abbey, and a great luncheon with the Lord Mayor at the Guildhall in London.

More importantly, King George had a meeting with Gladstone at 10 Downing Street, and at a dinner at Marlborough House he was introduced by his brother-in-law to statesmen of both parties, including Disraeli and Sir Charles Dilke, the new Under-Secretary for Foreign

Affairs. Both thought very highly of the King's ability, following a reasoned discussion on Greece's claims. It was, however, too late for Disraeli to revise his formerly dismissive opinion of King George. He was ailing and had less than a year to live.

In June 1880 a further meeting of the Powers at Berlin agreed upon a frontier very favourable to the Greeks, including Ioannina, Metsovo and Mount Olympus. This angered the Turks, and the Greek government under Kharilaos Trikoupis made the mistake of ordering a threatening mobilization. The irritation of the Powers led to a re-opening of the whole question and it was not until May 1881 that a settlement was finally reached. It gave Greece Thessaly, which the Turks no longer wanted, but in Epirus only the area around Arta, leaving Ioannina and Preveza to the Turks. A new Greek government under Alexander Koumounduros reluctantly accepted it. Indeed, they had no alternative.

Greece's nationalist ambitions were naturally still far from satisfied. Trikoupis had learned his lesson and proceeded to concentrate on domestic and economic reforms rather than foreign adventures. But the rival National Party, led by Theodoros Delyannis, took every opportunity to inflame public opinion against Turkey. Such an opportunity arose in 1885 when the Bulgars declared their independence and the union of their two provinces. Delyannis swept Trikoupis out of office on a wave of public emotion, arguing that if the Bulgars could defy the treaty of Berlin, so could the Greeks.

What they looked for was some compensatory territorial acquisition. At first King George backed their demands, for as a Greek patriot he considered this just and reasonable. But when he heard his subjects proclaim that if they did not get what they wanted then they would attack Turkey and seize it, he counselled caution. The indignant Greeks demanded general mobilization, to which the King did not agree, but he was powerless to prevent the situation.

King George appealed to the Prince of Wales, assuring him that there seemed no answer but for the Powers to secure Greece some Turkish territory; the Prince replied firmly that nothing could be done. Notwithstanding the desperate entreaties of the Princess of Wales, who feared for her favourite brother's throne if not his life, Greece must give way. Lord Rosebery, the Foreign Secretary, was against her. Serious consequences must follow if Greece remained intransigent. The King was helpless, and the Greek reply to this was to mobilize and move towards the Turkish frontier.

Ironically, the task of leading the Powers' naval blockade fell to the Prince of Wales's brother, Prince Alfred, now Duke of Edinburgh, who had been elected King by the Greeks some twenty years earlier. The Duke had been appointed Commander-in-Chief of the Mediterranean Squadron early in 1886, and he had been warned as early as March to prepare for a blockade. He wrote to the Marquis of Ripon, First Lord of the Admiralty (30 March 1886) that a proposal 'to blockade the whole coast of Greece against the Greek ships of war and commerce is considered by my foreign colleagues and myself in being easy to carry out.'[13]

By the end of April Lord Rosebery warned that there was no alternative but to go ahead with the naval blockade, followed possibly by bombardment of Athens with heavy guns and an armed landing. On 7 May the diplomatic representatives of Britain, Austria, Germany and Italy left Athens, leaving behind those of Russia and France. An allied fleet sailed into the Piraeus and for three weeks there was a risk of war.

The Duke of Edinburgh telegraphed to the Queen (1 June 1886):

I fear that the determination not to raise blockade until Greek Government has announced disarmament may produce revolution in the country, and not only endanger the throne but safety of King and Queen. I feel it my duty to say this as my opinion to you, as things are very critical.[14]

The crisis came to an end when the Greek army decided to demobilize. It was not, however, the last time in the reign of King George I that Greece would incur the wrath of the Powers.

CHAPTER THREE

'My father, hitherto infallible as the Deity'

King George I was fortunate in his family life. Between 1868 and 1888 Queen Olga gave birth to five princes and three princesses: Constantine was followed by George (born in 1869), Alexandra (1870), Nicholas (1872), Marie (1876), Andrew (1882), and Christopher (1888). A third daughter, Olga, born in 1881, only survived for three months.

King George of the Hellenes was a devoted father and he spent as much time with his family as the cares of state permitted. The children were brought up in a happy, homely atmosphere. They stripped the sides from four-wheeled carts and raced them downhill; they teased the head gardener, who had been in charge of the palace gardens since King Otho's reign; they fought mock battles with home-made swords; and, led by their father, took part in noisy roller-skating and bicycle races on the parquet floors, weaving in and out of the marble columns of the three large ballrooms which ran along the full length of the palace. Nor did they tire of games like hide-and-seek and leapfrog, and of playing practical jokes on their relations when they came to stay.

Not all their cousins found them ideal company. The Edinburgh princesses, whose mother was also by birth a Russian Grand Duchess, met them on some of their visits to Russia. The eldest, Princess Marie,* thought that 'there was an irresistible good-humour' about her Hellenic namesake, who was four months younger than her, 'but she had an exceedingly sharp tongue'. Although they later became close friends, in adolescence 'we heartily disliked each other, and as none of us was so ready with our tongue as she was she made us feel greatly at a disadvantage.' As for the princes, Marie wrote that 'they were decidedly rowdy and there were too many of them . . . so tremendously possessive and so loud'.[1] It comes as some surprise to find the eldest of the lively,

* Later Marie, Queen of Roumania.

high-spirited Edinburgh princesses describing her cousins disdainfully as 'so loud'.

King George never ceased to miss his native Denmark, but he was careful not to offend Greek susceptibilities by making it too obvious. One of the few discreet reminders of his ancestral home was the luxury of a Danish-style dairy in the grounds of his summer home at Tatoi, at the foot of Mount Parnes, in the wooded estate 15 miles north of Athens. He purchased the property in 1871 and here he built a small villa, looking out to a magnificent view across the Athens plain to the Saronic Gulf.

As the family grew, further accommodation became necessary, and between 1886 and 1888 a larger house nearby was added. In these friendly, rambling places, a contrast with the uncomfortable, old-fashioned palace in Athens, the family revelled in a more intimate, informal atmosphere. On the farm at Tatoi the family kept cows and pigs, which ate from troughs made of the finest white marble. They made their own butter and the poultry supplied them with eggs.

Everyone liked the turkeys best, finding them the most responsive of birds: when spoken or whistled to, they all answered together. As the family watched them one day, strutting around in their endearingly conceited, pompous way, Prince George suddenly addressed them in a loud voice with a salute by which Russian soldiers and sailors were generally greeted on parade by their superiors, and to which, according to military etiquette, they all had to reply together. The turkeys immediately answered Prince George's salute. King George appreciated the joke at once and roared with laughter, and although at first Queen Olga thought it showed a lack of respect towards the Russian army, she could not help joining in.

Foxes, badgers and weasels were encouraged to live in the grounds. Peacocks were kept in the gardens as well, though they gradually disappeared when the old trapper died. Red deer and wild boar roamed the forest, and though rarely seen in daytime the deer became less shy towards autumn; wandering into the garden at night, they helped themselves to the blooms adorning the flowerbeds right under the windows. They also wrought havoc among the young trees and vineyards, but the King admired them so much that he would not let anyone shoot them. He was never a keen sportsman; whenever his sons asked leave to go partridge-shooting on one of the Greek islands, he always replied, 'You can't shoot now, it is their breeding season', regardless of the time of year.

Tatoi was the one place, Prince Christopher noted, 'where we could live a real home life and forget, for a short time, that we were not supposed to be ordinary human beings!'[2]

The estate was entrusted to Danish agents, partly because the King had faith in their experience and competence for the job, and partly because speaking to them in his own language, he believed, kept him more in touch with his homeland. Most of the roads at Tatoi, stretching for nearly 50 miles, were laid out by his trusted agent Munter. The estate workers had houses provided for them, and the estate included its own grocery and inn, where visitors were not allowed to spend more than a couple of days. According to Prince Nicholas, the King 'hated the idea of Tatoi being over-run by strangers and foreigners'.[3] He had evidently fulfilled his pre-accession promise to 'become wholly Greek'.

King George was very proud of the pine trees at Tatoi and would never allow anyone to extract the resin from them for wine, as it disfigured the stems so badly. The forests provided the family with a Christmas tree every year, decorated and positioned in the Room of Heroes beyond the Throne Room. A large table was put out for presents for the King and Queen, with a smaller one for each child, and in due course, for wives and children. The nurses also had their own present table. On Christmas Eve at 6 p.m. everyone assembled in the Throne Room adjoining the one in which the presents were placed, and the lights were turned out. At the given time, King George rang a small bell and the doors were thrown back to reveal a blaze of light made brighter still by the darkness of the room in which they had been waiting. At the sight of the presents the children ran forward shouting with delight. Dinner began punctually at 8 p.m., after which the Queen took the children to hear vespers in the palace chapel and to 'thank God for the nice things He had sent us'. Before going to bed that night they were allowed a last look at their gifts, and took one or two of the most cherished to bed with them.

The acquisition of the Ionian Islands at the start of his reign had given King George two holiday homes on Corfu. The first was an imposing three-storeyed palace, formerly the residence of the British High Commissioner; the second was the more informal summer retreat, Mon Repos. To the children, it was 'an unfailing delight'.

Whenever a Danish ship berthed at the Piraeus, the King would go abroad, invite some of the officers and cadets to the palace, and be inordinately delighted whenever he was presented with freshly-baked loaves of brown rye bread which was unobtainable in Greece.

The Queen was less discreet than her husband about her enthusiasm for the country of her birth. If a Russian ship came near Athens she would go down three or four times a week to visit it. As most of her visits were unannounced, they sometimes proved a little embarrassing. There would be a frantic rush among officers and crew to provide her with a suitable welcome, and she would often stay so long that they were at a loss what to do to entertain her. She, too, invited the crew to the palace, where she gave them Russian tea and kept them talking for hours. She never really overcame her homesickness, and she felt that these visitors were her only link with Russia.

In the palace at Athens, her own rooms were hung with so many icons that one visitor said it was rather like entering a religious sanctuary. On the top floor a guest room was converted into an Orthodox Chapel, where she and her family worshipped, and she organized a choir to sing Russian church music. The house at Tatoi had been specially built to please the Queen. It was an exact replica of a Victorian-style mansion which stood in the grounds of Grand Duke Constantine's country estate at Pavlovsk.

Some of her family felt that she took her obsession with Russia to inordinate lengths. Though they had not a drop of Greek blood between them, the children were tactful enough to take their cue from their father and behave as if they had been Hellenic for generations. Prince Christopher, who was born at Pavlovsk, was the only one who inherited any of his mother's love for her country. The rest were so tired of her 'ramming Russia down their throats' that they became very pro-Greek. As an adult, Prince Andrew generally refused to speak any other language.

Royal princes and foreign observers agreed that the Athens of King George I was one of the most democratic towns in nineteenth-century Europe. Titles were not used and in the street the princes were addressed and called to by their first names, without the prefix of Royal Highness.

At the Court Ball in Athens there were none of the class distinctions which were second nature to the Austrian or German Empires. A foreign tourist, staying at the hotel in Athens, hired a carriage to drive him to the palace. The coachman asked him if he would mind going rather early, as he himself was going to the ball and had to go home and change. The gentleman laughed at what he thought was a joke, and was astonished to see his former driver that evening, resplendent in evening clothes, dancing with the wife of a minister.

E.F. Benson was greatly impressed by Athens, 'with its high-born princes, and its national pride, and its army dressed in Albanian costume (embroidered jacket, fustinella, like a ballet skirt, fez, white gaiters, red shoes with tassels on the toes like the seed of dandelions), its fleet of three small cruisers, its national assembly of bawling Levantines, and its boot-blacks called Agamemnon and Thucydides, was precisely like the fabulous kingdom of Paflagonia in the "Rose and the Ring", or some Gilbertian realm of light opera.' It amused him to see a bugler, stationed by the front door, who blew 'soul-stirring blasts in a great hurry whenever a royal personage emerged from within. Sometimes the royal personage was only a royal baby in its perambulator, and the slightly self-conscious nursery-maid hastened to convey her charge into the garden away from these trumpetings of advertisement.'[4]

King George granted an audience to any overseas traveller, who, through his legation, asked for quarter of an hour's conversation with him. Queen Olga was equally willing to talk to foreign ladies, and American women flocked to Athens eager to hobnob with royalty, as according to one of them, 'The royal family of Greece is the easiest royal family to become acquainted with.'

Naturally, this informality had its limits. Ladies visiting the Queen had to wear high evening dress with a lace mantilla or similar garment on the head. Gentlemen seeking a royal audience were expected to wear top hats and frock coats, but since few travellers carried these in their luggage, they were permitted to wear dress-clothes and white ties. They would be received in a room at the palace decorated with purple Victorian wallpaper sprinkled with gilt stars, and the King stood during the whole interview seesawing backwards and forwards from toe to heel. It was a movement as infectious as yawning, and only with great self-control did the earnest visitor prevent himself from following the royal example. The King would signify the end of the interview by giving a little bow, and his visitor a low one.

During his first twenty years on the throne King George had earned the respect of his people and indeed of Europe, even if foreign journalists were not always fully predisposed to acknowledge the fact. In 1886 an anonymous British commentator remarked with faint praise that he had

settled down into the position of an easy-going, elderly*
Constitutional King, who likes to live exempt from troubles and
responsibilities. He is growing bald, collects pictures, and is much
interested in getting good wine equal to Bordeaux out of his private
vineyards. His official dinners are more frequent, and are served up
by a French cook. He sometimes suggests an alteration in the
uniform of the army, but gives way at once if his responsible advisers
hint that a party question might be made out of the matter. He and
the Queen live much in the country, bring up their children
admirably, and are delighted to extend the most gracious hospitality
to any stranger of distinction who visits Greece. But they
ostentatiously eschew politics. Queen Olga as a Russian has but a
faint appreciation of the Parliamentary system; but, on the other
hand, she has not the spirit of a Russian Catherine or Elisabeth, so
that she has never attempted to shape her husband's course, or to
establish him in a commanding position above parties . . .[5]

The writer went on to take the King to task for remaining 'serenely and
severely indifferent' to the crisis of 1886, but in mitigation admitted that
the blame for the misgovernment of Greece lay not with him but rather
with the Powers that had set him on the throne, fearing Greek
aggrandizement at the expense of Turkey.

King George was perhaps never happier than at family reunions with his
parents at one of the country castles of his childhood, Bernstorff or
Fredensborg. Here they could all lead the patriarchal life so dear to their
hearts, with brothers, sisters, nephews and nieces, away from the cares of
state. King George, who was not prone to take advice readily (or so his
sons considered), would listen with humility while King Christian IX
propounded his views on politics; while the Princess of Wales would
receive many a stern lecture on the art of managing an errant husband.
'The discovery that my father, hitherto infallible as the Deity, actually
feared Grandfather was a surprise not unmixed with holy pleasure to
me!' noted Prince Christopher. 'It demanded a complete readjustment of
my philosophy.'[6]

Fredensborg Park was open to the public on certain days of the week.
It was so vast that visitors invariably became lost in the labyrinth of parks.

---

* Hardly accurate; he was only forty years old when the article was published.

One afternoon King George, Tsar Alexander III and the Prince of Wales were out walking when they met a man who asked them to show him the way out. They accompanied him to the gates, talking of the weather, crops and politics. When they took their leave of each other, the stranger thanked them, adding, 'I've very much enjoyed my walk with you gentlemen and I hope we shall meet again; may I ask you for your names?' 'Certainly', said King George. 'I'm the King of Greece, this is the Prince of Wales, and this is the Emperor of Russia.' 'And I am Jesus Christ', replied the man, as he fled from what was evidently a party of escaped lunatics, their hearty laughter ringing in his ears.[7]

Autumn found the family back in Greece, with the princes and princesses returning to their education. The princes had tutors from the university to teach them Ancient and Modern Greek, history, geography, literature and mathematics, and they would go to the university laboratory to learn chemistry.

Three foreign tutors came to teach them at the palace. The one they remembered most was Dr Otho Lüders, 'a man of exceptional severity, who used to pinch our ears between the nails of his thumb and forefinger – sometimes to the point of bringing tears to our eyes – or roar at us with a voice of thunder when we were stupid or disobedient.'[8] Some years later he became German Consul-General at Athens, and they all looked upon him as a friend. He was a regular visitor to the palace, though he never really shed his schoolmasterly demeanour and they found him somewhat over-punctilious in his observance of etiquette. There was also a French master, Monsieur Brissot, and an English tutor, Mr Dixon, but in the latter's lessons they paid more attention to his trimming his fingernails with a penknife than to their work.

English was the first language they learnt. They spoke it among themselves in the nursery and at all times with their parents, but when they entered the schoolroom King George insisted that they should speak Greek to each other, a habit which they retained for life. Inevitably, some subjects appealed to the princes more than others. Nicholas took piano lessons to the age of fifteen, but without much enthusiasm or aptitude; and botany meant 'incongruous Latin names to every shrub and blade of grass that we encountered by the wayside'.[9] On the other hand he revealed a natural gift for drawing and painting, which proved of inestimable value to him in the lean years ahead.

As befitted princes of Greece, they loved archaeology and eagerly accompanied their father on to the Acropolis when extensive excavations were being carried out in the 1880s, bringing to light the foundations of prehistoric temples. Prince Constantine was honoured when invited to become President of the Greek Archaeological Society.

The princes' day began at 6 a.m., when they were woken for a cold bath. After an early breakfast lessons took place between 7.00 and 9.30 a.m., followed by 'the regular breakfast' with their father and whoever else in the family was around at the time. (The Queen ate breakfast alone in her room.) Lessons continued from 10.00 a.m. until 12 noon, then they would go to the gym in the garden for physical exercises and gymnastics. Lunch was taken with the family, followed by another two-hour session of lessons, from 2 p.m. until 4 p.m., then an outing and back again at school desks for preparation. At 7.30 p.m. they said goodnight to their parents and went to bed. This went on until the age of fourteen, when the princes joined their elders and betters at dinner, being packed off to bed at 10 p.m. sharp. Woe betide any youngster who was a few minutes late. At the same time they would begin attending the military school, twice a week, for drill. They enjoyed this as it gave them a chance to meet other boys of their own age. When they came of age they joined either the army or the navy.

Prince George was particularly bad at his lessons in the schoolroom. The tutors found him slow and stupid, and made no attempt to hide their displeasure at his apparent lack of effort. He was more than happy to 'escape' at the age of fourteen to the Danish naval cadet school at Copenhagen, where he soon proved himself one of the best scholars and left as head of his class.

Prince Nicholas benefited from the education of his French-Swiss tutor, Monsieur Constant Guignard, who imbued in him a lifelong love of the French language, literature, drama and history. A charming man, an intelligent instructor and pleasant companion, Guignard was much more congenial than the well-meaning, but less likeable, Dr Lüders. His tutelage fostered a benevolent disposition in his pupil towards France that was to survive the duplicity that the family were to suffer from that country only thirty years later.

Prince Constantine came of age in 1884, on his sixteenth birthday. Henceforth, until his accession to the throne, he was recognized as the *Diadoch*, or successor. Although he had been Crown Prince by birth, until coming of age no special favours or distinctions had been paid to him that were not meted out to his brothers.

King George was by nature a strict disciplinarian. A sense of orderliness made it difficult for him to reconcile himself to the impulsive, irregular, slap-happy ways of his subjects. To instil some kind of discipline into his heir, he fought down the Glucksburg antipathy towards Prussia – for it had been Bismarck's Prussia which had gone to war against Denmark with such devastating effect in 1864 – and in 1884 he sent Crown Prince Constantine to study political economy at the University of Leipzig with Dr Lüders.

Later he attended Heidelberg University, where he shared a room and became close friends with his cousin Prince Albert Victor of Wales, who was four years his senior. Of the two, Crown Prince Constantine cut a more imposing figure and left with a better scholastic record; for 'Eddy' was a lethargic, backward individual who proved virtually ineducable, an unpromising soldier, and whose dissipated lifestyle weakened his constitution to such an extent that he readily succumbed to an influenza epidemic at the age of twenty-eight.

The princesses were educated by governesses and professors from the university, with special teachers for music and painting. They were trained as strictly as their brothers, for schoolroom discipline was supervised by the King. 'His keen eyes never seemed to miss anything', Prince Christopher recalled. 'No use for us to try to slip away from tedious Court functions, hoping to have a quiet little smoke in the corridor, for his eagle eye would detect some stealthy movement behind him and he would call to us just as we were reaching the door. His eyes would twinkle as we sneaked sheepishly back again.'[10]

During these years King George and Queen Olga also played host to their nephews from England, Princes Albert Victor and George of Wales. During an extensive cruise on HMS *Bacchante*, the young men stopped at Greece on their return journey back to England, sailing into the Piraeus in May 1882 to spend ten carefree days with the family at the palace and Tatoi.

From then onwards the future King George V of Britain was always devoted to his Glucksburg relations at Athens, in particular his Aunt Olga, whose affection and sense of humour made her virtually a second mother to him. When he teased her about her 'nautical entertainments', her open house for Russian sailors, she scolded him for not appreciating her friends as 'Russian sailors were all angels'. Without hesitation he retorted, 'Sailors are never angels. Some women are, but damned few!'

In June 1887 Queen Victoria celebrated her Jubilee. King George, Queen Olga, Crown Prince Constantine and Prince George were among the galaxy of European royalty who flocked to London. Among other guests were the German Crown Prince and Princess Frederick William, whose third daughter, Princess Sophie, was shortly to become part of the first family of Athens. 'Willy has brought with him two gigantic sons',[11] Queen Victoria noted in her journal (20 June). That evening, at the 'large family dinner' in Buckingham Palace, King George had the honour of sitting on her right, while his father, King Christian IX, was on her left.

On the following day the procession to Westminster Abbey took place. For the service of thanksgiving afterwards, King George and Queen Olga sat with the other foreign sovereigns on the right of the gilt throne in the choir, while their son in naval uniform was with foreign princes and princesses on the left.

At that time Prince George of Wales was serving in the Mediterranean naval station. Although he saw much of another uncle and aunt, the Duke and Duchess of Edinburgh – the Duke was then Commander-in-Chief at the Mediterranean – he was invariably homesick. Soon after Christmas 1887 he was granted the privilege of spending 'ten perfect days' with the royal family at Athens.

The invitation met with mutterings of disapproval from Queen Victoria, possibly because she feared that her grandson might imbibe his parents' pro-Greek, anti-German prejudices. 'Why may I not go and see Uncle Willy if you and Papa wish me to?' he wrote indignantly to the Princess of Wales (2 February 1888). 'It is the greatest bosh I ever heard.'[12] 'Bosh' or not, the visit went ahead, with Uncle Willy and Aunt Olga delighted to have him back, albeit for a short time. He particularly enjoyed the company of his cousins Alix and 'little Minny', who introduced him to figure-skating and painted headings for his notepaper. Though he was not musically-minded, they constantly engaged him in duets and part-songs with them. When the ten days were over he found the parting 'hateful'. In later years he would write regularly to his cousins Prince George and Prince Nicholas, and to Uncle Willy, who would address him with such written Danish endearments as *gamle pølse* ('my dear old sausage'), and *gamle sylte* ('my dear old pickled pork')[13].

Though King George could never hope to match the scale of Queen Victoria's Jubilee celebrations, he was proud when the kingdom came to mark the twenty-fifth anniversary of his own accession in the autumn of 1888, with an orgy of flag-waving, flower-throwing, fireworks, national dancing and other events.

Among the guests who came from abroad were the King's eldest brother Frederick, Crown Prince of Denmark; his brother-in-law the Prince of Wales; the Duke and Duchess of Edinburgh, who would have been celebrating the Jubilee of King Alfred of the Hellenes if the voters had had their way in 1862; and Queen Olga's cousins, the Grand Dukes Serge and Paul of Russia. The harbour and Gulf of Salamis were filled with warships from most of the maritime nations of the world. Djevad Pasha came at the head of a special Embassy from the Sultan of Turkey, ready for once to show goodwill to Greece, bringing two splendid Arab horses with jewelled trappings as a gift for the King, and the Shefakat Order in brilliants for Queen Olga.

Envoys came from England, France, Germany, Italy, Roumania, Serbia, and the Vatican, all bearing autograph letters of congratulation from their sovereigns. A thanksgiving service was held in the Cathedral at Athens, and the Municipal Council entertained the guests of Greece at a luncheon presided over by the royal family. Other court functions included legation balls, torchlight processions and illuminations, gala performances in the theatres, parades and reviews, royal salutes from mighty squadrons in the Gulf of Salamis, and from warships in the harbour.

At this time the first impending break in the family circle was announced. One of the Romanov guests, Grand Duke Paul, was there for a special reason. A younger brother of Tsar Alexander III and a constant guest at Athens and Tatoi for some years past, he had become engaged to the King's daughter Princess Alexandra. Another Glucksburg bond with one of the great thrones of Europe was being forged, with the King of the Hellenes's daughter about to become sister-in-law of the Tsar.

The wedding took place at St Petersburg eight months later, in the Chapel of the Winter Palace, with all the traditional glory attendant on an imperial Grand Ducal marriage. At the ceremony Princes Constantine, George and Nicholas acted as their sister's groomsmen, an important role in the Orthodox ritual for the bride had no bridesmaids, and it was the responsibility of the groomsmen to support the principals during the ceremony and hold the symbolic crowns above the heads of bride and bridegroom.

All the family went to Russia, not without sadness, for Alexandra, the most restrained member of the family, was a particular favourite of her parents. It was fortunate that none of them could foresee that the married life of this delicate Princess was to be tragically brief.

CHAPTER FOUR

'A good heart and good character'

While in Germany, Crown Prince Constantine of the Hellenes became deeply attached to Princess Sophie. The third daughter of Crown Prince and Princess Frederick William, son-in-law and eldest daughter of Queen Victoria, they were an enlightened, liberal couple, in principle opposed to much of what Bismarck stood for.

Tragically, just as the health of ninety-year-old Emperor William began to decline, it became apparent that Crown Prince Frederick William, his only son, also had little time left. During Queen Victoria's Jubilee celebrations in June 1887, it was well known at court that he was seriously ill with cancer of the throat. On medical advice he refrained from returning to Germany during autumn and winter, staying instead in the warmer climate of Toblach and San Remo, on the Riviera. His condition steadily deteriorated and a tracheotomy left him unable to speak. His father died on 9 March 1888 and he returned to Berlin as Emperor Frederick III, dying on 15 June.

The Emperor's illness had exacerbated the tragedy of his wife, now the widowed Empress Frederick, distrusted if not actively detested by Bismarck and the court clique which had cleverly turned her eldest son, now Emperor William II, against his parents. The perpetual support of her three youngest daughters, Victoria, Sophie and Margaret, had often been her only consolation. It was therefore with mixed feelings that the Empress viewed Sophie's betrothal to Crown Prince Constantine, announced on 3 September. 'If only the bridegroom were not so young,' she wrote in her diary, 'and Greece so far away and one of the elements in the unsolved and dangerous Eastern question! He is very nice and charming and well brought up.'[1]

Queen Victoria had no such reservations. Writing from Balmoral the following day to express her 'satisfaction' at the news, she wrote glowingly that 'Tino', 'a good, steady young man . . . comes from, and belongs to,

47

loving parents and a very united, loving family. And this is a priceless blessing. A good heart and good character after all go far beyond great cleverness.'[2]

After the wedding of Grand Duke Paul to Princess Alexandra the following year, the family went to Fredensborg for one of the Danish family reunions. Joining them for the first time, the Empress was interested to see the family at close range and reported in a letter to Queen Victoria (13 September 1889):

> Dear Tino and Georgy are certainly the finest of the young men, and also the most intelligent. Alix of Greece was sweet and dear, but like wax, so terribly anaemic. She and Paul seem very happy. The noise they all made, and the wild romps they had were simply indescribable . . . Once or twice I was obliged to laugh right out when they were all carrying each other. It was certainly a very novel and original sight, very absurd sometimes, and they seemed happier and to enjoy themselves more thoroughly than children of five or six. Tino and Georgy are as strong as two young Hercules! I only wonder no arms or legs were broken. The Queen of Denmark's furniture must be unusually strong – one sofa, I believe, had to have the springs renewed at different times . . .[3]

It was ironic that the Empress Frederick harboured such reservations on the instability of the Greek throne. Though her worst fears for her daughter were to be realized, her forebodings about her eldest son's behaviour as German Emperor would also bear bitter fruit in time. The Greek throne would outlast the German.

The wedding of Crown Prince Constantine to Princess Sophie of Prussia on 27 October 1889 was the first great international occasion in the history of modern Greece. It was a wedding which united five ruling houses – those of Greece, Germany, Denmark, Britain and Russia. The Danish contingent was headed by King Christian and Queen Louise; the British by the Prince and Princess of Wales; the Russian by the Tsarevich, Nicholas; and the German by Emperor William II, bringing with him the largest suite of all, plus the Empress Frederick, her eldest daughter and son-in-law, Prince and Princess Bernard of Saxe-Meiningen, her younger son, Prince Henry, and her unmarried daughters.

Athens was richly decorated with flags and wreaths of laurel leaves with words of welcome to the bride displayed on all the main buildings. The streets from the palace to the Cathedral were covered with a brilliant carpet of peasant costumes. Business was much neglected, as everyone took advantage of what was almost an unofficial public holiday. The anxious police took the precaution of asking the troops to keep a watchful if unobtrusive eye on proceedings, for good-natured crowd management was outside their experience.

Preparations for the wedding had given King George and Queen Olga many a problem. Unlike the other great European capital cities, Greece had no tradition of splendid royal ceremonial. King George was not particularly interested in royal pageantry, which in any case was beyond his limited means, but he felt obliged to provide some kind of grand spectacle for the benefit of his guests. It would certainly be expected, especially by the German Emperor and the Prince of Wales.

Royal and imperial guests and the key members of their suites were lodged at the palace, but many other distinguished guests and members of suites had to be found accommodation. Queen Olga suggested that they should ask private citizens in Athens. The response was enthusiastic and offers to lodge and entertain foreign guests poured into the palace. Perhaps some of the guests would not find the standard of entertainment they expected, but the offers were gratefully received.

Supplying enough coaches and horses was another difficulty. The King had a secondhand eighteenth-century state coach, which was allotted to the bride and groom, and some state carriages of varying condition, horses, grooms and footmen were promised. Yet there were still too few and he had to ask the Athens hackney carriage proprietors to help. At last the quota was complete and a strange collection of vehicles, with some very odd-looking coachmen and attendants, mustered in Kifissia Square for registration and inspection.

On one point, at least, the King was fortunate. A search in the palace storeroom revealed large bales of the blue and silver court liveries, enough for all the hired coachmen and attendants. But the fit of many of these splendid liveries fell far short of what was desired. The artistic Prince Nicholas scanned the long processions of carriages and drivers with disfavour on the wedding day. The appearance of many, in clothes that were either too large or too tight, was a sight impossible to forget. How fortunate, he recalled in his memoirs less than forty years later, that the cinema did not exist at that time to record the scene for posterity.

The wedding was a suitably spectacular affair. Ablaze with jewels and orders, the royalties drove in their borrowed carriages through sunlit streets to the new Orthodox Cathedral. The Crown Prince's best men were his brothers Prince George and Nicholas and his Russian cousin Nicholas, the Tsarevich; Sophie's bridesmen were her brother Prince Henry and her British cousins, Princes Albert Victor and George of Wales. The Tsarevich complained to his mother that these bridal attendants were 'half dead from the heat'.

To the Protestant members of the family the long ceremony seemed very theatrical, with hundreds of flickering candles, incense, jewel-studded icons, bearded and mitred bishops, and the crowns held high above the bridal couple, each holding a lighted taper as they walked three times round the altar. As Princess Sophie had not yet been converted to Orthodoxy, this sumptuous ceremony was followed by a short, simple Protestant service in King George's private palace chapel.

After a gala luncheon, the bride changed from her lavishly embroidered gown into a dress of white and gold. The couple drove to the little rented villa in Kifissia Road, close to the palace, which was to be their first home. To the Empress Frederick, it was 'a tiny place, smaller than Osborne Cottage (a good deal), but light and cheerful and comfortable – arranged like a little French villa.'[4]

That night there was an immense firework display in Athens, and the Parthenon blazed above the city in red fire, which changed suddenly to green.

The enthusiasm for the bride and groom was evident, particularly as the Greeks saw their marriage as another step towards the realization of their country's destiny. On his birth, Crown Prince Constantine had been hailed as the successor to the last Emperor of Byzantium. By taking as his bride a Princess Sophie, whose name was synonymous with that of St Sophia in Constantinople, Greece would surely once again know greatness. The 'Great Idea' would become a reality; how long would it be before all the Hellenic peoples would live, free and united, in a new Byzantium?

Nine months after the wedding, the Crown Princess of the Hellenes gave birth to a son. The Empress Frederick had arranged to be with her daughter for the birth, expected at the end of July. Events, however, forestalled her and she was at Gibraltar when she was told that the Crown Princess had given birth to a son prematurely at Tatoi on 19 July. Queen Olga arrived at Athens from Russia two days after the confinement, and the Empress at the end of July, bringing her two youngest daughters,

Princesses Victoria and Margaret. The infant prince, second in succession to the throne, was christened George on 18 August.

A fierce quarrel was soon to disrupt family harmony. Early in November the Crown Prince and Princess came to Berlin to attend the wedding of her elder sister, Princess Victoria of Prussia, to Prince Adolf of Schaumburg-Lippe. The Crown Princess had decided that, as wife of the heir to the throne, she would enter the Greek Orthodox Church.

She had intended to inform her brother Emperor William, as head of the family, of her decision. But he heard before she could tell him personally, and shortly before her sister's wedding she received a command from Dona, the Empress, to come and see her at once. Primed by the Emperor, the priggish Dona (who was expecting her sixth child) told her that, as head of the Lutheran Church, William would never agree to her changing her religion. If Sophie disobeyed him, she would 'end up in hell'.

Sophie told her to mind her own business and walked out in disgust. The Emperor angrily called on his mother to give her an ultimatum to the effect that, if Sophie entered the Greek Church without his permission, he would forbid her to set foot in Germany again. The quarrel cast a shadow over the wedding, held in the Schloss chapel, at Homburg.

He telegraphed to King George of Greece that 'Should she persist in her intention, I shall no longer regard her as a member of my family and will never again receive her. I beg you, as far as in your power, to dissuade her from her intention.'[5] The King replied with great restraint that he did not feel justified in influencing his daughter-in-law. Though too tactful to do so, he would have been entitled to point out that she was now not only married but also a Greek subject, and no longer under the orders of her elder brother. King George, the Empress Frederick wrote to her daughter, 'has the best of the argument, and I admire him for being so gentle and moderate, in spite of such provocation.'[6]

Sophie had never liked her brother and cared nothing for his outbursts. The Empress Frederick asked her to write him a conciliatory letter explaining her reasons for adopting the Greek faith. When he still would not give way, she sent her mother an open telegram saying: 'Received answer, keeps to what he said in Berlin, fixes it to three years. Mad. Never mind. Sophie.'[7]

The Emperor William's sixth son, Prince Joachim, had been born three weeks prematurely on 17 December 1890. Although the baby thrived, the father continued to nurse a grievance against his sister. Almost five months later he was complaining hysterically to Queen Victoria that if 'my poor baby dies it is solely Sophie's fault and she has murdered it'.[8]

The Greek royal family's annual holiday in Denmark, at Fredensborg, in the summer of 1891 was overshadowed by bad news from Russia. King George's beloved daughter, Grand Duchess Paul, was seven months pregnant with a second child when she became seriously ill. King George and Queen Olga hurried to her bedside and were just in time to see her breathe her last. After being in a coma for six days, she gave birth to a son, named Dmitri, and then died. King George, who had been particularly devoted to her, was distraught at her death.

The rest of the family followed later in a special funeral train. For three days and three nights the train rocked its way across Europe from Copenhagen to Moscow, where the body of the Grand Duchess lay covered by a cloth of gold lined with ermine in a special hall at the station. The coffin was put aboard the train and carried on to St Petersburg for burial. For several months after their return to Athens, King George and his family remained in mourning and no entertainments were held at the palace.

The 1890s were an unhappy time for the family. In January 1892 the King's nephew Prince Albert Victor, Duke of Clarence, died of influenza at Sandringham. Although the demise of this chronically backward, dissipated young man was a blessing in disguise for the British monarchy, King George knew how devoted the Princess of Wales had been to her eldest son, and he feared quite rightly that she would never really get over the tragedy.

The Duke of Clarence's brother, Prince George, was likewise devastated by the loss of his brother to whom he had been so devoted. Created Duke of York in May 1892, he took a long time to reconcile himself to events, not least the realization that as second in line to the throne he would have to leave his beloved Royal Navy. Early in 1893 the Princess of Wales took him with her on a Mediterranean cruise to visit her relations in Greece, her excuse being that he needed 'a complete change and rest before settling down in life', although she really wanted to have him to herself for a while before he married and was no longer hers any more.

Their visit to Athens gave them a disturbing insight into life at the court of King George. He had inherited one of the family failings: all the Danish royal family were inclined to treat their children as children, even when they were adults and had families of their own.

The Princess later poured her heart out to the Empress Frederick, who recounted much of the conversation in a letter to her youngest daughter, Princess Frederick Charles of Hesse (9 March 1893); King George, she said, 'does not & cannot remember that his sons are grown up now! He does not take them into his confidence . . . the consequence is that they are very bitter, and have become very antagonistic to him.' Crown Prince Constantine was never kept informed and had been 'unjustly used'. The King, thought the Princess of Wales, was a good father but 'rather tyrannical in the family'; when the sons were together or talking to Queen Olga, 'the moment he comes in the conversation ceases & every one is silent, or that they get up and go away.' Queen Olga was so upset at this state of affairs that she feared there would soon be two parties in the kingdom, one for the King and the other for his sons.[9]

For some years the King had kept a diary containing a detailed record of all he did, people he had seen, and conversations with them. One day he told his sons casually that he had burnt it. Aghast, they told him that he had thus destroyed an important document. He retorted that he did not wish to speak about himself, and any written record of private conversations might compromise other people.

Politics were taboo *en famille*, whether at home in Greece or on family reunions in Denmark. This golden rule had prevailed at the court of Queen Victoria ever since the contentious issue of the Schleswig-Holstein duchies in 1863 had provoked bitter verbal exchanges between the Prince and Princess of Wales on one hand, and Crown Prince and Princess Frederick William of Prussia on the other. King Christian IX (coincidentally the loser in the war which broke out a few weeks later over the ownership of the duchies) always took a similar line. When King George and his children were staying with him one summer during the late 1890s, somebody unwisely tried to bring up the potentially explosive subjects of the Dreyfus affair and Fashoda. In deference to Prince Waldemar and his wife Marie, daughter of the Duc de Chartres, the topic of conversation was swiftly changed.

A similar reticence marked family gatherings at Athens and Tatoi. King George never allowed family or friends to criticize his ministers in his presence. Only from the time of Crown Prince Constantine's marriage onwards would he ever discuss politics with him, as his eldest son and successor, and even then he retained a certain reserve. Legal provision had been made, shortly after his marriage, for the Crown Prince to act as Regent in King George's absence from Greece, on the understanding that both men could never be away from Greece at once. It was a measure which had the objectives of allowing the King to pay longer visits to Denmark and France with a clear conscience, and giving the *Diadoch* more chance to become acquainted with the machinery of government.

Nevertheless, King George's reserve hindered the Crown Prince's political experience and knowledge in his preparation for the throne. 'In later years,' Prince Nicholas wrote, 'this habit acted often as a brake on any desire we might have had to speak to our father with absolute frankness on political matters.'[10]

However, the last decade of the nineteenth century saw some positive achievements in Greece which her far-sighted King was quick to encourage. In August 1893 he opened the canal across the isthmus of Corinth, which had been under construction for eleven years. The opening of the canal cut the sea voyage from the Adriatic ports to the Piraeus by over 150 miles, revived trading communities along the Gulf of Corinth and helped to save ships from the frequently stormy waters off Cape Matapan.

A couple of years later the ancient tradition of the Olympic Games was revived. The first modern Olympiad was staged in the autumn of 1896 at Athens, with Crown Prince Constantine as President. King George had decided not to invite any foreign sovereigns to the festivities, as he could not face a repetition of the organization prior to that which had bedevilled him at the wedding of his eldest son.

Yet one insisted on coming. King Alexander of Serbia declared he had a confidential matter to discuss. King George had been warned that the King was after the hand of his daughter Princess Marie in marriage. She was unofficially engaged to one of her Russian cousins, Grand Duke George, but nothing could yet be said about this. King Alexander was accordingly invited under duress, but he made himself anything but welcome. At the youthful age of twenty he was surely the ugliest sovereign of his time, with his stumpy hooked nose, long thin neck, closely-cropped hair and weak gimlet eyes that peered through his pince-nez. These physical shortcomings were matched by his lack of moral reputation and his irritating habit of perpetually asking his hosts questions while watching the games.

When Spyros Louy, a shepherd who lived 7 miles from Athens, ran barefoot into the stadium to win the gruelling Marathon race, the spectators gave him an overwhelming reception. King George stood up to cheer with boyish enthusiasm befitting that of a man half his age. 'What nationality is the victor?' asked King Alexander. King George answered curtly that, judging by the cheers of the crowd, he must be either a Turk or a Bulgarian – but such sarcasm was lost on his slow-witted guest. Prince George, who at 6 foot 6 inches was known as 'the tallest Prince in Christendom', and his brothers all hurried down from the stadium to run beside Louy for the last thousand yards.

The Olympic Games were a triumph for Greece and boosted national pride. Yet such pride was a dangerous prelude to the perpetual demands of Greek subjects, still intent on freeing those of their countrymen still living under Turkish rule. In the event, the immediate result was the most severe crisis of King George's long reign.

The island of Crete, lying south of the Greek mainland, was the focus for discontent. Turkish-ruled Crete had a large and unresigned Greek population, in almost constant rebellion against Turkish misrule. Following the addition of Thessaly and a small part of Epirus to their kingdom, the Greeks were determined to liberate the rest of Epirus, and the whole of Macedonia and Crete, Homer's 'island of a hundred cities'.

Though the Sultan went some way towards recognizing their grievances, by appointing a Christian governor and making other concessions to his non-Muslim subjects, they were not appeased. In 1897 the majority of the Cretan people, most of whom were of Greek extraction, were Christians and desired union with Greece. The population of Crete numbered about 270,000, of whom no more than 70,000 were of the Moslem faith and thus looking for Turkish protection. The Sultan of Turkey had granted a large measure of autonomy to Crete in 1889, but later revoked the Pact of Halepa. The Armenian massacres of 1895 and 1896 had raised Cretan hopes that Europe might intervene on their behalf, but they were disappointed when the Powers instead sent warships to Crete to dissuade the Greeks from joining the islanders.

In January 1897 a more serious rebellion swept throughout the island. Macedonia was inhabited not only by Greeks and Moslem Turks, but also by peoples of Bulgar and Serb extraction. Macedonia thus became a focal point of Greek-Turkish dissension, and the cockpit of Balkan rivalries. In espousing the cause of Crete, the Greeks hoped to add not only that island but also Macedonia to the kingdom.

King George despatched a Greek force, under the command of his second son Prince George, who had received his naval training in

Denmark, to support the insurgents in their demands that Crete should be absorbed into the kingdom of the Hellenes and take possession of the island. Again, the Powers tried to smother the Cretan insurrection and prevent the Greeks from setting the Balkans alight. On 25 February 1897 the Powers announced their intention of giving Crete an autonomous administration under nominal Turkish suzerainty, and demanded that both Turkey and Greece evacuate their troops from the island. The Sultan was ready to comply, the Greeks were not.

Greece was spoiling for a full-scale war. King George counselled moderation, hoping that the matter would be settled peacefully, and the family were behind him. 'Nothing is so costly as war!' the Empress Frederick wrote to her daughter, the Crown Princess. 'Greece is beginning to develop and prosper after centuries of oppression and neglect. War would devour her slender means and throw her back.'[11]

Rather recklessly the Greek Prime Minister, Theodore Delyannis, urged on by his impatient colleagues and some of the army officers, sent fifteen hundred armed volunteers to sail from the Piraeus to Crete.

The allied Admirals in Cretan waters recommended that not only Crete but all major Greek ports should be blockaded. Britain agreed in principle, but refrained from sending warships to join those of the continental powers in the blockade. In the event the latter had no stomach either for the blockade of the Greek ports. The British decision left it open to them to send warships to Greece. They refrained from doing so, and thus the last chance of preserving peace vanished. Greek troops crossed the Thessalian frontier and on 17 April 1897 the Sultan declared war.

King George appreciated just how unprepared Greece was for an armed campaign, but in their patriotic fervour his people did not. The distraught Empress Frederick wrote to Queen Victoria (18 April):

Greece and the King were much in the position of a man whose home is set fire to and, the doors all being locked, he has to jump out of the window even at the risk of breaking his neck. They seem to have tried their outmost to prevent it . . . What my feelings are when I read of the encouragement given to Turkey by Germany and the German officers in the Turkish Army, you can imagine . . . Alas, William's personal hatred to Greece and enmity to the King and whole royal family is well known everywhere and does not improve matters. The Turks are a fearful foe, not for Russians or European troops, but for the Greeks. They are like wild beasts in their cruelty . . .[12]

Prince William of Denmark as a naval cadet, c. 1860

The entry of King George I into Athens, October 1863

The Royal Palace, Athens, from a pen and ink sketch by Prince Nicholas

Iron tray, c. 1875–80, showing King George I shortly after his accession

King George I and Queen Olga and their nephews, Prince Albert Victor and Prince George of Wales, 1882

Ceramic soup tureen commemorating the marriage of King George I to Grand Duchess Olga, 1867

Ceramic plate, probably issued to commemorate the wedding of Crown Prince Constantine to Princess Sophie, 1889. Their portraits flank those of King George I and Queen Olga; around the rim are medallions of the King's Prime Ministers

King George I, Queen Olga and their children, c. 1887. Standing at back: Prince Nicholas, Prince George, Crown Prince Constantine, Princess Alexandra. Standing at front: Princess Marie, Prince Andrew

HAMLET AT ATHENS.

KING GEORGE (*Prince of Denmark*).

"THE TIME IS OUT OF JOINT; O CURSED SPITE!
THAT EVER I WAS BORN TO SET IT RIGHT!"

'Hamlet at Athens' from Punch, *8 May 1897. As the artist observed, both King George and Shakespeare's tragic hero were Princes of Denmark*

King George I in later life

Prince George, c. 1900

Crown Prince Constantine

Crown Princess Sophie

The Greeks themselves surged in hysterical crowds throughout the streets of Athens, roaring patriotic songs and cheering themselves hoarse for the King. The ill-equipped Greek army had been reinforced by volunteers who streamed out from Athens to the front with ill-assorted weapons. Men marched across the Northern frontiers, under Crown Prince Constantine as a very reluctant Commander-in-Chief, commanding an army without a plan of campaign, already spread thinly along a difficult frontier, dominated by a numerous and experienced foe, superior in both organization and numbers. A flotilla under Prince George sailed to Crete to cut off Turkish reinforcements, and a force of Greek volunteers landed on the island.

The attempt to invade Turkish territory was a disaster. The Crown Prince's forces were driven back into Thessaly and his headquarters at Larisa were overrun by the Turks. By the end of April 1897 the Greek military position was hopeless and the war was irretrievably lost. Two short battles in the following month ended the campaign.

It was largely the efforts of the Prince of Wales, persuaded by his distressed wife, which converted Lord Salisbury towards adopting a firmly pro-Hellenic point of view. Both agreed that Germany held more influence with Turkey than any other European nation, and it was only right that the German Emperor should be encouraged to champion his sister's interests. When pressed, he let it be known that, notwithstanding family ties, it was internationally incorrect for him to interfere unless Greece requested him to do so.

Salisbury informed Queen Victoria that he hoped King George was 'in no real danger; and that the dynasty is safe', but blamed the 'fatuous' conduct of the Greeks, who refused to ask for mediation. Yet on 8 May the Queen sent a telegram to the German Emperor: 'For the sake of humanity an armistice must be proposed without delay, or thousands of lives will be sacrificed. Do what you can to urge the Powers to propose this for both contending parties. You have always expressed great regard for my advice; let me therefore urge this on you.'[13]

Flattered that his grandmother should plead with him, he reported to her the following week that 'after the King and the Government had begged for my intervention through Sophy', and after having officially notified to his minister and again through his sister that they unconditionally accepted the conditions he had proposed, he had ordered Baron Hans von Plessen, German Minister in Greece, to take necessary steps to restore peace in conjunction with the representatives of the other Powers.

Nothing could happen quickly enough for the Princess of Wales. On 18 May, reported the Queen's lady-in-waiting, Marie Mallet, the Princess 'came down last night in an awful stew about Greece, imploring the Queen to do something to stop the war and stay the hand of the triumphant Turks.'[14]

By this time King George had acknowledged the scale of his country's defeat and agreed to an armistice, involving the withdrawal of Greek troops from Crete and a complete ceasefire.

King George's dynastic affiliations proved some guarantee to his subjects that the Powers would not permit Turkey to inflict a crushing defeat on them. Peace terms were ratified by the Sultan in December 1897. Greece was ordered to pay an indemnity of approximately £4,000,000 to Turkey; minor frontier modifications were made, in Turkey's favour, but arranged so that no Christians who had not been Turkish subjects before the war should come under Turkey's rule. British policy ruled out any annexation of Greek territory by Turkey except for minor frontier rectifications. Crete was not handed back to direct Turkish administration, but remained under the occupation of the six Powers for another year.

Thanks largely to the intervention of the Prince of Wales and Tsar Nicholas II, Britain and the Powers had spared Greece from the worst consequences of defeat. British public opinion had always been overwhelmingly pro-Greek, chiefly because of continuing Turkish attacks on the Armenian population of the Ottoman Empire.

In June 1897 Britain was in the throes of celebrating Queen Victoria's Diamond Jubilee, and the Women's Liberal Federation formally protested to Lord Salisbury against the visit of a Turkish envoy to the festivities. The German Emperor was informed by the family that his presence in London for the Jubilee would not be welcome, ostensibly because the ageing Queen wished to make it primarily a celebration of British imperial glory and restrict guests from royal and imperial Europe, but in fact because he was particularly unpopular for openly championing Turkey in the struggle. Unknown to the public, Emperor William had privately expressed to the family how much he pitied Crown Prince Constantine, and would have gladly lent Prussian officers as instructors to the ill-prepared Greek army. This, the Empress Frederick told her daughter, 'was really nicely and kindly meant'. Nevertheless, as far as the public was concerned he was still aggressively anti-Greek.

Late in October 1897 a subdued Greek army returned to garrisons for demobilization; and Prince Nicholas, bringing the remains of his battery back to Athens, was not the only commanding officer who timed his return to reach barracks in the dead of night, to attract the least possible publicity.

The crowds in Athens, who had wildly applauded their reluctant King at the outbreak of war, now suddenly turned against him and the royal family. He was held responsible for the war which he had been powerless to prevent in the first place, while the hapless Crown Prince Constantine and his German-born wife were also blamed. They were jeered at and spat on in the streets and there were demands for him to be court-martialled. There were rumours that he was to retire into exile for a short cooling-off period.

This unpopularity, which marked the nadir of King George's fortunes during his reign, was dispelled by an alarming incident which proved a blessing in disguise. One February afternoon in 1898 King George and his daughter Princess Marie were driving in an open carriage as usual. Suddenly there came the crack of rifle shots from a clump of bushes and bullets zipped over the carriage. The coachman whipped the horses into a gallop, but it was several minutes before they were out of effective range of the marksman. King George ordered Marie to lie on the floor and stood up, defying his attacker as a clear target, until the bullets ceased to follow them. One footman was slightly wounded in the leg, but otherwise the shaken party were unhurt.

The news of this attempt on the King's life, and his brave conduct, spread like wildfire. A wave of furious indignation swept Greece. Suddenly the royal family were acclaimed as eagerly as they had been vilified. Messages of sympathy and congratulation on the escape poured into the palace, and a public subscription raised sufficient funds to build a church on the site of the ambush. The man responsible, Kardzitis, declared that he had no confederates. On his arrest he said that he wanted to shoot the King because he considered him responsible for Greece's defeat and humiliation. He was found guilty and executed. Crown Prince Constantine was reappointed Commander-in-Chief.

After an outbreak of violence on Crete in September 1898, during which the British vice-consul and some British soldiers were killed, the Powers ordered Turkish troops to leave the island. Tsar Nicholas II proposed Prince George as Governor-General of Crete, under the sovereignty of the Sultan. The Prince and Princess of Wales welcomed the idea with enthusiasm. Turkey and the remaining European powers all agreed, with the exception of Germany. Prince George, maintained the Emperor, was a 'tool' of Marlborough House, and could not be trusted. The Emperor wrote angrily to the Tsar, who filed the letters away calmly without taking any notice.

In December Prince George landed in Crete to take up his post amid scenes of demented enthusiasm. He was to be given a three-years' trial by the Powers. As a young man he had often been singled out rather cruelly as the idiot of the family. To be entrusted with such responsibility was a personal triumph, although even his most fervent well-wishers had few illusions that he would be able to make a success of such a contentious appointment.

In the summer of 1898 Queen Louise of Denmark, King George's eighty-year-old mother, became seriously ill and he came to stay with her. She spent most of her days out of doors; one of her sons would wheel her in her bath chair into the rose garden, where she liked to see and smell her flowers, even though she could no longer cut them herself. Her daughters waited on her with biscuits and jugs of milk. One day the Princess of Wales was carrying a tray of refreshments, a pekinese following at her heels. Prince Nicholas ran into it on his bicycle and it howled with pain. 'He has killed my dog!' the Princess shouted, dropping her tray in fury and hobbling after it. When they saw that the dog was not injured, Prince Nicholas gave a faithful imitation of her screams of distress and her limp. It reduced her to fits of laughter, and much to his embarrassment she asked him to repeat the performance *ad infinitum* until everybody had seen it.

Queen Louise rallied during August, but the following month she had a relapse. King George telegraphed for the rest of his family, who arrived just in time. Her son, daughter and husband took it in turns to hold her hand as she slipped away peacefully on 29 September 1898.

In March 1900, at the age of twenty-four, King George's second daughter, Princess Marie, was married to Grand Duke George, cousin of the Tsar. A passionate patriot, she refused to go to Russia for the ceremony, which took place at the Church of the Fortress in Corfu. The guests included Tsar Nicholas II and the Tsarina, and King George's sister, the widowed Dowager Tsarina. While there, the rest of the family were rather perturbed to hear rumours that 'Nicky' was now entirely ruled by his mother, who was said to be the real Tsar, and that 'Alicky' feared and detested her mother-in-law, who seemed to conduct her conversations over and through the silent Tsarina. Such family conflict did not help Grand Duchess George to love or respect her husband's country, and she continued to spend much of her time in Greece and Britain.

The next of the family to be married was Prince Nicholas. He had been a regular visitor to Marlborough House and Sandringham, where he was entertained by the Prince and Princess of Wales. At one time he had become rather fond of his cousin, Princess Maud, the youngest and most vivacious of the rather apathetic, listless Wales princesses, and was disappointed when she married another cousin, Prince Charles of Denmark.* Her rejection of him he attributed lightheartedly to the fact that, during an argument at Fredensborg, she had hit him with a bag full of dried peas and he had answered in kind with his walking stick, a retaliation which had sent her running tearfully to her enraged father, who told him in no uncertain terms that he must never hit a lady. All the same, he and Crown Prince Constantine were among guests at their wedding in London in 1896.

He did not share his sister's dislike of Russia; on the contrary, he was devoted to the country. On one visit he became betrothed to Grand Duchess Helen and they were married at Tsarskoe Selo in August 1902.

Prince Andrew would not be long in following their example. The third, and according to Meriel Buchanan,† the best-looking of all King George's sons, he was attached to the Hessian 23rd Dragoon Guards for training at Darmstadt. While serving there he became quite attached to Princess Alice, eldest daughter of Prince and Princess Louis of Battenberg. She was a striking young woman, though profoundly deaf since childhood. They became engaged in London, while Alice was staying with Queen Alexandra in April 1903, and six months later were married at Darmstadt. Among the sights converging on the church, it was agreed afterwards that none was more splendid than that of their Greek Majesties, with a military escort and three four-horsed carriages.

Meanwhile the succession in Greece was secure. The Crown Prince and Princess had three children by the end of the nineteenth century: George, born in July 1890, had been followed by Alexander (August

---

* Later King Haakon VII of Norway.
† Daughter of Sir George Buchanan, *Chargé d'Affaires* at Darmstadt and later British Ambassador at St Petersburg.

1893) and Helen (May 1896); two more followed during the first decade of the twentieth, a third son Paul (December 1901), and a second daughter, Irene (February 1904).

The elder children were particular favourites of their grandmother in Germany, the Empress Frederick. Whenever Crown Princess Sophie took them to stay at Friedrichshof, they were allowed to run riot. In her old age the Dowager Duchess of Brunswick, born Princess Victoria Louise of Prussia, the only daughter of Emperor William II, recalled with a tinge of jealousy how her Hellenic cousins were permitted to do whatever they wanted in front of their Grandmama. Even using her best silver tea trays as sleighs to slide downstairs was not frowned upon. One day 'Georgie' found some cowbells in the park; all the young cousins hung them up and made 'a fearful din'. Victoria Louise and her brothers knew instinctively that, had they taken the initiative in such a prank themselves, they would have been punished, but as the much-indulged Greek grandchildren were responsible, nothing happened.[15]

For all his love of making a noise, Prince George was inclined to be a serious-minded child, as if conscious of his destiny as the eldest son of a Crown Prince. The others were noticeably more extroverted, and Helen was something of a tomboy, being especially fond of swimming, gymnastics, riding and cycling.

Prince Alexander generally took the initiative in any mischievous escapades. One favourite game was to smoke cigarettes made of blotting paper; another was to fling cupfuls of petrol against the walls of their playroom and set it alight, thankfully without any harmful results. The only occasion on which they did any damage was when they filled several watering cans in the garden and brought them upstairs to sprinkle the 'lawn', which was actually the green carpet in their playroom. Water soon dripped through the ceiling and servants had to mount stepladders in the room below to puncture holes in the ceiling and let the water out.

All the children loved riding toy haycarts in the grounds at Tatoi, as their father and uncles had done. One summer day, when Paul was aged about three, they were coasting down a hill, Alexander steering the cart with his feet, and gaining speed every second. Suddenly the cart gave a sickening lurch and plunged off the track, dropping six feet into a tangle of bracken and bramble. A deathly silence ensued and Helen was terrified that Paul had been killed. Much to her relief he soon rallied, and let out such angry screams that the Crown Prince and Princess came running to see what all the fuss was about.

CHAPTER FIVE

'Steadfast obedience to the call of duty'

With the death at Osborne in 1901 of Queen Victoria (at whose funeral he represented his country), King George of the Hellenes had reigned longer than any other European sovereign except for Emperor Francis Joseph of Austria. His stature had increased with the passing years and he was warmly respected by all his fellow crowned heads. He continued to spend a few weeks each year in Denmark, where his brother ascended the throne as King Frederick VIII on the death of King Christian IX in January 1906, and every autumn he was a welcome guest of Emperor Francis Joseph at Vienna.

Relations with his brother-in-law, now King Edward VII, remained as cordial as ever, and King George shared in the general concern when King Edward's Coronation was postponed in June 1902 while he underwent an operation for appendicitis. Writing to wish him well (2 November 1902) for his birthday the following week, King George wrote:

When the passing year brought terrible moments of anxiety to us all concerning your precious life, we also had splendid proofs of your people's great loyalty and sincere love towards their King, which must have given you great satisfaction and comforted you during your dangerous illness and recovering. May God bless and protect you and grant you many many happy returns for your own happiness and for the satisfaction and content of your admirable and loyal people. I need not say that my thoughts never left you since I heard the beginning of your sufferings, and I thanked the Almighty from all my heart, when He gave you strength to go through that most dangerous operation, and made you strong and healthy after. Let me now thank you most sincerely for the splendid large golden medal, which Tino brought me as well as for the small silver coronation medal which you were kind enough to let Alix give me.[1]

In 1905 King George paid an official visit to London. Accompanied by Prince and Princess Nicholas of Greece, he arrived at Portsmouth on 13 November. Sir Frederick Ponsonby, King Edward VII's equerry, was appointed to look after them. He found King George 'a charming man, very shrewd, with a thorough knowledge of European politics and quite conscious of the slender ties that bound him to the throne of Greece.'[2] His buoyancy and naturalness charmed everybody. Climbing into a carriage beside the King, Ponsonby suddenly saw that, contrary to continental tradition, he would be sitting on the right, instead of the left, of the visiting monarch. 'Sit down,' King George ordered him, 'I know you don't have any nonsense of that sort in England.'[3]

A state banquet in St George's Hall, Windsor, the evening after their arrival was followed the next day by luncheon at the Guildhall, London. In his speech to the Lord Mayor, the King recalled previous visits to the capital, and also the fact that 'the liberation of Greece has inspired some of the most brilliant pages of your literature and the most glorious achievements of your diplomacy.' Like Great Britain, he went on, Greece 'looks to peace as the best guarantee of her progress, and, were it not that I am speaking in the capital of a Monarch whose reign will ever be memorable for the work of pacification which he has achieved, I should be tempted to say that I yield to no European Sovereign in my love of peace.'[4]

In March 1906 King Edward and Queen Alexandra came to visit the King at Athens. King Christian IX, a widower for seven years, had died in January at the age of eighty-seven. His death was scarcely unexpected, but the Queen felt 'very low' for several weeks and longed to be with her brother at this time of bereavement. The family gathering was joined early in April by the Prince and Princess of Wales, who were on their way home from India.

On their arrival King George appointed his brother-in-law an Honorary Admiral of the Greek Fleet. Though there were few honours and orders which had not already been conferred on him, King Edward was always keen to receive more.

Their time in Athens coincided with the Olympic Games, and naturally the King and Queen took great interest in the participation of British athletes. The stadium had been completely rebuilt in marble, and was crowded with spectators.

Queen Alexandra was asked to present the prizes. One of the victors, who had won a trophy in the shooting contests, was Metaxas, the court architect. When King George introduced him to the Queen, she spoke to him briefly in English. As he did not understand her, he assumed she was paying him a compliment and thanked her profusely. Turning to Prince Nicholas, who was standing nearby, Metaxas asked him to translate her words. To his astonishment it turned out that she had said, 'I am very pleased to meet you – my brother's house is falling to pieces.'⁵ The day before, when talking to King George on the palace verandah, a small piece of plaster had come loose from the ceiling and fallen on her dress.

Though King Edward was keen to avoid any controversial subjects as far as possible on what was mainly a family visit, one political issue had to be discussed – the presence of an international force in Crete. King Edward was insistent that British troops should not be withdrawn from the island. Prince George, he pointed out, 'leans on England more than any other country – and especially for advice'.⁶

Prince George's stewardship of Crete as the High Commissioner, which had been due to expire in 1901 but was renewed for a further ten years, was no easy task. While the majority of representatives in the Cretan Assembly were committed to union with Greece, a vociferous minority party aimed for the island's complete independence. It was led by the ambitious Eleutherios Venizelos, who was shortly to become a persistent thorn in the side of the Greek monarchy. Born in October 1863 (within a few days of King George's arrival at Athens) of Turkish, Jewish and Armenian descent, Venizelos, according to Prince Christopher, was 'a shabby young man with a fox-like smile and an amazing gift of oratory and a still greater gift of putting other people in his pocket'.⁷ He was a convincing talker, with an agile mind and a gift for convincing people who did not immediately agree with him.

Most of the Cretans found Prince George as affable and fair-minded as the father he so resembled in looks. Only a small minority of politicians, notably Venizelos and his followers, found fault with his 'arbitrary' rule. Unhappily their criticism was taken as gospel truth abroad. British troops remained on Crete for a time, but Britain and other countries were ready to believe that his high-handed rule was responsible for any trouble on the island. 'Prince George of Greece out-Sultans the Sultan', blazed one British press headline.

In March 1906 Sir Charles Hardinge reported that it was becoming difficult to maintain order on the island. He was unaware of Venizelos's subtle campaign of propaganda, in denigrating their royal representative as a useful factor in his party's independence campaign. As a Greek patriot, who supported the absorption of Crete into the kingdom of Greece, Prince George was anathema to him. Fanning the flames of rebellion, the independence party found it easy enough to persuade the Powers that their royal governor was to blame for Cretan unrest.

King George had every sympathy with his son, but as a model constitutional monarch, he felt unable to defend him against overwhelming ministerial disapproval. He was evidently all too aware of adopting what might be misinterpreted as arbitrary measures. Unfair though it seemed, he saw no alternative but for his son to resign his post of High Commissioner before matters in Crete became too dangerous.

Though it was a matter of sadness to him as well, King Edward had to agree. Three months later Prince George resigned his post, and the appointment of a former Prime Minister of the Hellenes helped to restore tranquillity to the island. King George was grateful to King Edward for his support with the problem. Prince George took it bitterly, and disillusioned with his homeland he retired to Paris, though he continued to spend part of each year in Greece. He soon found contentment; in 1908 he married Princess Marie Bonaparte, a great-great-niece of Napoleon I.

Though he kept his opinions to himself on the matter, the King had always shared the family's antipathy to Emperor William. In addition to the grievance which the Danish royal family harboured against the Hohenzollerns (the late Emperor and Empress Frederick excepted) for the war of 1864, he had deeply resented the Emperor's bullying behaviour towards his mother and youngest sisters. It therefore took considerable magnanimity on his part to entertain the Emperor on the regular April visits he made from 1907 onwards to the Achilleion, Corfu, which he had purchased from Emperor Francis Joseph, who had built it for his restless peripatetic Empress Elizabeth.

King George generally arranged to be at Corfu at the same time as the Emperor, or else arrive a day or two before him. Queen Olga, knowing there was not much love lost between them, once asked why he felt obliged to go to Corfu to meet the Emperor. 'If I don't,' the King replied, 'he'll think he's the King of Greece.'[8]

King George was as unimpressed by the Emperor's bombastic speeches as most of their contemporaries. After reading with some amusement a newspaper report of one of His Imperial Majesty's addresses extolling the Divine Right of Kings and the use of the 'royal mailed fist', he asked an aide for his opinion of the speech. 'I have heard of better speeches, Your Majesty', the man answered tactfully. 'Yes, but have you heard of any worse?' the King smiled.[9]

The Emperor always described his stay in Corfu as 'my favourite way of leading the simple life', though his hosts considered it anything but simple. He invariably brought with him an army of generals, equerries and military aides. Every motor drive was a procession of imperial cars, the All-Highest leading, followed by countless members of his suite. Queen Olga loathed heights and nothing would ever induce her to drive over the mountain roads. She was eternally sympathetic towards an elderly general, who she was told emitted such piercing screams from the last car, rounding a corner, that the Emperor heard him every time.

Just as marked was the impression the two regularly visiting crowned heads made on the children of Crown Prince Constantine. When King Edward VII and Queen Alexandra brought the royal yacht to Corfu, the ships' officers would always organize lively games for the children in the wardroom, and join in the fun themselves. On Emperor William's yacht there was less fun to be had, Princess Helen recalled, 'for the officers were not encouraged to indulge in undignified romping'.[10]

King George's own favourite holiday destination, outside Denmark, was Aix-les-Bains. He spent some time in France on his way to and from Denmark whenever possible. Like his brother-in-law in London, he had great admiration for the French. Xavier Paoli, whose duty it was to ensure his safety on French soil, considered him the most Parisian of foreign royals, in the elegant ease with which he spoke the language and 'in his turn of mind, which is essentially that of the man-about-town'. The citizens of Aix declared at one stage that there were only two sights worth seeing at the town – the Municipal Gardens, and the King of the Hellenes. His name figured everywhere as the patron of local concerts, balls and charities, and in shop windows his photograph was to be seen far more frequently than that of the President of the French Republic.

To the people of Aix, their most illustrious visitor was *'Monsieur le Roi'*. The laundresses, who worked in the open-air wash-houses which he strolled past on his way to the baths, always greeted him as *'Monsieur Georges'*. The King evidently had an ulterior motive for walking past their premises, for according to custom the laundresses provided what the more censorious described as 'a show of undraped bust and limbs' as they worked. The municipal council decided at one stage that the King of the Hellenes might be offended by the sight and issued orders to the girls to dress with more circumspection. The next time he walked past he was greeted gloomily by a group of familiar faces in unusually modest dress. At once he assured the Mayor that local customs should in no way be altered for his benefit, doubtless omitting to add that the 'cover-up' order had certainly not been for his benefit. The following day he was greeted with delighted cries of '*Vive Monsieur Georges!*' and the customary display of 'busts and limbs'.

King George's regular *pied-à-terre* in Paris was the Hotel Bristol. Afternoons would be spent on the boulevards, and at night, after dinner, he would visit the gaming rooms or theatre. Again, like his brother-in-law, he had a keen eye for actresses. No sovereign, it was suggested, 'aroused more affectionate curiosity in female circles than King George'.

Crete was at the centre of the next crisis during King George's reign. In July 1908 the Young Turks revolted in Macedonia. A counter-revolution in Constantinople led by conservative leaders loyal to the Sultan was overthrown by the military, and the Ottoman Empire was left in temporary chaos. Their Balkan neighbours and the Powers of Europe were quick to take advantage in various ways of the confusion: Austria annexed Bosnia and Herzegovina; and Prince Ferdinand of Bulgaria, proclaiming his country an independent sovereign state, assumed the title of Tsar.

At the same time, the Powers began to withdraw their troops from Crete, and in October 1908 the Cretan Assembly proclaimed the island's union with Greece. Motivated by the spirit of the 'Great Idea', and even more so by the glittering prize of high office, Venizelos abandoned his pro-independence views and fully championed the move. Yet the Powers would not rescind their agreement with Turkey that the island should remain under the sovereignty of the Sultan, much to the chagrin of the Greeks and most of the Cretans themselves.

Disaffection with this state of affairs came to a head in August 1909 when a group of disgruntled army officers in Athens, taking advantage of recent events elsewhere in the Balkans, announced the formation of a Military League and demanded the resignation of Dimitrios Rallis and his government. They declared that they were 'animated by feelings of the utmost devotion to the King and the Constitution', and that their main purpose was to reform and improve administration of the services.

However, the King was alarmed when they demanded a bill providing for a number of measures, including a request that the Crown Prince and all the royal princes – including the *Diadoch* – should be relieved of their army commissions. This move, they asserted, was for their own good; they were being relieved of responsibilities likely to injure their prestige, and in order to avert the discord and hatred which personal favouritism and the sympathies of the princes would inevitably have engendered among officers serving under them. To save their father the humiliation of having to sign warrants for their dismissal, they immediately resigned.

King George swallowed his pride and accepted, but he revealed the full measure of his bitterness to a newspaper correspondent some weeks later. It was humiliating for him, he said, to be forced by a military body to deprive his sons of their rank, for no other reason than that of their royal blood. In the demands for reform, he thought he detected 'a distinctly anti-dynastic movement', though it was some consolation to know that the majority of his subjects were faithful to him and his family. He promised to place himself at the head of any genuine reform movement, provided the constitution was safeguarded; reform, he insisted, must be brought about only by constitutional methods.

Not only the military made him feel bitter; he considered that the Powers had let him down by failing to back the union of Crete with Greece, on which his subjects had pinned their hopes, and none more so than the British government. In his blackest moods he even considered abdicating, but he knew that to step down from the throne in response to such a crisis would mean the ruin of Greece, the collapse of political stability, and the instant disappearance of such little sympathy as the Powers still had for the country.

The crisis lasted till December, when a minor but totally unforeseen incident played into the King's hands. A few days before Christmas he gave an audience to the leader of the Military League, General Zorbas, in which he regretted that the military leaders had not frankly confided their views to him from the start. On being told that the army and fleet still had the greatest confidence in him, he said that he would continue to discharge the duty of a constitutional monarch, as he had done for the last forty-six years, devoting himself to the welfare of his people, whose well-being was his only aim. Later that day Zorbas consulted with the other members of the Military League council, and on returning to the palace, told the King that they wanted to install a *Cabinet d'Affaires* in place of the present ministry.

This was in effect threatening an outright military dictatorship, and the King refused even to look at the list of persons from whom the Colonel suggested he could choose a Cabinet. The government had not resigned and there was no valid reason for discussing the question of a change of ministry. With this, the League knew that the King was determined to defend the constitution and their only hope lay in a *coup d'état*. Troops were confined to barracks, sealed orders were issued to their commanders, and there were fears of a coup overnight. The situation was defused by the revelation that Colonel Lapathiotis, Minister for War, had sent to the state printing press a list of promotions for a large number of officers. Zorbas and his council colleagues deemed the time ill-chosen, and Lapathiotis was dismissed. The League, somewhat chastened, withdrew their demands, and order was restored.

Several months later the Military League decided to place their trust in Venizelos, who persuaded King George to summon a National Assembly to revise the constitution, which met in September 1910. The Military League agreed to its own dissolution, Venizelos became Prime Minister, and Crown Prince Constantine was reinstated as Commander-in-Chief.

Venizelos was fired with the spirit of the 'Great Idea'. Once he had become Prime Minister, he applied himself to two important tasks: the revision of the constitution and the reorganization of the army. If Greece was once again to know greatness, she must have a stable government and a strong army. King and Prime Minister were united in their belief that the humiliating defeat of the Greco-Turkish war of 1897 must be avenged. Greece must prepare for war.

As Commander-in-Chief, Crown Prince Constantine devoted himself to military preparations, while Venizelos applied himself to the diplomatic. Before she could face Turkey on the battlefield again, Greece must come to an understanding with her Christian neighbours, Bulgaria and Serbia. By the summer of 1912 Venizelos had arranged military alliances between the three Balkan states, and by the autumn they were ready for war.

The Prime Minister and the King-in-waiting made an ideal partnership. Venizelos proclaimed that he had perfect faith in him, telling parliament in June 1911 that he considered the Crown Prince to have 'exceptional military abilities such as few senior officers possess'. In the past the ambitious politician had shown that he had less than total respect for the royal family, and he would do so again without scruple; but he was ready to acknowledge not only the Crown Prince's military abilities, but also his prestige and popularity among other officers in the armed forces.

Indeed, Prince Constantine was dedicated to the army. His admiration for the military prowess of Germany, where he had received his training as a young man, was undimmed. After the Greek military humiliation of 1897, he resolved privately that never again would his country's fighting forces be found wanting. He despised Greek officers who had fallen short of such standards and, being reluctant to suffer fools gladly, he was inclined to make enemies among those who did not share his unswerving devotion to the task.

At the same time he harboured no blind admiration for Germany. To his personal dislike of the German Emperor William was added the latter's partisanship of Turkey during the previous war, and the open knowledge that Turkish officers were also trained by a sympathetic Germany. His admiration for the German Reich, tempered with a perfectly justified questioning attitude towards the country's foreign policy, was to cost him dearly in the future.

King George returned from his Danish holiday, to the gathering storm at Athens, on 9 October 1912. Queen Alexandra was horrified by a rumour that the British were about to occupy Crete, 'one of the most unfair acts England could do towards Greece'. In distress she reminded her son King George V that 'England put my brother there and are bound to keep him there.'[11] He was given a tremendous welcome as he came back to his kingdom, but the mood of the people was very different from what it had been fifteen years before. This time the Athenian crowd was serious, restrained, filled with a sense of national purpose and harbouring no illusions of easy victory.

Montenegro declared war on Turkey on 8 October, Serbia and Bulgaria followed with the dispatch of 'unacceptable' ultimata, and massive concentrations of troops on their frontiers. Turkey declared war on them on 17 October, and Greece declared war on Turkey the following morning.

Remembering what had happened the last time his troops had crossed the Thessalian frontier, King George accepted the need for a war of liberation with some reluctance. He was too old for active campaigning, but he was tireless in carrying out the duties of inspecting troops, visiting hospitals, and keeping up morale.

Under the command of Crown Prince Constantine, the army bore little resemblance to the enthusiastic but inept force of 1897. Well trained and equipped, with the best artillery in the Balkans, it conformed to good discipline. The allied force consisted of 120,000 Greeks, 400,000 Serbians and 500,000 Bulgars. Against the larger but less organized Turkish forces, it won one victory after another.

In November 1912 Salonika, the capital of Macedonia, which had been ruled by the Turks for over four hundred years, was liberated. Crown Prince Constantine, with his brothers and eldest sons, Princes George and Alexander, now junior officers attached to their father's staff, rode into the city at the head of the First Division, and the whole army followed behind, with torn and mud-smeared colours borne before each battalion. The mounted head of the great column clattered into the city and the Greek inhabitants swept forward around their Crown Prince, weeping, dancing and screaming. When he sat on his horse before the Konak Palace, the whole army paraded past him. As he entered the palace, the Turkish governor handed over his sword. It was the most glorious moment in the history of modern Greece.

The disappointed Bulgars had promised themselves Salonika, and it had never occurred to them that the Greeks might arrive there first. The Bulgarian Commander-in-Chief, General Theodorov, declared that since the Bulgars and the Greeks were allies, they ought to occupy jointly the eastern and western halves of Salonika. Crown Prince Constantine replied tactfully but firmly that, by the laws of war, a city fell to the control of the first conqueror to enter it; under the circumstances he could not permit the Bulgarian forces to enter Salonika, but if the Bulgarian princes or General Theodorov himself wished for shelter, he willingly offered it to them.

The highly sensitive dispute was saved by the arrival of King George on 12 November. He realized that the Powers were perturbed by the delicacy of the situation, and that moves might be made to cajole the Greeks to leave the city in order to appease Bulgaria. However, he had decided that the triumph belonged to Greece. If he stayed firm in Salonika, it would be difficult to move him.

Followed by Crown Prince Constantine and Venizelos, the King rode in triumph though the acclaiming streets. The great victory was celebrated with a *Te Deum* in the Byzantine Cathedral, and he took up residence in a detached villa about 2 miles from the harbour and centre of the city, looking out on the sea across the road where the tramway ran.

In Athens he had always walked around the streets unguarded by detectives, with just an aide for company. He proposed to do the same in Salonika. It was a bold decision, for Salonika was a polyglot city, with not only Greeks, but also Bulgars and Turks, who detested the sight of any Greek. Although apparently oblivious to the dangers, he was persuaded to take two members of his Greek bodyguard, following discreetly a dozen yards behind. Nearly every afternoon he would stroll along the road, which took him past the headquarters of the Bulgarian army.

Queen Olga and her daughters-in-law, Helen and Alice, came to Salonika to help with hospital organization. They spent much of their time travelling between Athens and Salonika, every mile of the way by Greek train, as King George proudly pointed out to everyone.

On 19 December 1912 Tsar Ferdinand of Bulgaria arrived in the city. He was determined to show King George that he was not coming as a guest; on the contrary, he considered he had an equal right to Salonika. He left the train at a station nearby and drove rapidly by car to the Bulgarian Consulate in the city. He had planned to take the Greek King and Crown Prince by surprise, but they were warned of his approach. When told that he was inspecting Bulgarian troops outside their headquarters, King George announced that they must go there to receive him.

It was a clever piece of one-upmanship, and Ferdinand received them with good grace. He had evidently conceded defeat for the time being, and the monarchs had lunch and a private conference next day. During the meal, noted Prince Nicholas, Tsar Ferdinand 'charmed us with the elegance of his speech, his wit and rare intelligence; both his erudition and historical knowledge are remarkable.'

The sovereigns avoided the delicate question about who was to have Salonika. More forward than her husband, Queen Olga endeavoured to persuade Ferdinand firmly that Salonika would have to form an integral part of the Greek dominions. Tactfully, Ferdinand remarked that it would be a matter for future discussion between their respective governments.

In January 1913 Crown Prince Constantine, who had acted as governor of Salonika, decided to take command of the Greek forces in Epirus, where the fighting against the Turks was not prospering. King George asked Prince Nicholas to become the new governor of Salonika. It was the Prince's first taste of responsibility and it would have been difficult to find a harder one. The city was inhabited by so many nationalities, including Turks with whom the Greeks were still at war, as well as the large Bulgarian army, who were proving increasingly intractable. Under Constantine's command, Janina, the capital of Epirus, fell to the Greeks. Turkey was defeated; Constantinople and its outskirts remained its only European possession.

In this time of triumph for Greece, King George felt that many of the disappointments of his reign had been balanced. He was full of optimism for the future; a time of peace and prosperity seemed assured. The war was coming to an end, and it was agreed that the three small daughters of Prince and Princess Nicholas could safely come and join their parents in Salonika.

Captain Walter Christmas, a close friend and later his first biographer, was astonished at the change in the King, whom he had last seen sitting in his summer house at Copenhagen the day before he left for Athens during the previous autumn. Then, he had looked unusually careworn:

> His face was scored with deep lines on each side of the mouth, and his clear blue eyes, usually so lively, were veiled in the deepest gravity, almost in melancholy. Now [at Salonika] I saw before me a slight, active figure, with the elasticity of youth, dressed in a tight-fitting khaki uniform; the face beamed with pleasure, the eyes sparkled with life, and about the mouth, half-hidden by the fair moustache, played the smile I remembered so well, in which kind-heartedness, humour and a hint of good-natured mockery were wonderfully combined.[12]

The multi-lingual King George could move with ease in conversation from Greek to Danish, English, German, or French, as the occasion demanded. It was a particularly valuable asset when he wanted to make announcements to assembled company which needed to be kept a secret from some people. At lunch on 18 March 1913 he told his sons in English – which none of the Greek officers present understood – that in October he would celebrate the Golden Jubilee of his reign. Already the people of Athens were preparing to mark the anniversary in fitting style. Continuing in Danish, he said that he would take advantage of the occasion to abdicate. Fifty years was long enough for any King and he felt he was entitled to a little rest in his last years. Prince Constantine, he continued, had gained considerable popularity at home and abroad as a military commander; he was the right age to ascend the throne; and 'he possesses a vigour I can no longer boast of'.

That afternoon the King took his customary stroll through Salonika, accompanied only by his equerry, Colonel Frangoudi, with two Cretan gendarmes following a few yards behind. Walking through the busy, crowded streets, they passed a small, rather squalid café, the 'Pasha Liman', from which emerged a ragged man, looking at them closely as they passed. At the old White Tower, which marked the end of their walk, the King and his equerry turned. The man was still there when they passed the café a couple of hours later, at around five o'clock in the afternoon. As they did so, he pulled a revolver from his pocket and shot King George in the back, at a distance of less than a yard away. He was taken at once to the nearest hospital, but death had been almost instantaneous.

Frangoudi seized the assailant by the throat, disarmed him and held on to him until two policemen arrived. Meanwhile Prince Nicholas, who had had lunch with his father, was the first member of the family to be informed. He was sitting in the garden behind the palace when he was amazed to see a private soldier running down the path. The man was sweating and appeared frantic. Nicholas's instant reaction was amazement that he had got past the guards. Indignantly he got to his feet, when the soldier shouted breathlessly, 'They have struck the King!'

Instinctively he knew at once that the worst had happened. Another thought was uppermost in his mind: had a Bulgar been responsible? Whatever the assassin's nationality, the Greeks would surely believe it was an aggrieved Bulgarian and the last thing they wanted was for innocent citizens in Salonika, of any country, to be slaughtered in a wave of revenge. When he and the soldier reached the scene of the attack, they found people standing around a pool of blood, while Greek soldiers were running about in all directions, brandishing revolvers and bayonets. A policeman assured him that the murderer was a Greek, and Prince Nicholas instructed an officer to announce the news publicly.

The man, named Alexander Schinas, declared on arrest that he had killed the King because he refused a demand to give him some money. He was variously reported to be mentally deranged and perhaps an alcoholic as well. It was widely believed that he had been a tool of the Bulgarians or perhaps the young Turks. On 6 May, while awaiting trial, he committed suicide by throwing himself out of a window on the second floor of the Prefecture.

After leaving the scene, Prince Nicholas hastened to the hospital where his father's body lay. To him fell the melancholy task of informing the rest of the family.

King Constantine, as he now became, was at the army headquarters in Janina when he received a telegram telling him the news. His youngest brother Prince Christopher was with him. They went to Athens immediately, where the new King solemnly took the oath of allegiance to the constitution, and then left for Salonika on the royal yacht. In a proclamation to the army, he announced that 'The impious outrage upon the sacred person of the King deprives us all of our leader in moments very critical for the whole Hellenic nation. I am now called by Providence to succeed my father of imperishable memory on the throne on which he had so long shed lustre and honour.'[13]

Venizelos accompanied them, and Prince Christopher, who sat next to him at meals, had to fight down his distaste for the man. It was difficult, he later recalled, 'to reconcile his loud protestations of sympathy with his fox-like smile and certain aspects of my father's death.'[14]

The previous evening the brothers had had a strange experience which they could never explain. A lady attached to the Red Cross in Janina was interested in spiritualism and persuaded them to take part in an experiment in automatic writing. The three of them sat at a table covered by a large sheet of white paper. For over half an hour they waited solemnly for something to happen. Suddenly the pencil which Christopher and the lady were holding between them gave a violent jerk and began to write. It flew over the paper at such a rate that they could hardly keep their fingers on it, then it stopped abruptly. A message was left for Constantine, promising him fame and glory, the winning of two wars, and after that much sorrow. Below it was written the word 'Death' several times, and then 'Tomorrow'. The rest was illegible. The following day, King George was assassinated.

Crown Princess (now Queen) Sophie, seven months pregnant, was resting quietly on a sofa when a Marshal of the Court came to tell her. At first she feared that something had happened to her husband, until he told her that 'His Majesty has met with a serious injury.' Instinctively she realized that her father-in-law was dead. Accompanied by her daughter Princess Helen, she went at once to the palace to comfort Queen Olga, who wept quietly, saying that it was the will of God.

At eleven o'clock that night Prince Nicholas and a small group of generals carried the body of King George on a stretcher from Salonika hospital to the palace. He lay uncovered in his uniform so that the people might see him as he passed slowly along. As they walked down the road in the dim light of the street lamps, all the doors were open and the householders of many nationalities in a kind of dreadful awe knelt outside with lighted candles in their hands.

Queen Olga was summoned from Athens, and King Constantine from the war zone. At the site of the murder, the widowed Queen had a simple shrine set up and in it she lit a lamp to the memory of the husband whom she had helped through so many troubles. All the family gathered to accompany the King's body as it was carried back to Athens by sea.

For three days the coffin, draped in the Greek and Danish flags, lay in state in the Metropolitan Cathedral. It was then taken to his beloved Tatoi. Half a mile from the summer palace rose a little hill known as Palaeolcastro, from which King George and Queen Olga had often watched the sun set over the plain of Attica. On this hill, which King George had chosen as his last resting-place, a chapel was being built; Queen Olga had always feared that as soon as this mausoleum was completed, death would find an occupant for it. Here, King George was buried.

'Too horrible, I was devoted to him & he will be a great loss to Greece', King George V noted in his diary after hearing the news at Windsor. 'Motherdear [Queen Alexandra] is fearfully upset by this fresh sorrow.'[15]

As Queen Mary observed, at Marlborough House Queen Alexandra was 'in a great state of mind at the death of her favourite brother'.[16] However, when a Danish friend sent her an enormous laurel wreath, asking her to arrange for it to be laid on the King's tomb, practical considerations prevailed. 'Too much trouble to send it out to Greece,' she told one of her manservants, 'put it on dear little Beauty's grave in the garden.'[17] Beauty was a favourite pekinese dog who had recently died and been buried in the garden at Sandringham.

Throughout Europe, tributes were paid to the sovereign who had reigned for nearly half a century over a country where few had held out much hope of success for him. In London, *The Times* wrote:

The tragedy of his death at the hand of an assassin is heightened by the fact that he has been slain in the hour of victory – of victory in great part due to his sagacity and to his steadfast obedience to the call of duty. We have but to contrast the place which Greece holds in Europe today with that which she held a very few years back to realize what she owes to the judgment, the firmness, and the self-abnegation of the King whom she has lost.[18]

CHAPTER SIX

'A beautiful and longed-for summer'

By the assassination of King George, the Greeks lost a trusted sovereign, whose moderating influence had helped his factious subjects to work in harmony, and whose insight into foreign politics had been of inestimable use to his ministers. In his place, they gained one who lacked his father's experience in statecraft and perhaps his tolerant outlook, but who had two important advantages – his Orthodox faith, and the fact that he was a Greek by birth. Moreover, he bore the name of the founder and last Emperor of Byzantium. Many hoped, if not expected, that he would acknowledge Greek aspirations by taking the title of Constantine XII.

In one field – the military – he had had more experience than his father. Having been made a scapegoat by the Military League for Greek reverses in the short and inglorious war against Turkey in 1897, he had learned the lesson well. As the conflict of 1912 had shown him, if not the nation as well, the moral was that military undertakings should never be attempted without adequate and efficient forces. When he ascended the throne, his military prestige stood high, and the country regarded him with pride and affection as the man who had already realized some of their most cherished dreams.

It was inevitable that the Bulgarian army would attempt to attack the Greeks before long. The Greek army was concentrated around Salonika in readiness, when the Bulgars struck without warning in total darkness on 29 June. Had they succeeded, they might have left Bulgaria as the supreme and unchallenged power in the Balkans; but instead it brought the country swift, overwhelming disaster. The Graeco-Serbian military agreement, which had started with a private meeting at Salonika between Prince Nicholas and Crown Prince Alexander of Serbia just before the death of King George, was initially intended as a bulwark against the threat of Bulgarian aggression; it had led to a firm understanding at the peace conference called by the Powers in the spring after the defeat of

Turkey. Between them, Greece and Serbia took advantage of the powerful bargaining position which their united front had given them, to lay claim to territory to which Bulgaria felt herself entitled. As a result of Venizelos's demands, Salonika and its environs were confirmed as part of Greece, and most of the Aegean Islands were added to her territory as well.

The new Bulgarian attack came simultaneously in three areas: one against the Greek positions around Salonika, one against the Serbians in the north of Macedonia, and one in the middle to serve as a wedge between the Greeks and Serbians. Venizelos was shaken by the news, but he underestimated his King, who led his army against the Bulgarians and routed them in a battle at Kilkis. With Serbian and Roumanian forces also advancing on Bulgaria, her defeat was complete and she appealed to Tsar Nicholas II to mediate.

In August the war came to an end with an armistice signed at Bucharest. Greece had gained considerably from the two Balkan wars: Southern Epirus, Macedonia, and the islands of Crete and Samos, nearly doubled the size of her territory. Yet there were disappointments at the same time: two Greek islands in the Aegean Sea, Imbros and Tenedos, were reserved for the disposition of the Powers, while the Dodecanese remained in the 'temporary' possession of Italy; parts of Macedonia still belonged to Bulgaria, and the creation of a Bulgarian outlet to the sea was also a cause of Greek resentment; so was the establishment of the new kingdom of Albania, including the Greek-speaking area of northern Epirus, which the Greeks had actually occupied during the war.

None the less, Greek national pride was satisfied at having avenged the defeat of 1897. It was a good start to the reign of King Constantine I, who seemed more dynamic and purposeful, less aloof, than his father. By the summer of 1913 Greece had emerged as a significant Mediterranean power. Under the leadership of Venizelos, the hitherto elusive vision of the 'Great Idea' appeared to have moved beyond the vapourings of romantic nationalists to the realms of possibility.

When he returned to Athens on 5 August, in the dual role of conqueror and King and moreover one who had succeeded to the throne through personal tragedy, Constantine was given an emotional reception. Arriving at Phaleron on board his battle cruiser, *Averoff*, escorted by the entire Greek fleet with Prince George, the new *Diadoch*, they were met by Queen Sophie with state carriages and a display of fervent emotion from the huge crowds in Athens. Together, in an open landau, they drove through hysterically cheering crowds into the capital.

The scene which took place each time King Constantine passed one of the stands erected for the wounded soldiers was perfectly Hellenic. The King would rise in the carriage and rigidly salute the stand, and the troops supporting each other and waving hundreds of little flags wept and howled rather than cheered, tears pouring down their cheeks.

At the palace Queen Olga was waiting for her son. The crowds saw that, on this day of glory, she had put aside her black crepe and appeared clad from head to foot in white.

Aged forty-four at the time of his accession, King Constantine was quiet and restrained in character. By nature the military commander, cool and unruffled at all times, he was patient but determined, with a sense of purpose which was sometimes mistaken for obstinacy. He was popular with his soldiers, not least as he was said to have 'a full vocabulary of Greek oaths', which he did not hesitate to use when the occasion demanded.

Much as King George had been beloved and respected, he had long preserved a kind of patriarchal aloofness, which could not be penetrated by any Greek. Now the army recognized that they had a King who possessed the common touch, for King Constantine was renowned among his subjects for his courtesy and friendliness.

He was so popular at the beginning of his reign that hardly a dwelling in Greece did not have a coloured picture or a photograph of him, as a kind of holy icon. A piece of music, *The Son of the Eagle*, was composed in honour of his victories in the Balkan wars, and frequently played or sung in Greece during the first few months of his reign. He was persuaded to become *Koumbaros*, or godfather, to every sixth child born in his kingdom, and to every child born to the wife of one of his soldiers. In the Greek Orthodox Church the godfather assumed a relationship to the child and his or her parents that was spiritually closer than the tie of blood. Thus the parents, on meeting the King, would greet him 'with the unembarrassed friendliness of brotherly kinship'.

To every soldier who had served under him in the Balkan wars, he presented a photograph of himself. It showed him in a plain khaki uniform and dusty boots, smoking a cigarette. Each picture carried the handwritten inscription: 'To my gallant fellow soldiers of two glorious wars'. It was signed CONSTANTINE B. (the B, meaning King, always followed the royal name). To many of its enraptured recipients, this scrawled B looked more like IB, which in Greek numerals stood for XII.

Had he inadvertently or deliberately signed himself Constantine XII? Was he destined to fulfil the prophecy that forecast he would lead his people back to Constantinople and there, under the great dome of St Sofia, wear the imperial crown of Byzantium?

Among his brothers, the closest was Prince Nicholas, who was constantly at his side in the years of stress. With the burdens of kingship, it was inevitable that King Constantine and Queen Sophie should be at a distance from the rest of the family to some extent, but it was agreed that, whenever the family was in Athens, they should all gather at Nicholas's house for dinner on Tuesdays and at the palace on Thursdays.

King Constantine and Queen Sophie had moved into the new palace, built beyond the grounds of the old one. Crown Prince George, twenty-three years of age, went to live in his parents' old house in Kifissia Road. Here his frequent guest was his young uncle, Christopher. In age they were only two years apart. Christopher was rather taller, but otherwise they were physically similar, being dark, swarthy and monocled, dressed normally in tight army tunics. They were a popular spectacle as they walked about, almost invariably in step, and the object of affectionate amusement.

At the time of her husband's accession, Queen Sophie was expecting her sixth and last child. A third daughter, Katherine, was born on 4 May; all the officers and men of the two services became her godfathers.

The King and Queen lived very simply. In their limited spare time they were keen gardeners, and they converted the kitchen garden beside the palace into a model English country-house garden, with large lawns, cypress avenues, pergolas, ponds and herbaceous borders. The King prided himself on his knowledge of botany, while the Queen was particularly interested in arboriculture and made it one of her missions in life to help in the re-afforestation of Greece. Trees in the country were under constant threat from fires in summer and damage by wild goats, and she formed a society of which Prince Nicholas became Vice-President. Its aims were to organize nurseries from which young trees could be taken and planted in the countryside where needed, especially on the bare hills around Athens.

In addition Queen Sophie devoted herself to social welfare, taking a keen and active interest in hospitals, soup kitchens, district nursing, schools for domestic training, and kindergarten education. The Union of Greek Women owed much to her inspiration and encouragement.

For the first few, comparatively untroubled, months of King Constantine's reign, he and Venizelos appeared to be in perfect accord with each other. The Greeks seemed to have a well-matched partnership with which to steer the ship of state. Greece had had a king for the last eighty years, and despite the ignominious failure of King Otho it seemed that many of the aspirations of the Hellenes had at last been achieved. Large Greek communities still remained under 'alien' rule, but at this time nobody was impatient for further conquests. It was a time for consolidation. King, ministers and government alike were united in being intent on repairing the ravages of war, assimilating the newly acquired provinces and cementing national unity in an ambitious plan of reconstruction. All that was needed was a prolonged period of peace.

Unfortunately, a prelude to the troubles which were to pursue King Constantine for the rest of his life took place in the autumn of 1913. Within three weeks of returning to Greece, he travelled to Germany, as a personal guest of Emperor William II at the annual army manoeuvres. On 4 September he arrived in Munich, accompanied by Queen Sophie and most of their children. Queen Sophie and the four younger children went to stay at Friedrichshof, the large country mansion bequeathed by the Empress Frederick on her death in 1901 to her son-in-law and youngest daughter, Prince and Princess Frederick Charles of Hesse-Cassel.

King Constantine and Crown Prince George continued to Berlin. While there, the King hoped he might be able to negotiate a substantial loan for funds to develop the port of Salonika and to construct a railway northwards from Larissa into Greece's new territories. As the Germans were providing the Ottoman Empire with considerable capital, they were reluctant to help, and the German Foreign Ministry expressed no interest in aid to Greece. All the same, the optimistic King Constantine was keen to make a good impression on his hosts.

Emperor William was equally intent on turning the visit of his brother-in-law to advantage. All too conscious that the protecting Powers of Greece were also the three entente Powers, he appreciated the tactical value of attempting to create a partnership with Greece by flattering her King.

King Constantine had never had any warm feelings for the Emperor, since the fuss that had been made over the then Crown Princess Sophie changing her religion. Nevertheless, he was prepared to let bygones be bygones, and in his overwhelming desire to please everybody, he was totally unprepared for the trap set for him.

After dinner on the eve of the manoeuvres, the Emperor cordially invested him with the Order of the Black Eagle, presented him with an embossed leather case containing the baton of a German Field Marshal, and made him the Colonel of the 2nd Nassau Infantry Regiment. Crown Prince George, whose initial studies at the Greek Military Academy had been followed by two years with the 1st *Garderregiment zu Fuss*, interrupted by the outbreak of the Balkan war in 1912 and his return to join his father's staff, was simultaneously invested with the Grand Cross of the Order of the Red Eagle with Swords. Then came a congratulatory speech, in which the Emperor recalled proudly that His Majesty the King of the Hellenes was a pupil of the German military system, that he owed his success as a commander in the Balkan wars to that system, and, finally, that Germany surely had a valuable military ally in Greece in the years to come.

Taken by surprise, and discomfited at having to make an impromptu speech, yet flattered at the honour just paid him, King Constantine replied as tactfully and courteously as he could. He expressed his gratitude at such compliments, alluded to his military training in Germany, and referred to the experience and studies from which his own son and many Greek staff officers had profited in the German Empire. The observance of such courtesies between brother sovereigns was only to be expected.

The incident, which seemed harmless enough to the innocent King Constantine at the time, was blown up out of all proportion. A photograph of King Constantine in German Field-Marshal's uniform, complete with spiked helmet, was widely published alongside reports of his presence at manoeuvres with the Emperor and the German military high command. With it went a draft of his speech, the emphasis of the wording altered slightly by the wily Emperor. As the dinner and speeches had been made on a Saturday evening, it was regarded as significant that nothing was published in the press until Monday afternoon, thus allowing plenty of time for alteration. To this, King Constantine made no objection at the time. He could hardly have done otherwise.

In France the reaction was one of dismay. Government and official circles in Paris had been looking increasingly askance at the German Emperor's sabre-rattling and foreign policy initiatives. Twice in the last eight years, at Tangier in 1905 and at Agadir in 1911, his behaviour and words had brought the major European countries perilously close to war.

Moreover, they were disappointed that King Constantine had paid so much tribute to German military training in reply to the Emperor's speech, feeling he should have spoken more of France's share of guns and military organization in the Balkan victories over Turkey, who had drawn her military inspiration from Germany.

Even in Britain some people expressed regret that the nephew of Queen Alexandra, who hated the German Emperor more implacably than any other member of the royal family in England, should be seen apparently 'flirting' with the All-Highest. When chided by his secretary for having agreed to the draft, the King answered sadly, 'How was I supposed to know that the thing would be telegraphed all over Europe?' That King George V was also a German Field-Marshal, and Emperor William a British one, was conveniently overlooked.

As he was due to visit Paris later that month, the French attached no malice aforethought to his words, giving him the benefit of the doubt and regarding his behaviour as carelessness. It was hoped that his visit to their capital would help him to remove the impression produced by his Potsdam speech.

In Athens the official newspaper *Hestia* declared that, as the King was not accompanied by a responsible Greek minister, his pronouncements had no official bearing on government foreign policy. Greece's position, as far as her relationship with the rest of Europe, was one of 'absolute abstention from any dependence on either of the groups of the Great Powers; but such abstention does not exclude a feeling of gratitude towards those Powers which have supported the rights of Greece, and to the list of those Powers must now be added Germany.'[1]

Yet the debate about what King Constantine had actually said and intended continued to run and run. Trying to drive a wedge between France and Greece, the German press mischievously made matters worse by exploiting his speech and Greece's defensive reaction to it to the full, declaring that the King had made it clear that Germany and Greece had common aims and common enemies.

A week after the manoeuvres it was confirmed that he would arrive in Paris on 21 September, to be received by President Poincaré. A dinner to be given in his honour would

afford King Constantine an opportunity of completely effacing the impression made in France by his speech in reply to the Emperor William. General Danglis, the Greek representative of the French

Army Manoeuvres, in the course of conversation with a representative of the *Temps*, said that in his opinion King Constantine in declaring that the success of the Greek Army was due to German training was undoubtedly referring to the German tactics of the enveloping line adopted by the Greek Army at the battles of Sarandaporos and Yenidje-Vardar and finally at Yanina. The value of this method of attack was recognized by the French Army, as it had been used by General Chomer in these manoeuvres. Greece, he declared, could never be sufficiently grateful for the Services of the French Mission under General Eydoux.[2]

If this was meant to be an olive branch to the offended French, it did not have the required effect. On the following day the press announced a sudden change of plan for the Greek royal family. King Constantine would accompany Queen Sophie and the children to Eastbourne. This was in the nature of a private visit, for the young princes and princesses attended private schools there. Prince Paul, then aged eleven, had always been interested in the sea and was showing interest in a naval career. The King, who believed that, despite Germany's increasing naval strength, Britain still had the greatest navy in the world, wanted to find out whether he could send his youngest son as a cadet to Osborne or Dartmouth.

They arrived privately at Dover on 17 September and proceeded to Eastbourne, where Queen Sophie was to stay for a fortnight. The next day they received the Deputy Mayor and Chief Constable of Eastbourne.

On 19 September, two days earlier than scheduled, King Constantine arrived in Paris. Perhaps mindful of the possibility of angry demonstrations, the authorities had not revealed the exact date and hour of his arrival, and only on the announcement of his departure from London was it evident that he would be in Paris that evening. Only a few spectators were there to see him, and most were probably unaware of his identity. It was a modest start to what would be a low-key visit.

After attending morning service in the Greek Church at La Rue Bizet, Paris, on Sunday 21 September, the King went to the Elysée. At a lunch with Poincaré, toasts were cordially exchanged, in the course of which the French President said he trusted His Majesty would believe that France, 'whose feelings are unchangeable, will remain the loyal and true friend of Greece she has always been'. In his reply, King Constantine spoke effusively of France's assistance and active sympathy.

Yet the French papers next morning regarded the King's speech as colourless and lacking in the accents of enthusiasm and gratitude which France wished to hear, compared with his emphatic praise earlier that month of German military might. His speech was accepted as the ritual ending of an incident the effect of which, it was admitted with regret, had not been effaced by the King's 'stilted and laboured' phrases. The German press readily seized with scorn on French reaction, declaring that 'if there were in France anything like reasonableness they would be satisfied with the very friendly and conciliatory words in which the King replied to the certainly remarkably cordial words of M. Poincaré', and noting that the French appeared to expect from King Constantine 'a sort of apology, or at least an indirect correction of his Berlin speech'.[3]

The King's remaining days in Paris included nothing more spectacular than a private lunch with Prince Roland Bonaparte, his brother's father-in-law, and a meeting with Monsieur Pichon, the French Minister for Foreign Affairs, at the Quai d'Orsay that afternoon.

However, he was also given an opportunity to explain himself in an interview with *Temps*. Greece, he insisted, intended to follow a policy of firmness, frankness and independence. The friends of Greece, among whom the best was France, would be the first to advise her to adopt this course. Greece must be mistress of her own destiny and play her part for herself. The peace of Bucharest had shown her that the conditions of Near Eastern politics had been profoundly modified, and that Greece was able to deal directly with her interests. It was in this spirit that Greece intended to serve her sons. By doing so, she would respond to the general wishes of France, 'which had been the first at her cradle and which maintained a friendship the efficacy of which all Greeks joined with him in appreciating'.[4]

All the same, by the time the King returned to Athens at the end of September he was angry and disillusioned. With the best of intentions, by trying to be friendly and reasonable to all nations, he had unwittingly placed himself in a position where his most dependable allies did not altogether trust him. During the years ahead, when he most needed friends and allies, he would not find them; and France would take vengeance on Greece, and on King Constantine, with devastating effect.

Had King George not been so reticent with his sons about politics and affairs of state, King Constantine might not have been led so easily into the German Emperor's trap.

Despite this regrettable overture to the King's reign, the first few months of 1914 appeared deceptively carefree and prosperous in Greece. Business and the arts flourished, the people still basked in the afterglow of the previous year's triumphs, and travellers from abroad were impressed by the atmosphere of national pride and confidence in the country. In June King Constantine told Prince Christopher that 'I think that at last we can look forward to peace.'[5]

In retrospect, during his years of exile Prince Nicholas recalled the season as 'like a beautiful and longed-for summer that had at last come after a severe and dreary winter. Alas, it was only a summer preceding a winter that never ended, both of us and our beloved country!'[6]

Later that summer, as holiday-makers of every nation lazed blissfully in the June and July sunshine, dismissing the assassination of the Austrian heir Archduke Francis Ferdinand and his morganatic wife at Sarajevo as another anarchist outrage but little more, the royal family of Greece were scattered throughout Europe. Queen Sophie was in Eastbourne with the youngest children, a routine she had followed for several years. Prince George, who lived mainly at St Cloud but still regularly came to Greece to see the family, was at Bernstorff, sailing with his uncle Prince Waldemar of Denmark, a widower of some four years' standing. Prince Nicholas and Queen Olga were in St Petersburg, while the Anglophile Crown Prince George and Prince Christopher were in London. The latter had just become unofficially engaged to Mrs Nancy Leeds, an American widow whom King George had met shortly before his assassination and found charming, and had tacitly given his blessing as a future daughter-in-law. They hoped to be married almost immediately, but in the end they had to wait for nearly six years.

Gravely concerned at the march of events in Europe, King Constantine stayed in Athens with his daughter Princess Helen. On 28 June they were watching a display of Greek classical games in the city stadium, when an aide brought the King a telegram. He read it and turned to his daughter, telling her that the Archduke and his wife had been murdered. Crumpling it up slowly, he added, 'Now we can expect trouble.'[7]

On 4 August, six weeks later, Prince Christopher was staying with his aunt Queen Alexandra at Marlborough House. He stood at the window at midnight to watch the immense crowd in front of Buckingham Palace, counting the seconds as the ultimatum to Germany expired. Great Britain and Germany were at war.

Queen Sophie hurried back to Greece to be at her husband's side, leaving the children in the care of their nurse at Eastbourne to return later. Prince and Princess Nicholas were in Russia, visiting her widowed mother, Grand Duchess Vladimir. They returned as soon as possible, travelling through Roumania where they stayed briefly with Crown Prince and Princess Ferdinand.

During the war years the Greek royal family would stand united; but family unity was perhaps the only blessing vouchsafed to them throughout one tragedy after another.

CHAPTER SEVEN

'It is imperative that we should remain neutral'

As the clouds of war were gathering over Europe in the last days of July 1914, King Constantine received a telegram from Emperor William II, asking what he would do in the event of war in Europe. There could be no doubt from the Emperor's tone as to what answer was expected, but the King replied that Greece would remain neutral. On receiving this refusal to join Germany, the Emperor spoke of his secret pacts with Bulgaria and Turkey and declared that if Greece did not join them she would be treated as an enemy. But King Constantine stood firm. He did not trust the Bulgarians, did not like the Turks, and he rejected the idea of opposing Russia, so giving her an excuse to exploit her ambitions in the southern Balkans.

Where family ties were concerned, King Constantine and Queen Sophie had close connections with both sides. While they regarded German military power as superior, they were by inclination more pro-British. English was the language they spoke together at home, they spent most of their annual holidays in England, and the younger children had regularly received part of their education in English schools.

Like her mother the Empress Frederick, Queen Sophie had always been passionately fond of Britain. Though she was the German Emperor's sister, relations between them had improved but little since he had remonstrated with her for daring to enter the Orthodox Church without asking his permission. Like her husband, she was on far better terms with King George V and Tsar Nicholas.

King Constantine felt himself under no obligation to join his brother-in-law, merely because he held a German Field-Marshal's baton. Entreaties not to throw in his lot with the 'Serbian assassins', whose murder of Archduke Francis Ferdinand and his wife at Sarajevo in June had triggered the crisis, had no effect. He was neither pro-German nor pro-Allied, he insisted to friends and detractors alike, merely pro-Greek.

To Prince Nicholas, he made his allegiance clear:

It is extraordinary. Does [Emperor William] take me for a German? And, because he has given me a German Field-Marshal's baton, does he imagine that I am under any obligation towards him? If that is so, I am ready to return the baton at any time. Besides, he seems to forget his geography and that Greece, twenty-four hours after she had declared herself Germany's ally, would be reduced to cinders by the Allied fleets. What folly! Whoever heard of such a thing? No. We are Greeks, and the interest of Greece must come first. For the present, at any rate, it is imperative that we should remain neutral. But as to joining Germany, such an eventuality is and always will be an impossibility.[1]

The Balkan wars had left Greece victorious, but exhausted and depleted. King Constantine, his General Staff, and most of the Greek people were of the same opinion. To consolidate what they had won, they needed a long period of peace. Moreover, to declare on the side of Germany would render Greece and her long coastline vulnerable to attack from the combined British and French fleets.

Venizelos thought otherwise. He maintained that war would be over within a month, and if Greece wished to be on the winning side she should join the entente – Britain, France and Russia – without delay. Finding little agreement from his ministerial colleagues, he approached the various Allied ministers in Athens. On behalf of their respective countries, they answered that they felt it undesirable for war to be carried into the eastern Balkans.

The Great Powers were desperate to woo Greece. The treaty with Serbia imposed no obligation on Greece to intervene in a war against a non-Balkan power. But should Turkey enter the war, Greek interests would become directly involved. This would provide a chance to destroy the Ottoman Empire, liberate several hundred thousand Greeks from Turkish rule, and even perhaps to achieve the dream of enthroning a Greek King again in Constantinople, the old Byzantium. To Venizelos, who had already declared sympathy with Allied aims, the opportunity was too good to miss, whatever the risks. Cautious neutrality was incompatible with the vision of the 'Great Idea'.

The prospect of reigning in Constantinople as Emperor Constantine XII was inviting, but the King would not let himself be dazzled. Unlike

Venizelos, he knew that the Tsar's ministers would never permit the Greeks to enter Constantinople and become masters of the Straits. Participating in military gambles that might expose his country to invasion from the north was a chance he was not prepared to take. Influenced by a prudent military outlook that his impetuous Prime Minister lacked, he wanted Greece and her economy to remain clear of military obligations until the army had recovered from the two recent Balkan wars. Short of equipment and supplies, it was in no state to resist a combined German-Bulgarian attack. He had not forgotten the causes of the defeats of 1897.

Such reasoning carried little weight with Venizelos. His offer of Greek aid against Turkey in exchange for promises of concessions in Asia Minor had been made at a critical hour in the fortunes of the entente, when the outcome of the battle of the Marne in September 1914 was in doubt. Though he was acting merely on his personal authority, the entente accepted his gesture as the basis of their attitude to Greek participation in the war.

As the chief protagonist of neutrality, the King found himself drawn into the party political arena. Encouraged by the situation, his opponents started to widen what had originally been a difference of opinion between two strong personalities into a rift with an ideological significance that eventually split the country into two rival camps. They found an easy opening to challenge the King by suggesting that his desire for neutrality was born of unpatriotic motives.

It was all too simple for the supporters of Venizelos to suggest that the country's politics, and indeed the sovereign, was dominated by dynastic links with Emperor William. Queen Sophie, it was claimed by those who shared the views of Venizelos, exercised a strong pro-German influence over the King and court, and over certain of his ministers.

In January 1915 Sir Edward Grey, British Foreign Secretary, proposed that Greece should cede recently acquired territory to Bulgaria in return for compensation in northern Epirus and the even more attractive, if vague, promise of 'important territorial concessions on the coast of Asia Minor', which with its large Greek population was a major bone of contention. Grey was reluctant to be more specific, for he was also wooing Italy, which likewise cast a covetous eye on parts of Asia Minor.

Venizelos was willing to accept Grey's proposal. The King and his advisers wanted genuine assurances before giving up land so recently won. Matters were further complicated when the entente forces launched the ill-fated Dardanelles campaign in February 1915. Venizelos was keen to take part, although Constantinople, the eventual objective of the landings, had already been promised to Russia in the event of success.

Reluctantly, King Constantine agreed to the plan when it was first presented to the Crown Council. The British Minister in Athens reported that King Constantine was prepared to show 'benevolent neutrality' towards the Allies, in addition to authorizing the use of Mudros as a British base of operations, and allowing Greek naval and military participation in the campaign. However, at once he found himself at odds with Ioannis Metaxas, Chief of the General Staff. Arguing that the army was in no state to fight a protracted campaign against powerful, well-equipped enemies, Metaxas threatened to resign, and the King changed his mind.

Venizelos tried to regain his consent by reducing the Greek commitment from an army corps to a single division. He thought it vital that Greece must make her presence felt in Asia Minor, and the least the nation could do was to send a token force to march victoriously into Constantinople with the Allies.

King Constantine held firm; the Greek army could not afford the losses that such a campaign would surely bring. Parts of the Dardanelles had been attacked in November 1914, thus giving Turkey and Germany adequate warning of further operations later. British strategists realized it could only succeed through the combined efforts of an Anglo-Greek force, and she hoped to secure Bulgarian cooperation at the same time. No European statesman – or at least none outside the Balkans – appreciated that Tsar Ferdinand's personal grudge against Greece and Serbia, who had thwarted his territorial aspirations in war only two years earlier, was the significant factor in the foreign policy of Bulgaria. The entente were still optimistic of securing Bulgarian support, at least until they learned that the latter had just received a loan from Germany.

The object of the entente's attack, King Constantine knew, was to reach Constantinople. He recognized that the Dardanelles could never be forced by a fleet alone. There would have to be a simultaneous attack by land and sea, and a very large army would be needed to see it through. If Venizelos was to send any Greek divisions to help the Allies, the Bulgarians would fall on their left flank. One Greek division after another would be sent, until the Greek army was annihilated.

Angered at what he felt was excessive use of the royal prerogative by his sovereign, Venizelos demanded the verdict of the Crown Council. Backed by the entire Greek General Staff, the Council voted with the King. On 6 March Venizelos resigned in fury and the King asked Dimitrios Gounaris, an old opponent of Venizelos known for his German sympathies, to form a government.

King Constantine was already unwell, and the strain of events exacerbated his condition. In a high fever he took to his bed shortly after the crisis, with pleurisy and pneumonia. For several weeks it was doubtful whether he would survive. Two ribs had to be removed and blood poisoning set in as a result of the anaesthetic used. Bulletins were issued three times a day and displayed on placards throughout Athens; those fixed to the gates outside the palace were read by large crowds that silently and unceasingly gathered, anxious for any news in the change of their sovereign's condition. There were rumours that he had been stabbed by Queen Sophie with a knife, during an argument in which she had attempted to persuade him to declare on the side of her brother in Germany.

A warship was sent to Tinos to bring the miraculous holy icon of the Virgin and Child from the shrine of Panayia Evanghelistria to the royal sickroom. Thousands of other sick people had been cured by it before, and perhaps it would do the same for the apparently dying King. By the time it was brought to him, he had already been given the last rites. With his ebbing strength, he venerated the sacred image and fell into unconsciousness. Late that same evening, he rallied. The icon remained beside his bed, until he was pronounced out of danger a week later. As a thanksgiving for her husband's recovery, Queen Sophie gave a magnificent sapphire to enrich the icon.

Nevertheless, a further operation was necessary. Athenian surgeons hesitated to take such a responsibility, and sent for a Viennese specialist. Preferring to avoid the major operation that might either have cured him completely or killed him, he made a local incision that removed the immediate danger, but left a permanent aperture which allowed the accumulating poison to escape from under the ribs.

While the King was recovering, the Allies continued to press Gounaris and his government to cooperate, still offering vague concessions in Asia Minor. Standing by his sovereign, Gounaris demanded in return a guarantee of the integrity of Greek soil from Bulgarian attack, which they would not concede.

Prince Nicholas, the closest of the King's brothers, realized that Greece was desperately isolated. Even Russia appeared to be against the Greeks, not merely because she refused to join the entente, but because she was afraid that Greece would do so. On no account would she permit a single Greek soldier to enter Constantinople.

Though no longer Prime Minister, Venizelos retained his majority in the Greek Parliament in a general election held in June 1915. Still convalescing, the King returned to affairs of state in July. Under pressure, he accepted the resignation of Gounaris the following month and reappointed Venizelos as Prime Minister.

In September 1915 Bulgaria, aligned with the Central Powers, attacked Serbia. This raised the question as to whether Greece was bound, as Venizelos and his supporters insisted, to go to Serbia's aid under the terms of the June 1913 treaty. They asked the King to proclaim a general mobilization in Greece, which he refused to do. Under the threat of Venizelos's resignation, he finally signed the decree, but encouraged his General Staff to treat it as a purely defensive measure involving no commitment to Serbia. Venizelos retaliated by renewing his invitation to Britain and France to send troops to Salonika in support of Serbia. King Constantine dismissed him, just as Anglo-French forces were beginning to land.

The breach between both men was now irreparable. According to historian C.M. Woodhouse, even if the King's judgement was correct, 'he was straining at the constitution and seeking to impose extremely doubtful interpretations on it'.[2] As Commander-in-Chief of the armed forces, surrounded by staff officers who like him were convinced that the Central Powers were invincible, he was in a strong position to undermine his Prime Minister's policies. Whether King George I would have taken such measures is a moot point, but King George was fortunate in never being called upon to make such a fateful decision.

Greece was still technically neutral, but the Anglo-French forces still established a front at Salonika. Relations were deteriorating fast between Greece and her nominal Allies, Britain, France, Russia and Serbia. The Allies could not, and Greece would not, help to prevent Austria and Bulgaria from overrunning Serbia, the remnants of whose army escaped across the mountains to take refuge in Corfu. More bad news came in the shape of reports about the treaty of London, signed in April, which assigned the Dodecanese definitively to Italy, promised Italy an 'equitable share' in the eventual division of Anatolia, and arranged a partition of Albania more favourable to Italy than to Greece. In anticipation, the Italians were allowed to take over the occupation of northern Epirus from the Greeks as soon as they entered the war in May 1915. To emphasize their displeasure, the Allies demanded (yet did not enforce) the demobilization of the Greek army, instituted a partial blockade of Greece, and declared military law at Salonika. The last measure was justified by fear that the Austro-German and Bulgarian forces would attack Salonika once they had disposed of Serbia, though this never materialized.

In December 1915 the British government finally admitted the failure of their Dardanelles campaign and withdrew their troops. This withdrawal shook Greek confidence in the Allied cause further, though it enabled the Allies to strengthen their hold on Salonika. The Greeks thus saw their King's judgement vindicated. By refusing to be swept into war, they knew that he was sparing them unnecessary military humiliation and needless loss of soldiers' lives in pursuit of a hopeless cause.

King Constantine judged the time right to dissolve Parliament, though Venizelos still unquestionably held a clear majority. He suspected that the failure of the Allies, who had shown themselves interfering and ineffective, would contribute to the emergence of an anti-Venizelist majority. Venizelos advised his followers to abstain from the election, in which the poll was thus barely a quarter of that with which his party had won the summer election. Alexander Zaimis, the previous Prime Minister, had been succeeded by Skouloudis, who lost his seat but still remained in office.

The King's government now felt justified in pursuing more active collaboration with the Central Powers. Orders were given to senior commanders in Macedonia not to oppose any Bulgarian advance that might take place. An official protest was lodged against the help provided by the Allies to the remnants of the Serbian army, first in landing them on Corfu and then in transferring them to Salonika. To emphasize the hostile action of the Allies in admitting the Italians to northern Epirus, King Constantine proclaimed the annexation of the area in April 1916, though he was unable to make it effective. By far the gravest of the acts committed was the surrender to the Bulgarians in May of the frontier fort of Rupel on the River Struma, which opened up the whole of eastern Macedonia to attack.

In August Roumania joined the war on the side of the Allies. After a few victories the Roumanians were defeated and under enemy occupation by the end of the year, being finished as a combatant power. The Bulgars overran eastern Macedonia and Bucharest was under enemy occupation. Perhaps King Constantine felt himself vindicated again by events, though the Western Allies were stirred to firmer action. In June 1916 they had presented an ultimatum demanding total demobilization of the Greek army, the dismissal of Skouloudis's government, and the dissolution of Parliament. Reluctantly the King gave way, though his General Staff effectively evaded the decree of demobilization and the elections were repeatedly postponed. Venizelos declared that it was no longer possible for his party to cooperate in the government of the country.

The family could not understand how the peoples of the Allied countries could believe such groundless allegations of treachery against King Constantine, and why nobody in power ever challenged them. Not for some years did they learn how powerful Allied censorship had been in forbidding the publication of his own statements, or the ministers loyal to him. In desperation, he tried to speak to the United States through American journalists, but their dispatches were similarly suppressed in the name of Allied censorship. How different the situation might have been a few years later, Princess Helen would reflect ruefully, had radio broadcasting been available for him to put his own and his country's case directly to the world.

Threats on the King's life were made from time to time. General Sarrail was advised in December 1915 to have him 'made away with by assassins', and four months later the French Minister in Athens outlined a scheme for twenty men to abduct him and confine him aboard a French warship.

A much more serious matter was an attempt on the life of the King and his family. Just before dawn on 14 July a wall of distant fire was seen creeping towards their estate at Tatoi. Prince Christopher was staying with his brother Nicholas at Kifissia, and woke that morning, certain he could smell burning. As nobody else immediately noticed anything, he thought he was mistaken until Queen Sophie telephoned her sister-in-law Helen from Tatoi, 6 miles away, to say that a fire had been reported and the King had gone to investigate.

The wind blew straight towards the royal residence, advancing through the tinder-dry trees more quickly than anybody could have anticipated. It had been a dry, hot summer, and the earth was parched. At noon the King set out with a party in cars to observe the fire. They found themselves in an area of exhausting heat. Suddenly, half a mile from the house, roaring tree-high flames seemed to engulf them.

The King remembered a goat track which he hoped would still be safe. It was a slender chance, but their only one. Calling to the others to follow him, he started down it with his son Paul. The flames leapt and crackled on either side of them as they ran; the smoke was so thick that they could hardly see the path ahead. They were on the edge of the forest, a few feet from safety, when the King tripped over a tree root and sprained his ankle. Two soldiers, seeing what had happened, ran to the rescue and carried him away, but only just in time. A moment later the two fires met and the road was closed.

The three cars burst into flames. Blinded and lost in the smoke, a group of aides, soldiers and chauffeurs tried to fight their way to safety. Too panic-stricken to keep to the path, they ran wildly until they were overcome by thick smoke, and sixteen of them perished in the flames. Queen Sophie carried three-year-old Princess Katherine in her arms for nearly 2 miles before they were clear of the flames.

A dense pall of black smoke in the sky was visible many miles away, and a red glow had spread over the whole horizon. By evening a belt of fire had engulfed the forest. People were running wildly in all directions, some trying to fight the fire, others carrying out furniture and pictures. The King's house and most of the surrounding buildings had been burnt to the ground, and he was sitting in front of Queen Olga's house some yards away, surrounded by furniture. One of his feet had been bandaged. When he had gone out to investigate, none of them (including Queen Sophie and Princess Katherine) had realized until it was almost too late that the flames which had broken out in several places were closing in on them more and more, cutting off their retreat. In the horror of finding themselves trapped, they scattered in all directions, trying first one path and then another, only to find the way blocked by fire.

Finding his brother almost helpless, Prince Christopher offered to go up to the clock tower, overlooking the entire forest, to see whether the main road into Athens was still clear. Reaching the platform, he saw that the whole pine forest was a mass of flames for miles around, but the road was still clear. He was about to climb down, when to his horror he saw a great tongue of flame coming straight for the tower. He jumped down the staircase and had only run a few yards when an explosion threw blazing wood in all directions. A collection of jars, containing various snakes and reptiles preserved in spirits, had turned the tower into a huge torch.

By nightfall, Tatoi was burnt out. Queen Olga's house had been saved as it was thickly surrounded by evergreens. Even ten years later, observed

Prince Nicholas bitterly, the house with its encircling green wall resembled 'the oasis in the midst of a desert'. Nothing was left of the deciduous trees in the forest but blackened stumps, beside the pathetic corpses of several thousand animals.

While investigating next day, the police discovered empty petrol cans at three different places in the forest. It confirmed suspicions among the family and their aides that the fire was no accident.

Blame was laid at the door of the Secret Police Service, a 150-strong 'Franco-British Police' force, an unofficial corps of private detectives which had been created with the consent of the British and French Legations. This body had been responsible for a calumny that the royal family, or sympathetic associates, had taken part in the re-victualling of German submarines off the Greek coast, and that wireless apparatus had been installed at Tatoi, for communicating with enemy submarines, as well as with headquarters at Berlin and Sofia. Shortly before the fire, workers on the estate recalled having seen a French aeroplane flying low over Tatoi, evidently on a reconnaissance mission. They also reported that a car carrying four unknown individuals had been seen driving slowly along isolated tracks, eluding the guards and returning to Athens.

Anonymous letters threatening their lives were so common in those days that they grew to expect them as a matter of course. One Tuesday, the day of the week on which the King dined *en famille* with his brothers in Kifissia, the King's aide came to tell Prince Christopher that he had received an anonymous letter that morning warning that, in consequence of a plot to assassinate the King, all the wines in the villa at Kifissia had been poisoned. The Prince warned the butler to take the strictest precautions that night, to serve no wines except old bottles that had been in the cellars for years, and to examine every bottle himself. White and shaking, the servant went to the cellar, where he began trying out every bottle. Fortunately none of the wines was poisoned, and apart from an understandable difficulty in standing upright by the time evening came, the zealous butler was none the worse for his duties.

In September 1916, Venizelos left Athens for his native Crete, accompanied by Admiral Koundouriotis, Commander-in-Chief of the Navy. At Khania he proclaimed a revolutionary movement, calling on the Greek people to return to their alliance with Serbia, to enter the war against the Central Powers and Bulgaria. After an enthusiastic reception in Crete, he went to Salonika the following month to establish a provisional government, in opposition to that of the King in Athens. Large numbers of supporters joined him there, including officers, politicians and officials, but he was unable to obtain recognition from the allies. The Russian and Italian governments, both of whom now had troops on the Salonika front, were implacably hostile to Venizelos. The Russians objected to the anti-monarchical character of his movement, especially as King Constantine's mother was a Romanov, while the Italians saw Venizelos as a potential rival to their claims in Asia Minor. The British and French, while supporting the cost of Venizelos' armed forces, still feared that recognition could precipitate civil war and thus divert allied troops from their main task.

King Constantine had had a valuable British supporter in Lord Kitchener, 'a soldier and an idealist like himself'. As Secretary of State for War, Kitchener had visited the King in Athens in November 1915, trying to persuade him to join the Allies, only to be told that the British and French were exceeding their brief in their casual breaching of Greek neutrality. Kitchener realized that he was talking to a fellow soldier forced to work with idealistic politicians who knew nothing of military matters, for whom he felt little respect, and the two men instinctively liked and trusted each other. 'I spoke to him as one soldier to another,' said the Field-Marshal after the interview. 'He is in the right. When we want the Greeks we can have them on our side.'[3] Had Kitchener not been lost at sea in July 1916, and had there been another point of view to counter that of David Lloyd George, an ardent admirer of Venizelos and Kitchener's successor as War Minister, the King's fate might have been a happier one.

Yet the King was not without sympathy in the British government. The Foreign Secretary, Sir Edward Grey, appreciated his plight, and he was concerned at the virulent anti-Greek propaganda in Britain and France. He shared the opinion of King George V that, as Britain had entered war in defence of Belgian neutrality, it was unethical for them to impose their will on another small neutral state, especially as Britain would be in no position to protect Greece if matters were to go badly.

H.A.L. Fisher was one of the first historians who would not accept without question the official view of King Constantine's apparent perfidy towards the allied cause. Twenty years later, he remarked that 'the rights of neutrals were little regarded' during the war. He cited not only the German invasion of Belgium, and unrestricted U-boat warfare, but also 'the interference of the British Navy with neutral trade, the appropriation of Corfu as an allied sanatorium, and the blockade of Greece by the French Navy' as 'in varying degrees actions for which no legal purist can find a defence.'[4]

A constant thorn in the King's side was the writer Compton Mackenzie, who had come to Greece to work in counter-espionage during the war. The King was infuriated by his interference; while the other allies and Germans took sides in the rift between him and Venizelos, they did so as foreigners serving their own countries' purposes. Mackenzie joined in as a 'supernumerary Greek', devoting himself ruthlessly to the pursuit of British interests, combined with those of a Greater Greece whose territory would include the coastline of Turkey, and become the controlling power of the Eastern Mediterranean. Mackenzie and Venizelos were two of a kind, and the King sent his brother, Prince Andrew, to Paris and London in 1916 to ask their governments to control their respective intelligence establishments. The Prince convinced King George V that Mackenzie's organization was plotting to destabilize and overthrow King Constantine. Under pressure from his sovereign to withdraw him, a British envoy was sent out to see the situation for himself, but he returned with a recommendation that Mackenzie should be left where he was, in view of his highly effective secret service work in Greece.

King Constantine had another ally in Paris, the brother closest to him in age, Prince George. He and his wife were such intimate friends of Aristide Briand, the French Premier, that in French political circles and the press, Briand was suspected of trying to negotiate with Venizelos to put George on the Greek throne. The rumour was unfounded, for Prince George had never forgiven Venizelos for hounding him out of office in Crete, and angrily attacked the Premier when he believed France was humiliating his country and his brother.

He sensed the resolve of the French and British statesmen to get their own way in Greece in the face of all obstacles, and at one stage had been inclined to advise King Constantine that for better or worse it would be wisest to accept the Allies' invitations, and place the entire Greek army and Navy at their disposal without any stipulations. Caught between divided national loyalties, his wife Princess Marie established a military hospital at Salonika in November 1915; and she always insisted in private conversation that, whatever the views of Greek ministers towards Germany, her brother-in-law would never take the side of Emperor William in Berlin.

The French government and her emissaries were far more hostile to King Constantine than the British. If it was revenge for his speech at Potsdam in 1913, the debt was paid back with interest. Overall allied command had been entrusted to General Sarrail, an unashamed republican who had no respect for any of the crowned heads of Europe. Once he was established at Salonika he wished to proclaim a formal state of siege, and was only dissuaded from doing so by orders from Paris. Under him and the commander of the allied naval squadron, Vice-Admiral Dartige du Fournet, the allies demanded control over the railway to the north, the surrender of certain warships, the disarmament of the land batteries at Salamis and Piraeus, and the departure of the enemy legations. Offering an olive branch to the Allies, the King suggested the surrender of a quantity of guns and other equipment and the withdrawal of his troops to the Peleponnese. The Allies agreed to accept a smaller quantity of arms, but as soon as they had done so, the pro-German faction in Athens launched such a campaign of propaganda against the allies that Constantine felt impelled to withdraw his offer, and issued a protest against actions already taken by the Allies.

King Constantine was perpetually on the conscience of King George V, who wrote to Grey (4 September):

Are we justified in interfering to this extent in the internal Government of a neutral and friendly country, even though we be of the guarantors of its Constitution? Are we acting up to our boasted position as the protector of smaller Powers?

I cannot help feeling that in this Greek question we have allowed France too much to dictate a policy, and that as a Republic she may be somewhat intolerant of, if not anxious to abolish, the monarchy in Greece. But this I am sure is not the policy of my Government.[5]

Neither was it the policy of Tsar Nicholas II, who had expressed his personal anxiety over affairs in Greece to King George V, regretting that the protecting Powers were immersing themselves too much in her internal affairs to the detriment of King Constantine.

To the Tsar, King George wrote (1 October) that the situation in Greece was 'most difficult to understand', following the revolution headed by Venizelos; 'Tino seems to do nothing and one is afraid that unless he declares war on Bulgaria he will have to abdicate, which is the last thing that you and I want.'[6]

CHAPTER EIGHT

'I beg you all to accept my decision with serenity'

By the autumn of 1916 King Constantine's position was becoming steadily more untenable. King George V's apprehensions that he might be forced into abdication were well justified. In November Venizelos took it upon himself to declare war on the Central Powers. King Constantine still clung to neutrality, while the French attitude became ever more menacing.

Believing that a show of force would bring the King to reason, Admiral Fournet landed a small Anglo-French force to march on Athens. Next he presented King Constantine with an ultimatum, demanding compliance with certain drastic conditions, including the surrender by the Greek army of much of their equipment and material. He returned to his flagship believing that the King would consent, provided it was made clear that he had only surrendered to force.

A few days later the Admiral presented himself at the palace again, to announce that a 'peaceful demonstration' of several thousand Franco-British troops was to be made on Athens. Their only object was to fetch the munitions which the King had promised them. They would not use force, but certain strategic positions outside and inside Athens would be occupied in strength until the war material had been handed over and removed.

On 30 November a message was sent to the Allies from the Greek royal government, stating that an allied march on Athens, with the object of occupying with arms any part of the city, would be regarded as a 'hostile act'. At the same time Greek troops were posted at all the strategic points in and around Athens. Two orders were given to these troops: they were on no account to surrender their ground to Franco-British parties; and they were not to fire first.

Shortly after daybreak, on 1 December, detachments of French and British marines disembarked and marched on Athens. At about 11 a.m. a shot was fired. Which side was responsible was never established, but

King Constantine believed that a republican extremist had done so in order to bring matters to a head. A British major later reported that the French were firing blanks in order to disperse an angry pro-Constantine crowd. Within five minutes battle was raging, Venizelists joining the Anglo-French forces and firing on their own countrymen's patrols who were still loyal to the King. At the first shots King Constantine sent senior Greek officers from the palace to stop the Greeks firing at all costs. They succeeded in restoring peace, and the Allied ministers with their staffs hurried to the palace, summoned to an emergency conference.

While they talked, firing broke out again. The Admiral, who was with French troops in the Zappeion, signalled to the ships in Phaleron Bay to bombard Stadium Hill, beyond the palace. Shells screamed over the palace, brushed masonry from the roof, and crashed into the royal gardens. Queen Sophie and her younger children had to take shelter in the cellars for two hours.

By 7 p.m. firing had stopped. The Greeks reported heavy casualties, and over two hundred British and French officers and men had been killed or wounded. King Constantine agreed to hand over a certain amount of arms, and as a gesture of contrition the Greek garrison paraded in front of the Allied troops, drawn up in formal array, and saluted the British, French and Italian flags in military apology.

On 6 December King Constantine addressed a telegram to King George V, justifying his actions by pointing out that the Allied landing had been repulsed as it was known to be part of a Venizelist conspiracy.

Whatever King George's personal feelings, he found himself obliged to support the entente cause. The Allied powers, he replied, had confined their demands upon Greece to the observance of a benevolent neutrality, but they had received 'indubitable proof of action on the part of the Greek Government, both damaging to their naval and military interests and of direct assistance to the enemy's forces'. Demands in conjunction with the Allied powers would 'include reparation for the unprovoked attack made by your troops and guarantees for the future'.[1]

After the attack the Allies withdrew their troops, but conferred official recognition on Venizelos's provisional government, to which French and British diplomatic representatives were accredited at Salonika. They declared a strict blockade of Greece and all foreigners were warned to leave the country. British and French women, including many governesses and children's nurses in Athens, were ordered to go otherwise their passports would be cancelled by the Consulates. Kate Fox, governess to the daughters of Prince and Princess Nicholas, stubbornly insisted on staying and no reprisals were taken against her.

The Allies were quick to demand repatriation from King Constantine's government. Dissatisfied with the lack of immediate response, they presented new demands to the King, including the reduction of the Greek army to the bare minimum necessary to retain order. But they were careful not to sever relations with the King altogether; they continued to recognize both rival governments of Greece, largely because the British and French ministers were still unable to carry the Italian and Russian governments with them. By the end of January 1917 the government in Athens had sufficiently complied with the Allies' conditions to justify a return to normality. Yet it was less a declaration of peace, more an uneasy truce. Some of the King's ministers were becoming increasingly pro-German; feeling themselves vindicated by the Allies' behaviour, they had no scruples about making friendly overtures to the Central Powers.

By February 1917 King Constantine was virtually a prisoner of the Allies. The blockade of Greek ports was so effective that for nearly three months not a single bushel of wheat was imported into regions of the country still loyal to the King. Allied agents offered the starving Athenians smuggled bread if they joined the Venizelists. Many of them remained faithful, claiming that they would rather die for their King than betray their allegiance to him. Fish was becoming scarce, for all vessels of the fishing fleet were boarded by patrol boats. If the fishermen refused to declare for the Venizelists, their boats were seized without compensation and the crews put ashore.

Public opinion against the Allies hardened with every act of violence committed against the loyal civilian population. The campaign of shame reached new heights in February, when French cavalrymen shot down in cold blood the Superior and four monks at Zidani monastery, merely because they declared their loyalty to King Constantine.

The British government remained largely unaware of and indifferent to events in Greece. The country lay within the French sphere, and Britain offered no resistance to the views and plans of her ally. The royal family knew that France was mainly responsible for their sufferings, but they were distressed that Britain, the foreign country that had always stood firmest in their affections, should be party to such victimization. As Princess Helen said, 'it was as though some dear, trusted friend had cold-bloodedly pushed a dagger in one's back.'[2]

Prince Nicholas expressed matters a little differently:

England . . . after the failure of the Dardanelles expedition, had silently given the laurels to her French Ally, whose decisions, despite occasional hesitations, she invariably ended by accepting.[3]

A further blow to King Constantine was the succession of David Lloyd George to the Premiership in Britain in December 1916. The fiercely radical Lloyd George, whose private utterances showed how little respect he had for his own sovereign, could hardly be expected to have any more sympathy for the King of the Hellenes. His memoirs, published some twenty years later, were positively vitriolic when discussing the head of state who had striven to remain neutral:

The history of our dealings with Greece is a dreary picture of paralysing indecision. The Greek people are with us, and have indicated their sympathies repeatedly by their votes, but the King is now, and always has been, the Kaiser's friend and the Entente's foe. He has never missed an opportunity of serving the former and selling the latter. He gave valuable information to the enemy as to our troops, our positions, our intentions, and our movements. . . . He has fooled us all round the ring and made us the laughing stock of the East whilst we were writing lawyers' letters to his military advisers.[4]

Venizelos's movement continued to grow in strength. Most of the Greek diplomatic and consular representatives abroad declared in his favour, as did all the more important islands. Even the hostility of the Italians and Russians began to wane. Only the veto of the Tsar had prevented the French and British from deposing King Constantine, and with the Russian revolution in March 1917 the King lost his most powerful advocate abroad. The Italian government's attitude was modified as a result of the treaty of St Jean de Maurienne in April, which gave Italy considerable freedom of action on the Adriatic seaboard, and the prospect of a sphere of influence in Anatolia after the destruction of the Ottoman Empire. Both countries were thus more well disposed towards Venizelos.

By now the King and Queen were virtually ready to throw in their lot with Germany. Neutral Greece had suffered no harm at German hands, but she had been bullied mercilessly by the Allies, France in particular. The Allies had deliberately undermined King Constantine's position, they had encouraged Venizelos in his rebellious stand, they had bombed Athens, and when their belligerent tactics had still not forced Greece to abandon her neutrality, they had blockaded the country.

Above all they had persistently connived at a campaign of abuse on the heads of a much-loved King and Queen. It was no wonder that Queen Sophie, in particular, was prepared to forget past disagreements and to call on her brother in imperial Berlin for help. Several telegrams, dated between December 1916 and February 1917, were sent from the Queen to Emperor William, enquiring when his armies would be ready for a decisive offensive in Macedonia, as the timely interference of the Germans could alone deliver Greece from a grim situation, rendered all the more hopeless by lack of provisions and munitions and by the pressure of the general blockade. As she asked bitterly, could Belgium have suffered more at German hands? Or, as Prince Nicholas said, 'if your house is broken into and plundered and finally set on fire by persons whom you considered to be your best friends, have the latter any right to call you a "traitor" because, in despair, you opened your window and screamed for help?'[5] After the Allied blockade, many other Greeks felt the same way.

In May the supporters of Venizelos held a demonstration in Salonika calling upon the Allies to repudiate and depose the King. Ministers in Athens recognized that it was inevitable they would soon do so.

Alexander Zaimis was recalled to form a more conciliatory government and he tried to oblige the Allies, but their tolerance was exhausted. On 10 June Monsieur Charles Jonnart, the Allied High Commissioner, informed Zaimis that the Allies required the King's abdication on the grounds that he had violated his oath to rule as a constitutional monarch. He must abdicate and leave the country immediately.*

---

* According to Arthur Gould Lee,[6] Jonnart proclaimed himself High Commissioner of the Protecting Powers of Greece. The Allies had not appointed anybody to such a post, and his mission was apparently part of a bluff which, however, completely deceived Zaimis when he was summoned for an interview. Prince Nicholas did not dispute the appointment, but quoted several documents to prove that Jonnart 'went far beyond the powers with which he had been entrusted by the Governments of the Allied Powers'.[7]

Crown Prince George was unacceptable as a successor to King Constantine, ostensibly as he had served in the German army before the war and had identified himself too closely with his father's pro-German sympathies. In fact, the Allies ruled him as ineligible to succeed as he had been educated for the succession, and would therefore be less amenable as a sovereign than his unprepared brother. If the Greek people wished to recall King Constantine after the war, they would be at liberty to do so.

Should the King refuse to obey this ultimatum, a further bombardment of Athens would take place and the dynasty would be driven out of Greece for ever. To any charges that the Allies were interfering excessively in Greek internal affairs, they could answer that they had every right to do so as they were the protecting Powers who had originally helped to establish the independence of the sovereign state of Greece by the London Protocol of 1830.

Zaimis came white-faced and haggard to the palace to deliver the message. For over an hour he conferred with the King, trying to find a way out of the situation. Although failure to comply with the order meant another bombardment of the city, if their popular King abdicated there was the grave possibility of an uprising and civil war.

King Constantine had been increasingly prepared for, and perhaps even resigned to, such an ultimatum. At once he summoned all his ministers to a Crown Council, and they listened to his speech with dismay. He was going to leave, he told them calmly; Athens would become a bloodbath within days if he did not comply. He named Prince Alexander, his second son, as his successor, on the understanding that he himself would return to Greece on the conclusion of hostilities. To the horrified Alexander, the King explained gently that he should regard the throne as a trust which he was holding during the absence of his father and elder brother, neither of whom would sign any act of renunciation of succession.

The ministers rose with the tears running down their cheeks. Each man clutched the King's hand and kissed it almost frantically before walking slowly out.

Prince Nicholas, who knew nothing of what had taken place, found his brother with Princes George and Alexander in the garden after the Crown Council. Their faces were pale and set. Smiling sadly, King Constantine broke the news to him.

That afternoon King Alexander took the oath of allegiance secretly in the ballroom in the palace. It was a sad ceremony, shorn of all the glory of magnificently robed clergy, congratulatory courtiers and cheering crowds. The Archbishop of Athens hurried through the streets to administer the oath and was smuggled into the palace by a back door. The only people present were King Constantine, the Crown Prince and the Prime Minister. The new King, aged twenty-three, was dazed and bewildered; tears were in his eyes and his voice faltered over the responses.

Early in the afternoon Prince Nicholas, who had returned to his villa, arrived back at the palace with Princess Helen. Andrew and Alice came shortly afterwards. Inside, the family wandered about aimlessly. Outside, the streets and squares of Athens began to fill with wan-faced people, gathering in small groups, stunned and leaderless.

Prince Christopher wondered where the crowds were who had cheered King Constantine with such frenzy on the day he had taken the oath at his accession. His answer was

a wail of anguish coming from outside the windows. Hundreds of men and women, having some vague idea of what was happening, had stolen up to the Palace, where they had heard the news that their beloved King Constantine was leaving the country. One by one they took up the cry . . . that age-old lament in a minor key with which the Greeks proclaim death or disaster.[8]

News of the King's imminent departure was to have been kept secret, but it had spread rapidly throughout the city. The crowds were determined that he should stay. They pressed closer to the palace, shouting, 'He shall not go!' When at length the King and Queen and their children emerged to enter the waiting cars, people flung themselves down on the road to prevent the cars from moving forward. The royal party was obliged to return indoors. Each time they tried to leave, the same thing happened.

The family remained virtually under siege overnight. None of the Princes was allowed to leave, 'lest by some means we should spirit away King Constantine'. Inside the palace, the tension was almost unbearable. Servants clustered together in frightened groups, while in the early hours of the morning everybody tried to get some rest, sleeping anywhere they could, three or four in a room, on sofas and armchairs. The King's own page slept across his door on the floor. They awoke in broad daylight, most of them stiff and cramped, threw on their clothes and hurried to the windows. The palace was surrounded by a larger crowd than ever.

Prince Nicholas attempted to humour them, speaking to them through the gates and begging them to let the rest of the royal family inside go back to their own homes and wash. 'There's enough water here, isn't there?' was their retort. As the hours passed, the lamentations turned to hysteria and there were cries to the effect that it would be better to kill the King than to let him leave Greece. One desperate man seized him and tried to throttle him by pulling at his necktie, until Prince Andrew grabbed the man and made him release his grip.

At length, the royal family hit upon a ruse. Word was circulated that the King was on the point of leaving by the back gate of his private garden. Carriages and cars were sent there to keep up the illusion and the crowd followed. In the ensuing confusion, nobody noticed other cars slip quietly into the garden round the other side. Quickly, the royal family surged out and made a dash for them. Queen Sophie, still recovering from illness, lagged behind and had to be seized by two of the princes. They were in the cars just in time, for there were angry shouts as the crowds realized they had been tricked. As the King, Queen and family drove off, they could hear the wooden railing cracking in the general stampede, but by then they were on their way to safety at Tatoi.

A stunned silence fell upon the crowd, then everyone looked upwards. The sky had darkened and rain began to fall, an occurrence so rare in a Greek summer that the people, deeply superstitious at the best of times, immediately hailed it as a bad omen.

At Tatoi the reaction was different. Alexander came to take his leave of his parents. He was closeted for nearly an hour with his father, who explained the sorry situation to him in detail and impressed on him kindly but firmly that he merely held the crown, which rightly belonged to his father and then his eldest brother, in trust until normal circumstances were restored. Late in the afternoon the royal party stood sadly around the grave of King George I in the little churchyard above the treetops, saying goodbye to the part of their private home which held so many sacred memories.

Numbed by despair, people came to bid farewell to their King. All day long they came, in a steady stream. Smart cars bearing Ministers and society people, lorries laden with workmen, peasants in their rough country carts, farmers on horseback, and city workers on bicycles all joined the procession out of loyalty to their sovereign. Many had brought small gifts and bunches of flowers. They crowded around the King in the garden, knelt at his feet and repeatedly begged him to stay with them. The princes thought they were like bewildered children; it was hard to make them realize that he was only leaving them for their own good. Groups of professional men and trade union delegations thrust into the King's hand declarations of loyalty and support and wishes for his early return.

At daybreak next morning the royal cars were bumping along a dusty country road, lined with silent people and vehicles of every description. They entered the small fishing village of Oropos, where the royal yacht *Sphacteria* had been brought to take them abroad. An ancient vessel that had belonged to King George I, it had been condemned more than twenty years before, but was kept in service as a utility vessel, and King Constantine refused to travel in a French ship. There had been no time to clean it and the living quarters were crawling with vermin.

Jonnart had been so taken aback by the demonstrations of public sympathy towards the family that he ordered they should depart from somewhere less obvious than the Piraeus. In order to minimize public solidarity, he also demanded that they should sail at two o'clock in the morning, but King Constantine insisted that he and his family would not comply with such a humiliating order.

An exhausted, emotional gathering of loyal citizens darkened the hillsides around the village. No shouting greeted the royal family, only the fluttering of white handkerchiefs. Flowers lay thick on the landing stage, and a line of children from one of Queen Sophie's orphanages stood watching sorrowfully.

It had been arranged that the family's destination would be neutral Switzerland. The Isle of Wight had been suggested as a suitable place, but fearful of repercussions after the outcry which had greeted his government's plan to give sanctuary to the deposed Tsar Nicholas, his wife and children, King George V had let it be known that he 'strongly disapproved' of such a choice. As the party climbed on board the yacht, men and women pressed so close that a number in front were pushed into the water and had to be rescued by other boats.

Nicholas, Andrew, Helen and Alice watched them depart before returning to Kifissia, Andrew and Alice going back to their family in Athens. Nicholas was well aware that the Venizelists and the Allies regarded him as the evil genius behind King Constantine. For the sake of his nephew, now King, he knew with sadness that it would be in their best interests to see as little as possible of each other.

As King Constantine and his family left, his proclamation to his people was published in the official government journal. He declared that

Even far from Greece, the Queen and I will ever retain the same affection towards the Greek people. I beg you all to accept my decision with serenity, trusting to God whose blessing I invoke on the nation. And that this sacrifice for the country may not be in vain, I adjure all of you, if you love God, if you love your country, if, lastly you love me, not to cause any disturbance, but to remain submissive. The least disorder, even if prompted by a lofty sentiment, may to-day lead to the most terrible disaster. At this moment the greatest solace for the Queen and myself lies in the affection and devotion which you have always shown to us, in the happy days, as well as in the unhappy ones. May God protect Greece!

CONSTANTINE R.[9]

CHAPTER NINE

'A city of the dead'

As Prince, Alexander had never expected to succeed to the throne, and he had therefore been given no experience in state affairs. Deeply moved by the way in which his parents, brother and friends had been thrust into exile, he bore a natural resentment against the men who had seized control of Greece with foreign aid. He knew that the task his father had given him was to keep the dynasty alive through the difficult period ahead, and he devoted himself doggedly to the task.

His task was made harder by the constant reminders of bullying ministers that he was the son of a traitor. Incessant indignities were heaped on him: portraits of his parents in public buildings were torn down; many of their oldest friends were thrown into prison; all the old palace servants who had served his father were dismissed; and other petty spiteful acts included cutting out from school books the records of King Constantine's achievements as a military leader.

Some individuals were only too eager to throw in their lot with the new regime. One of the most notorious was George Mélas, whose lifelong ambition, he claimed when presenting himself at court shortly after war broke out, was to serve the King. Prince Nicholas obtained him a post in the household, checking appeals and petitions from soldiers and others who had suffered as a result of the war. Each had to be verified and answered, with some form of pension or remuneration made according to need. Mélas had nothing to do with King Constantine's private or state correspondence, but in 1918 he published a series of articles, later a book, attacking his master's 'treachery' and calling Prince Nicholas his 'evil genius'.

King Alexander was an independent-minded character, not given to self-pity. He shouldered the unwelcome responsibility of being a puppet king as quietly and efficiently as he did everything else. A prisoner in his own palace, his orders were disregarded and he was surrounded night and day by spies. If he showed the slightest preference for any human being, that person disappeared from his household. Only the known enemies of his father and the royal house were permitted to be in his service. They kept up a steady propaganda and lied to him persistently about his family, but it was useless for him to protest; no one listened. The few friends who were able to see him said that his face had grown prematurely lined and sad.

He wrote to his parents frequently, but the letters never reached them. From the time he bade goodbye to his mother on the day of his accession until the day of his death, she never heard directly from him.

Resolving to make the best of a bad job, he met this miserable situation with feigned indifference and a bold show of independence. Already he had chosen a property to the north of Athens, an estate surrounded by woods and farmland, which he intended to purchase and retire to when his father was restored and he could resume life in peacetime as a country squire and farmer.

In every way he was a contrast to his elder brother George, who had been strict and serious, with a high sense of his destiny. A lively, careless and good-natured young man, Alexander had often been seen cruising around the estates on his motorcycle, or driving his car around the country at high speed. He was one of the first people in Greece to acquire a car, and shortly after his accession to the throne King Constantine had been presented with a petition from drivers of the horse-cabs in Athens, asking him to forbid Princess Helen to go in Prince Alexander's automobile, as he drove at such a speed that 'we do not like to see our young Princess with him in case there is an accident.'[1]

Most male members of the family were fascinated by the finer details of the internal combustion engine, and some of his happiest hours during a carefree youth had been spent dressed in dirty overalls, taking his vehicles to pieces and putting them together again, or engrossed in a motorcycle manual, the only kind of book which appealed to him.

The royal family in exile had received a solemn promise before their departure that Venizelos would not return to Athens. Yet nobody was surprised when he returned a few days later. Allied representatives were waiting at the harbour to receive him when he landed. The streets were lined with steel-helmeted troops and he drove through them with an escort of six cars, whose occupants could scarcely be seen for the soldiers standing on the running boards, rifles in hand. The Greeks themselves remained in their own houses behind closed doors and shuttered windows. When the 'hero' appeared on the balcony in Constitution Square, after taking the oath of office before the new King, there was no one to cheer him but a few loafers and the shrill voices of schoolchildren given a half-day holiday to mark the occasion.

King Alexander treated him and the rest of the ministers with chilly reserve. He had his own way of dealing with the duties of kingship. One day his attention was drawn to the fact that he had added his name to a state paper without reading its contents. 'My father read papers before signing them, and is in exile', he retorted. 'My grandfather signed papers before reading them, and died a King.'[2]

Prince Christopher, who had remained behind, described Athens in the days that followed King Constantine's departure as

> like a city of the dead. No one went out in the streets, all the theatres and shops were closed. Those of us of the Royal Family who remained behind lived in an atmosphere of suspicion. Everyone known to have been faithful to King Constantine was put under arrest. Men and women in all walks of life – statesmen, lawyers, writers, officers of both Army and Navy – were mysteriously denounced, brought before a tribunal and sentenced, some to years of imprisonment, others to banishment in remote islands.[3]

Houses were ruthlessly searched for any evidence of sympathy towards the previous regime, while parties of armed men loyal to Venizelos ransacked cupboards and drawers for photographs of the exiled King and his family. It was made a punishable offence to sing *The Son of the Eagle*, the song composed in celebration of the King's victories in the Balkan Wars, heard nearly as often as the Greek National Anthem during the four years of his reign. One of these armed parties heard the song being sung enthusiastically from a house one day, broke in through the front door and rushed upstairs. There they found an old woman sitting alone in an armchair, beating time to the song which emanated from her parrot. Without a word of explanation, they wrung the bird's neck and marched out again.

Though they did not dare to admit it for several years, some of the French – who were primarily to blame for this sorry state of affairs – already saw that they had exceeded their brief. Jonnart had come to Greece completely ignorant of the country's internal affairs, and he later declared that had the mood of the Greeks, who were devoted to King Constantine, been known in Britain, then the decision to dethrone him would never have been taken. This, he wrote to the French Prime Minister, 'has been a far from glorious page in the history of France'.[4]

King Constantine and Queen Sophie left for Switzerland via Italy. Arriving at Taranto, they continued their journey by train on a personal railway coach placed at their disposal by King Victor Emmanuel. After staying at the Palace Hotel, Lugano, for a week, they travelled on to St Moritz. In September they moved to the Villa Werli, Zurich, which they rented from the proprietor of the Dolder Hotel. For the next two years they divided their time between Zurich and the Carlton, St Moritz, until they went to Lucerne in November 1919 and installed themselves at the National Hotel. Even in neutral Europe, calumny and hatred had pursued the family. The Swiss government insisted that they could only stay in German Switzerland, and on their arrival at one town a demonstrator shouted '*Vive la France!*' as he threw stones at them, one hitting the King on the head.

The family were soon followed abroad by Prince Nicholas and his family. A representative of the French High Commissioner was sent to call upon the Prince and recommend that he should go to stay with his family on the island of Spetsai. It was important that the young King should 'settle down', and the presence of his uncles was thought to be 'disturbing him'. Spetsai was close to Nauphlia, the headquarters of the exiled Greek army. Prince Nicholas consulted a friend about the advisability of going there, and was warned that any trouble among the Greek troops would lead to accusations that he was responsible. The best thing he could do was to go and join his eldest brother in Switzerland before the Venizelists attempted to kidnap him, and he did not need telling twice. With a sigh of relief, the French High Commission granted him permission to leave; he and his family, and Prince Christopher, left for Switzerland at the beginning of July. Before long, they were joined by Prince Andrew and his wife and daughters.

The difference between the family's new life in exile and their routine in Athens was acute. Though they had never lived in ostentatious luxury, their private incomes were stopped and they had to depend on borrowed money. Fortunately their household servants had followed them from Greece and served them all out of pure devotion. Months went by without their being paid any wages, but they never complained.

Yet the introspective King Constantine, haunted by a sense of failure, found it extremely difficult to adjust. He fretted and brooded over the past incessantly, sitting around with his head and eyes down. When Spanish influenza took its toll on a war-weary continent early in 1918, weakened by worry, the King fell ill. On the Saturday before

Easter, Prince and Princess Nicholas were advised that his condition was alarming. By the time they reached his villa at Zurich, the doctors had practically given up all hope. They went to Midnight Mass on Easter night in one of the rooms of the Dolder Hotel, two steps from his villa, which had been converted into an Orthodox Chapel. During Mass the doctors slipped in quietly to tell them that his condition had suddenly improved.

Once recovered, he appeared to take on a new lease of life, and the family saw him smile again. He found some comfort in literature, and particularly admired Rudyard Kipling's 'If'. Princess Helen would recall him quoting verses to the family 'during our most difficult times, for there was always a passage that fitted the situation to perfection'.[5]

A further worry was the fate of Queen Olga, who had gone to Russia at the beginning of the war to establish a military hospital near Pavlovsk. She was there when the revolution broke out, but it was imagined that she would be safe among people who had known her since childhood. However, it was reported to the Bolshevik Commissioners that arms were being stored at Pavlovsk, and a detachment of soldiers and sailors from the Red Forces was sent to investigate.

Communications were so bad that it was a long time before she learnt what had become of her family in Greece. As soon as she heard the fate that had befallen her son and daughter-in-law, she wanted to join them at once, but not for several months did the Danish Legation help her obtain permission to leave Russia. She managed to depart just in time, being luckier than the rest of the Romanovs who had failed to escape and were now mostly prisoners of the Bolshevists, condemned to eventual execution. She entered Germany on the eve of military defeat, and was reunited with the family at an emotional gathering early in 1919.

Her only surviving daughter Marie, married to Grand Duke George, had been unable to leave England and return to Russia to be with him after the outbreak of war. She made Harrogate her home and, like her mother, she devoted herself to nursing, setting up three military hospitals in the area. For the first two and a half years they were financed jointly from her own purse and by donations from the Russian imperial family. After the revolution, they were maintained by a grant from the War Office. She was a popular figure with the soldiers, many of whom continued to correspond with her after being nursed back to health and leaving hospital. Her husband suffered the same fate as many of his relations; he was captured by the Bolsheviks and shot without trial in January 1919.*

Shortly after the family began their exile, Emperor William extended a carefully-timed invitation to his sister and brother-in-law. Knowing that King Constantine had been consulting King George V as to the possibility of enrolling Prince Paul as a naval cadet in England, a chance which now seemed remote, he suggested that his fifteen-year-old nephew would be welcome in the German Naval Academy if he was still interested. King Constantine agreed – he was in no position to do otherwise – and soon Prince Paul was on his way to Kiel. Not long after he had been accepted as a cadet, German naval morale began to crumble as the inevitability of defeat dawned upon them. A mutiny in the German High Sea Fleet quickly spread to the Naval Academy at Kiel, and Prince Paul was one of many abandoned naval cadets left to make their own way home.

At length the exiles reconciled themselves to their lot, but the greatest cross they had to bear was the impossibility of communication with King Alexander. In 1918 Queen Sophie heard that he was going to Paris. She was thrilled at the thought of being able to telephone him there, and for days she could talk of nothing else. When the day came she put the call through to the hotel where he was staying, and waited. At length, the voice of the Greek minister answered and said, 'His Majesty is sorry, but he cannot come to the telephone.' Queen Sophie walked away quietly, saying nothing, 'but the disappointment in her face wrung one's heart'. Long afterwards, the family heard that he was never even told of the call.[6]

Another worry to the family was King Alexander's marriage. While still second in succession to the throne, he had fallen deeply in love with Aspasia, daughter of Petros Manos, the Master of the Horse in King Constantine's household, whom he had known since childhood. When there had been little prospect of his succeeding to the throne, it was of no consequence, but once he became King, his obstinate attachment to the girl posed a grave difficulty. At his farewell meeting with King Constantine at Tatoi, he revealed that he had become secretly engaged to Aspasia and asked his permission to marry her. His father was non-committal and asked him only to wait until the war was over. To this, Alexander agreed.

* Princess Marie married Admiral Pericles Ioannides, of the Greek navy, in December 1922.

The Greeks, being a democratic race and recognizing no hereditary aristocracy, looked askance on the prospect of a Greek woman becoming their Queen. As all communication between King Alexander and his parents was cut off in exile, they had no chance of registering their disapproval. For once, they were in full agreement with Venizelos, who warned the King that his people would not approve of marriage between a King and a commoner of their own race. King Constantine desperately wanted his son to wait, as he had promised, wanting to tell him that if only he would be patient, 'I will be best man at your wedding'. Queen Sophie was completely opposed to his marrying a commoner, and was anxious that her husband's health would be jeopardized by the worry.

Yet King Alexander was determined. His sense of responsibility was frustrated by the cavalier treatment meted out to him by his government, and the knowledge that he was a mere cipher King. Princess Helen, who had been closer to her brother than anyone else in the family, was the first to appreciate that he would probably never have taken such a serious step if he had not looked upon himself as merely a temporary occupant of the throne.

His resolve to marry was hardened by a visit from the Duke of Connaught, who visited Athens in March 1918 to invest him with the insignia of the Knight Grand Cross of the Order of the Bath, on behalf of King George V. Britain was anxious to extend the hand of friendship to Greece, now that she was officially an ally.

After completing his mission, the Duke asked him for a private audience the next day. King Alexander had been told that the court's real intention was to arrange a marriage between him and King George V's daughter, Princess Mary, aged twenty. He spent a sleepless night worrying about it, aware that such a proposal would be impossible to refuse without giving offence. Much to his relief, all the Duke wanted to do was meet Mlle Manos, about whose legendary beauty he had heard so much. The King arranged an informal meeting, and the elderly Duke, whose wife had died the previous year, was greatly charmed by her. Before his departure, he told King Alexander with a mischievous twinkle in his eye that, had he been a little younger, he would have proposed to her himself.

Late one night in November 1919 King Alexander enlisted the help of Aspasia's brother-in-law, Christo Zalocostas. A palace chaplain had agreed to perform the marriage ceremony of the King and Aspasia, but he lost his nerve at the last moment. When he failed to appear at the appointed

time, Alexander had to go and fetch him by force in the middle of the
night to Zalocostas's house. Terrified at the consequences, the chaplain
gabbled his way through the service, signed the marriage certificate, and
left as soon as he could. Though he had been sworn to secrecy, he went
to the Archbishop at once and confessed everything.

There was consternation when the secret was discovered. The King had
married without asking the consent of his father or the head of the
Church, and the marriage was intensely unpopular in Greece. Feeling
ran so high that initially Mlle Manos, as she was still known, had to leave
Athens. Yet there was nothing anyone could do about it and, at length, it
was agreed that the marriage was to be recognized as legal, but that the
King's wife was not to be given the rank or any of the privileges of a
Queen. She was to be known simply as Madame Manos.

Six months later, they were finally permitted to go to Paris for their
honeymoon, on condition that she did not travel with him and that they
did not appear together on formal occasions. This stern rule was not
strictly obeyed, and while the King was at the wheel of his car in Paris
with his wife beside him, they emerged unscathed from what could easily
have been a fatal road accident. Soon after their return to Greece, they
knew she was expecting a child.

Greece had declared war on the Central Powers in July 1917 and took
part in the final offensive in September 1918 with British, French and
Italian troops, fighting in Macedonia and advancing into Serbia and
Bulgaria. By late September the campaign was over and the Bulgars asked
for an armistice, thus cutting Turkey off from her Allies in Europe.
Turkish capitulation in October was soon followed by the armistice,
which brought armed conflict in Europe to an end after four and a
quarter years, and Greek troops took part in the Allied entry into
Constantinople.

Although he resented the behaviour of the Venizelists, King Alexander
watched with some pride the emergence of the French-drilled Greek
army. He visited the Macedonian front and was popular with the British
officers. One of them gave him a large Alsatian dog which had been
found in a captured enemy trench. Nobody else could approach this
savage animal, but they took an instant liking to each other. He took it
home and named it 'Fritz', and from then on they were virtually
inseparable. The dog would follow him at heel everywhere or ride in his
car.

Flushed with pride at the end of the war in 1918, Venizelos was determined to play the national hero and statesman on the international stage. He sent Greek troops to take part in the expedition against the Communists in Russia, where they were heavily defeated. No less ominously, this red herring distracted him from the threat of Turkish nationalism and her thirst for revenge for humiliation under Mustafa Kemal. At the Paris Peace Conference, Venizelos asked for northern Epirus, Thrace, Smyrna and surrounding district, and the Dodecanese to be added to Greece, and sought to keep the future of Constantinople open by making it an international city. These claims created difficulties with the Allies, deeply divided among themselves about the future of the former Ottoman Empire. Britain, France and Italy all had their own claims and interests in the area, and all distrusted each other. Nevertheless, with the support of Lloyd George – who was opposed by several members of his divided Cabinet, the Foreign Office at Whitehall, and the War Office – Venizelos was authorized to occupy Smyrna in May 1919 and northern Epirus in December.

In August 1920 the treaty of Sevres was signed. Greece was to receive the whole of Thrace, including Adrianople, the Gallipoli peninsula and the northern coast of the Sea of Marmara, subject to an International Commission for the Straits; all the Aegean Islands, excluding the Dodecanese, which were subject to a separate convention with Italy; and Smyrna, with its hinterland, for an initial period of five years, after which a local assembly might vote for either Greek or Turkish sovereignty. Venizelos was not alone in believing that within a few years, King Alexander would become sovereign of a greatly enlarged Hellenic kingdom astride the Aegean.

For Greece, the treaty of Sevres seemed too good to be true. In fact, it was never ratified. Had it been applied to the letter, it would have deprived Turkey of her independence and virtually annihilated her. The Allies decided to retain the Sultan of Turkey in nominal control at Constantinople. With the encouragement of the increasingly isolated Lloyd George, in October 1920 Venizelos ordered Greek troops at Smyrna to advance against the army of Kemal Ataturk.

Prince Christopher had been engaged to Mrs Nancy Leeds since before the outbreak of war. The situation was complicated by the fact that while a prince of any royal house could marry a commoner, the concept of morganatic marriage did not exist in Greece, and any member of the

Prince and Princess Andrew, 1906

The Crown Prince and Princess and their children, c. 1910. From left: Prince Paul, Prince Alexander, Prince George, Princess Helen, Princess Irene

Ceramic plate, c. 1913–15, with equestrian portrait of King Constantine I. Reflecting contemporary sentiment, it is inscribed 'CONSTANTINE XII'

King Alexander

Prince Christopher

Prince Nicholas

Princess Nicholas

The daughters of Prince and Princess Nicholas. From left: Princess Olga, Princess Elizabeth, Princess Marina

King George II, c. 1922

Queen Elisabeth, 1922

King George II and his family, c. 1922. Standing, left to right: Princess Irene, Prince Christopher, Admiral Ioannides, Prince Paul. Seated, left to right: Princess Marie (widow of Grand Duke George of Russia, married Admiral Ioannides in December 1922), King George II, Princess Helen (Crown Princess Carol of Roumania)

Princess Katherine

King Paul, Queen Frederica and their children, 1947. Left to right: Crown Prince Constantine, Princess Irene, Princess Sophie

King Paul and Queen Frederica, inspecting troops at Lamia, 22 May 1948

King Constantine II and Queen Anne-Marie, leaving Athens Cathedral after their wedding ceremony, 17 September 1964

royal family wishing to marry could only do so after obtaining the consent of both the King and the head of the church. While not opposed to the marriage, King Constantine was reluctant to give his approval on account of the precedent it might create. Finally he suggested that the best thing would be for his brother to change his nationality back to Danish, thus enabling him to marry a commoner, renounce his claims to the throne, and relinquish the title of Royal Highness. Christopher hesitated to do so, as changing nationalities would result in further delays, and at a time when his family was going through such trouble in Greece, it seemed hardly the opportune moment to desert them in such a way.

Mrs Leeds came to Switzerland every winter, as Prince Christopher was unable to cross the frontier to meet her anywhere else. By the beginning of 1920 they decided that it was futile to wait any longer. King Constantine consented to the match, on condition that his brother telegraphed to King Alexander at Athens. It seemed an absurd situation for Christopher to have to ask his own nephew for permission to marry, but he sent the wire and King Alexander, naturally, granted it immediately.

The couple were married on 1 February 1920 at the Russian Church in Vevey. There was some adverse comment in the press, suggesting that the Prince had married a rich widow very much older than himself (she was a mere four years older) in order to lay claim to a 'vast Leeds fortune', which would be used for political propaganda, for buying arms and ammunition to support insurrections against the existing regime in Greece and to restore King Constantine to the throne. In order not to expose her to any unpleasantness, King Constantine refrained from attending the wedding.

A few months later Prince George became engaged to Princess Elisabeth of Roumania, eldest daughter of King Ferdinand and Queen Marie. The young couple had initially met before the war, and George proposed to Elisabeth three years later. Elisabeth had been put off him mainly by the discouragement of her great-aunt Queen Elisabeth, widow of King Carol I. Thoroughly pro-German and anti-British, she persuaded her namesake that she could do better. The somewhat short, monocled Prince George reminded contemporaries of 'a proper Englishman'. Influenced by the Queen's prejudices, Elisabeth dismissed him with barely a second thought, saying that God started him but forgot to finish him off.

In Switzerland George asked her again to marry him. She could not make up her mind at first, but after consideration accepted him. Perhaps she realized that her own personal and physical qualities were less than dazzling. She was fat and plain, with what her mother had to admit was a 'brutal, almost cruel, reckless' side to her. The girl's grandmother, the Dowager Duchess of Coburg (who did not share her daughter Queen Marie's passionately pro-British outlook), said that George 'ought to beat her, then she would like him'.

Virtually stateless, homeless and penniless, with an uncertain future ahead of him, George had little to offer Elisabeth, beyond his lineage. None the less, Queen Marie of Roumania was delighted with the match, and King Constantine and Queen Sophie were glad to see their eldest son's prospects as good as settled. Queen Marie invited him and his two eldest sisters, Princesses Helen and Irene, back to Roumania to stay when the engagement was to be announced and made public.

While they were staying, Crown Prince Carol of Roumania arrived home. An unstable young man, he had already made a marriage with a commoner, Zizi Lambrino, which had been dissolved. Helen at twenty-four was tall, slim, elegant (considerably prettier than her future sister-in-law), innocent and somewhat lacking in confidence as a result of her suffering over the humiliation of her parents and years of exile. Treated with great sympathy by the family, she and Prince Carol became deeply attached.

Before the engagement could be announced, there was another change in the fortunes of the Greek royal family. In a sense it was for the better, but it was precipitated by tragic circumstances.

On 2 October 1920 King Alexander called at the house of his vineyard keeper on the estate at Tatoi. Two pet monkeys were playing in the garden, and at the sight of his dog Fritz, they ran up screaming. One attacked it, and the King went to break up the fight. While trying to separate both animals, the second monkey attacked him, biting him severely on the legs and in the stomach. Helpers came running from the house to tear the animal off him, leaving a deep wound in his leg into which they forced an oil-stained bandage in an attempt to stop the bleeding.

The keeper's wife cleaned the wound at once, as did the doctors when the King returned to Athens, but they did not cauterize it. At first he seemed more concerned by the absurdity of the situation than the discomfort, and he asked his doctors not to talk to anyone about the incident. Nevertheless, high fever set in that evening, and next morning his condition was so serious that eminent European specialists were summoned from abroad. Violent septicaemia had set in and the poison was coursing rapidly through his bloodstream. In hopeless efforts to drain the poison, the surgeons seemed to be making a vicious wound even worse. Symptoms of jaundice appeared, followed by pneumonia in the right lung and dysentery. There was talk of amputating the leg, though none of the Greek doctors was prepared to take responsibility for authorizing such a drastic operation.

A medical correspondent from Athens reported guardedly (14 October) that 'the condition is referred to as "cellulitis", and is of a dangerous character. Operative measures and vaccination are practised, and are, on the whole, fairly satisfactory so far as the majority of cases are concerned . . .'[7]

King Alexander's case was to be anything but satisfactory. His cries of pain could be heard by the Evzone guard round the house. In moments of lucidity he would listen to the sound of visitors' cars and find some distraction in identifying them as soon as he could hear the engine approaching. He could even joke with the doctor who was dressing his leg, saying that he was using such a lot of bandage that he must have shares in the company. But delirium set in on 19 October and 'cerebral crisis' four days later. One specialist after another was summoned from abroad, but there was nothing they could do. At length the doctors would not allow the dressings to be changed any more, in order to spare the dying man unnecessary suffering.

In his agony, King Alexander called out for his mother. Desperate with anxiety at the telegrams from Athens, which arrived several times a day, Queen Sophie begged for permission from the Greek government to come and nurse him. The answer was a blunt refusal. Queen Olga was at Lausanne with Prince Nicholas and his family, and Queen Sophie asked her to go to her grandson, believing that the Greeks would not refuse her entry. She was right, and a permit was granted for Queen Olga. Her ship, however, was delayed by rough seas and she arrived twelve hours too late.

On 25 October, in his final delirium, the King thought he saw his dead grandfather walking down the hill at Tatoi where he was buried. He called for his driver and asked if the brakes of one particular model had been repaired, as he wanted to go for a drive. His hands curled round an imaginary steering-wheel as, in his mind, he took himself on a final journey around the lanes of the estate, then his arms dropped back. Shortly after 4.00 in the afternoon, he was dead. He was twenty-seven years of age.

That day the doctors had telegraphed to his parents that nothing could be done. Yet Queen Sophie still refused to give up hope, asking her doctor continual questions and staying up till late at night to ask if any message had arrived. The doctor and Prince Nicholas were the first to see the telegram announcing King Alexander's death that evening, but in order to allow them a few hours' rest, they kept the news from King Constantine and Queen Sophie until the following morning.

CHAPTER TEN

'Poor excellent honest Tino'

Once King Alexander's condition was recognized as hopeless, Venizelos and his ministers were confronted with the problem of who should succeed him. Any suggestions that 'should any change unfortunately occur in the occupancy of the Greek throne, a situation might arise that would entail the disappearance of the dynasty'[1] were firmly denied. The National Assembly emphasized that it did not demand the removal of the dynasty, only the definite exclusion of King Constantine and Crown Prince George. His closest associates affirmed that constitutional monarchy in Greece had no stronger supporter than Venizelos, 'who believes it to be the institution best adapted to the political needs of the Hellenic people'. While it was likely that a regent would be appointed, probably either Admiral Koundouriotis or Monsieur Zaimis, the possibility that the Venizelos cabinet would contemplate the establishment of any form of republican government was remote.

During the King's last unhappy days of delirium, the most commonly held view was that in the increasingly likely event of his death, the crown would be offered to the youngest brother, Prince Paul, subject to the conditions that he should swear to observe the constitution and regard the exclusion of his father and eldest brother as irrevocable.

Two days after his death, the body of King Alexander was conveyed to the Cathedral at Athens to lie in state, and there his funeral was held, with Queen Olga as the sole representative of the family. He was buried near his grandfather, in a simple grave on the hill at Tatoi.

In due course other members of the family were buried there as well. Significantly, the inscriptions on the tombs of the other Kings recorded their regnal names, followed by the designation 'King of the Hellenes, Prince of Denmark'. That on Alexander's reads 'Alexander, son of the King of the Hellenes, Prince of Denmark. He reigned in the place of his father, 14 June 1917 to 25 October 1920.'

Meanwhile, on 29 October the Greek minister, M. Kepetzis, arrived at Lucerne and asked for an audience with Prince Paul. The Prince was astonished to be greeted by the obsequiously bowing minister as 'Your

Majesty King Paul I'. It was explained that, by the death of his brother, the crown was now his; Crown Prince George was unacceptable to the Greek people and it was impossible to recall his father.

Paul pointed out that he was being placed in a painful position, which he would need to consider, and would give his answer later that evening. He consulted his father and they decided that under such circumstances he could not accept the crown. Accordingly, the Prince wrote to Kepetzis the following day, asking him to tell the Greek government 'with the request that the Greek people may also be informed' that the throne did not belong to him, but to his father, whose heir according to the constitution was his elder brother George. 'Furthermore, neither of them has renounced these rights, but both were obliged to leave Greece in obedience to their higher sense of patriotic duty.'[2]

Venizelos was disappointed, if not surprised. New elections in Greece were planned for the following month. Fresh from his triumphs at the Peace Conference in Paris, he expected an overwhelming mandate. But with Prince Paul having refused the throne, the election issue became partly one of personalities – the dictator against the King in exile. On 14 November the elections produced an overwhelming victory for the King's supporters, led by M. Ralli, the new Prime Minister.

The defeat of Venizelos (even in his own constituency) reflected partly war-weariness, partly feelings of resentment and humiliation at the flagrant meddling in internal Greek affairs by France and Britain, and disgust at his vengeful and arbitrary behaviour and that of his supporters during the previous three years. Disgusted and shattered, he went into self-imposed exile, and Ralli went to Tatoi, begging Queen Olga to accept a Regency until King Constantine returned.

She promptly sent a telegram to her son, signed by herself as Regent. His official reaction was one of shock. Then he declared that he could not return to Greece unless the people recalled him directly by a national plebiscite.

It was accordingly announced that the people would be asked to vote on 5 December whether they wanted King Constantine to return. Throughout the month of November, the reports he received from Greece were so optimistic that he felt the result was never seriously in doubt. By the beginning of December the Hotel National was crowded with packing cases labelled 'Bagages de Sa Majesté le Roi des Hellenes', and the press proclaimed that it was 'an open secret' that he planned to go to Athens once the result of the plebiscite was known.

In Athens Gounaris, leader of the majority party in parliament, and widely expected to assume the premiership once the result was announced, made it clear to the rest of Europe whose decision the matter was:

The question of the return of King Constantine is a purely internal one which concerns the Greek people, who are alone entitled to decide it. I cannot see why foreign Governments should interfere in the internal affairs of our people, obliging them to change their mind about a King who is most adored and beloved. Such action would be contrary to the principles of independence and self-determination which inspired the acts of the Entente Powers after the war.[3]

The British minister from Berne called on King Constantine, assuring him that the British government would offer no objection to his resumption of the throne. The King felt that this was a tacit acknowledgement by Britain of her misjudgement in the past.

Nevertheless, two days before the vote in December, a meeting between senior ministers of the British, French and Italian governments at 10 Downing Street issued a joint declaration to the Greek government. It stated that while the Powers had no wish to interfere in the internal affairs of Greece, they felt bound to declare publicly that the restoration to the throne of Greece of a king whose disloyal attitude and conduct towards the Allies during the war caused them great embarrassment and loss could only be regarded by them as acceptance by Greece of his 'hostile' acts. Such a step would 'create a new and unfavourable situation with regard to relations between Greece and the Allies, and the governments of the latter reserved to themselves complete liberty in dealing with the situation thus created'.[4] It was a thinly veiled warning that, under the leadership of King Constantine once more, Greece could expect no Allied support in her war against Turkey. A leader in *The Times* the following day confirmed the official Allied attitude by warning that the people remained free to bring back King Constantine and 'the ex-Emperor William's sister', but only at the price of the forfeiture of goodwill in the attainment of their 'secular aspirations', and the Allied governments would not hesitate to remind them.

What effect such coercion had on the result, it is impossible to say, but if it was an attempt to order the electorate to reject the King, whose enforced departure had been marked by emotional demonstrations of overwhelming sympathy, it misfired badly. The plebiscite gave him an overwhelming victory of 1,010,788 votes in favour, 10,883 against.

Before his return he indignantly told a correspondent from *The Times* that his policy would soon show that the Allies were wrong in imagining he favoured Germany, or that he intended to pursue a different foreign policy to that of the Venizelos government. He denied suggestions that Greece was to become a home for 'undesirable and dispossessed sovereigns'. 'Why the devil should I invite the ex-Kaiser?' he was quoted as saying. 'I am accused of being pro-German because the ex-Kaiser is my brother-in-law. I am not pro-German, and if I was so, for that reason it would surely be evident that I am so no longer, since the German Government has got rid of my brother-in-law.'[5]

The cruiser *Averoff* was sent to Italy to bring him back home. The British Admiralty issued instructions that no vessel of the Royal Navy should salute her on her passage. King George V thought this departure from customary naval courtesy seemed unduly vindictive, and ordered that British ships should withdraw discreetly out of sight of *Averoff* instead.

Entering Athens with Queen Sophie and Crown Prince George, the King returned amid emotional demonstrations of loyalty and affection. The crowds who called out '*Erchetai!*' ('He is coming!') swept onto the railway tracks as his train arrived and brought it to a standstill before it reached the terminal platform. When he stepped out, so tall and imposing in his bemedalled uniform and plumed helmet, they went wild with enthusiasm.

For half an hour the royal family battled against the excited crowd in order to reach the open carriages drawn up outside the station. The drive to the old palace was a triumph, with church bells clanging, flowers raining down on them, and tumultuous cheers. First they went to the Cathedral, where an official *Te Deum* was sung and thanksgiving prayers were offered by the Archbishop, then on reaching the palace, the King was lifted shoulder-high and carried indoors.

He was deeply moved by this riotous show of Greek affection, but Queen Sophie was less convinced. She had been bitterly hurt by her son's death, as well as their treatment during the war years. Recalling the demonstrations that had accompanied her husband's return into Athens as a war hero in 1912, she wondered whether the excitement was too exuberant to last. Her fears were to be confirmed all too soon. Prince

Christopher watched her during their return procession and caught her evidently brooding over the death of her son, 'a sacrifice to the schemes of others. I looked at his mother's grief-stricken face, smiling bravely at the cheering crowds, and knew that her heart bled in secret.'[6]

For some time after his return to Greece, King Constantine could not show himself in public without provoking frenzied demonstrations of loyal devotion. Much as he appreciated them, he soon found them mildly embarrassing. To the family, he commented wryly that he was beginning to feel like a guest made uncomfortable by over-lavish hospitality.

Yet he had little conception of what lay ahead. From the moment of his return the King and his family were to become the scapegoats for every misfortune which befell Greece as a result of the irresponsible policy imposed on the nation in their absence. A conference at London in February and March 1921, to which delegates from Greece and Turkey were invited, proved inconclusive. It left the almost bankrupt Greece still irrevocably committed to a hopeless war in Asia Minor.

It was an impossible situation. The Allies made no secret of their disapproval of his restoration and the electoral defeat of Venizelos, and true to their threats they withdrew their support for Greek military action. Such an eventuality had been foreseen by the King in 1915, when he was being urged to commit his country's forces to the Dardanelles campaign. As he told Prince Nicholas at the time, it would be absurd to expect any military assistance from the entente in Asia Minor after the war in central Europe was over. Not only would Greek presence alone clash with the interests of the Powers themselves, but 'everybody will be so exhausted by the time the war is over, that it will be quite out of the question for another campaign to be undertaken for our personal benefit.'[7]

Nevertheless there was some understanding among the Allies for King Constantine's position. General Sir Henry Wilson, who as Chief of the British Imperial General Staff was in a better position to appreciate the practical military aspects of Greece's situation than all the British and French politicians put together, had told Venizelos to his face that 'he had ruined his country and himself by going to Smyrna', but such words were of no practical support to the monarch, who was left to pick up the pieces afterwards. He would have preferred to bring the troops home, but to give up the territory already won from Turkey and so expose Smyrna's large Greek population to the angry Turks, thirsting for revenge, would be to risk losing his crown again.

Yet to continue to fight the Turks without Allied support would mean almost certain defeat. His position was further complicated by the fact that everyone on his General Staff was anxious to deal the enemy a quick, knockout blow before they had time to build up their army, and by the knowledge that it was his refusal to join battle during the war of 1914–18 that had cost him his throne.

First, though, came both marriages uniting the houses of Greece and Roumania. They had been firmly encouraged, if not engineered, by Queen Marie of Roumania. That neither were love matches did not disturb her, for she had not been in love with Crown Prince Ferdinand when she married him in 1893, and the marriage had turned out satisfactorily.

King Constantine told his daughter Helen that any engagement between her and the Crown Prince was a matter for her to decide. Queen Sophie, who temperamentally had little if anything in common with her flamboyant cousin Queen Marie, was upset and made no attempt to hide her feelings. She was particularly disturbed at the prospect of a marriage between the sophisticated, philandering Prince Carol and the unworldly, unspoilt, home-loving Princess Helen, with her simple upbringing.

She urged her daughter to be cautious, but Helen would not be dissuaded. She later recalled that she was 'attracted' to Prince Carol, 'and felt that later I could come to love him'. What really made her decide to accept him, however, was the death of her favourite brother Alexander. As he was no longer there, she felt she could not bear to face Athens and Tatoi again. If she went to live in Roumania, she would no longer be in the places that 'would constantly wound me with memories'. At the same time, perhaps she realized it was her only chance to escape from the uncertainty of life as a potential exile, and as Crown Princess of Roumania, later Queen, she would make a better life for herself. Little did she realize, she later admitted, how true were the warning words of her mother. 'Had I listened, I would have been spared years of misery.'[8]

Crown Prince George was betrothed to Carol's sister, Elisabeth, and had been in Bucharest when his brother died. Both weddings were celebrated in March 1921. King Constantine and Queen Sophie did not attend their son's wedding in Bucharest, but were present at Athens for the wedding of Carol and Helen at the Metropolitan Cathedral. After a honeymoon at Tatoi, they left for Roumania.

While Queen Marie was in Athens (without King Ferdinand) for her son's wedding, her hosts were subjected to an embarrassing and humiliating experience. A large royal party was walking outside when Lord Granville, British minister in Athens, came towards them. The Allied Powers had still refused to recognize King Constantine, and Granville had never yet paid an official call on the King. An informal meeting of this nature, however, was surely different. Granville had been an old friend of the King and Queen and they intended to greet him cordially, but he ignored them. Going up to Queen Marie, he bowed and shook her hand warmly. Then, without any sign of recognizing the others, he turned and left. The King and Queen were appalled, particularly as so many other people were present.

Later that year Beverley Nichols, a young English journalist, was asked to go to Athens under the special protection of the Greek royal family. Here, he was told, he would be given access to secret archives, as a result of which he would be expected to write a book containing 'sensational information' that would restore the prestige of King Constantine after years of calumny, and persuade the English and French governments to recognize him. 'King Tino' was widely regarded in both countries as an arch-traitor, 'a sort of miniature Kaiser, who by his treachery and his double dealing had imperilled our cause throughout the whole of the Near East'.[9]

Nichols got on very well with the Greek royal family, and was convinced at once that the legend of 'Tino's' treachery was false, owing more to ruthless propaganda and wartime hysteria than to any reasoned argument. He had several private meetings with the King and fully accepted his version of events, especially regarding his reservations in taking part in the débâcle of the Dardanelles and the subsequent Allied failure at Gallipoli.

As for Queen Sophie, Nichols would never forget his first sight of her, 'for she had the saddest face of any woman I have ever seen. Standing there, dressed entirely in black, a bowl of lilies by her side, her face rose from the shadows like one who has known every suffering.'[10] She told him that her greatest wish was to return to England, and that her most fervent dream was that her daughters should marry Englishmen.

Nichols abandoned his idea of writing a book, ostensibly as he considered there was no story. Yet he was impressed by their magnanimity towards Britain, their lack of ostentation, their apparently cheerful acceptance of reduced financial circumstances, and the pride that prevented them from accepting help from the King's wealthy American sister-in-law, Princess Christopher.

Similarly impressed was Mrs Philip Martineau, an Englishwoman much in demand in royal circles for her expert knowledge of gardens. Having come from the glittery Roumanian court, she was immediately struck by the simplicity of life in Athens. Initially she had attempted to refuse the royal summons, mindful of the reputation Queen Sophie had as an aggressive German *Hausfrau*. It astonished her to find instead a small, fragile, sad-eyed woman, dressed in deepest mourning for her son Alexander, in an extraordinarily English setting. Though she had an air of regal majesty, she was certainly not the virago of Allied propaganda. This, Mrs Martineau decided, could hardly be the belligerent German who was reputed to have taken a knife to her husband in order to make him reject the Allies.

During her visit to Greece, Mrs Martineau was shown the typically English garden at Athens and the Queen's scheme for the afforestation and landscaping of Athens. She was also shown part of the forest at Tatoi, still recovering from the arson attack of 1916. When asked what had prompted such action, the Queen, 'numb with pain', replied that it was because she was rumoured to have a private wire to her eldest brother, the then German Emperor, concealed there.

King Constantine, noted Mrs Martineau, looked ill and tired, with dark pouches under his eyes. Although placid by temperament, he was 'very bitter about his treatment', as might well be expected.

On 25 March 1921 the widow of King Alexander gave birth to a daughter, named Alexandra. The first grandchild of King Constantine and Queen Sophie, she had the distinction of being the only member of the Greek royal family who had any Greek blood in her. The King and Queen had come to terms with their earlier reservations about their tragic son's marriage, and in particular Queen Sophie was devoted to her daughter-in-law, who had done more than anybody else to make the last years of his woefully short life happy, and to her grandchild. At her insistence the former Mlle Manos was granted the title Princess Alexander, and the baby girl recognized, like the other female descendants of King George I, as a Princess of Greece and Denmark.

Meanwhile, to inject some morale into the Greek forces, the government decided that King Constantine must go to the theatre of war in Asia Minor and take over supreme command. The soldiers still believed that the victor of the Balkan wars could once again bring them to victory against all odds.

Yet the virile Crown Prince of 1912 had been a very different man from the tired, prematurely aged King of 1921. In May, while attending a *Te Deum* in the Cathedral at Athens on the eve of his departure, the stifling heat caused the dormant wound left by the incision to remove two ribs during his attack of pleurisy in 1915 to reopen. Blood spread over his white tunic and he had to sit down in order to hide the sight from the congregation. Yet he still set off for Smyrna as planned without giving himself a chance to rest and recover.

Thanks to outside help, the Turkish army was better equipped than that of the Greek. It was also becoming numerically superior, with a new factor appearing in the Graeco-Turkish struggle, namely the leadership of Mustafa Kemal, who turned the defeated Turkish armies into a first-class fighting machine. Stretched beyond limits to keep 350,000 half-clothed and half-starved fighting men at the front, Greece was in no position to pit herself for long and entirely unaided against a military genius.

On 10 June a son was born to Prince Andrew and Princess Alice at Mon Repos, Corfu. Male children in the youngest generation had been very few, for the baby Prince had four elder sisters, of whom the youngest was already aged seven, while all of Prince Nicholas's three children had been girls. Sixth in succession to the throne, he was named Philip and the entire town of Corfu stood sponsor at his christening.

Shortly afterwards, Prince Andrew left for the front to take command of the 12th Division army corps. Like his eldest brother, he had no illusions of glory and considered himself unsuited by experience and temperament to lead. However, King Constantine was Commander-in-Chief and required Prince Nicholas and Crown Prince George to remain beside him on his staff, and the reluctant Prince Andrew was the obvious choice to take over an active command in the field to inspire the troops. Modest about his abilities, he was experienced and far-sighted enough to notice at once the deficiencies in equipment and the lack of training among the men. He was soon to appreciate another unforeseen if hardly unexpected danger – the divided political loyalties among the officers, kept alive by the propaganda of political exiles in Constantinople. Many of them chose Prince Andrew as a convenient target, at one stage going so far as to put out a story that he had died of wounds in order to undermine confidence in Athens.

King Constantine spent most of his time in the war zone talking to staff officers, personally presenting decorations to all the officers and soldiers who had distinguished themselves on active service, or reading during the occasional moments left for relaxation. Queen Sophie was there as well, visiting hospitals daily and seeing to the soldiers' welfare. Their presence helped to raise the morale of his soldiers, but the King could do little more. They marched with renewed spirit against a stubborn foe, but the odds against them were tremendous. The unfamiliar countryside, parched, rugged and almost roadless, was a formidable obstacle. Dysentery and fever were rife, summer dust was swept up by the hot winds, and chronic shortages of food and water made conditions worse.

On one occasion as they moved up to the front in Asia Minor, the King's train came to a stop beside a returning hospital train. In an instant the grim, silent hospital train burst into life. Wounded people swarmed from the doors and windows, limbless men, smothered in bandages, crawled and rolled in the dust in frantic efforts to drag themselves to the King's side.

At first, the tide ran in favour of the Greeks. In July 1921 they won a battle at Eski-Shehr, and in recognition of Prince Andrew's role he was promoted to Lieutenant-General and given command of the Second Army Corps. Back in Athens, news of the victory conjured up dreams of the resurrection of the Byzantine Empire. Had any Greek counselled self-restraint and moderation, it was said, both rival supporters, royalist and Venizelist alike, would have considered him a traitor to his country. So General Papoulas, acting Commander-in-Chief, ordered an immediate advance on Ankara. Prince Andrew opposed this move on practical grounds, aware that it seemed a hopeless objective without reinforcements, but speed was essential as the advance and battle had to take place before the rains began in September. Mustafa Kemal personally supervised the Turkish retreat, aware that every mile he withdrew further weakened the Greek line of supply, and dug in to prepare for a counter-attack. The battle of Sakaria, which lasted for three weeks during August and September 1921, resulted in Greek defeat.

When news reached Athens there was an immediate demand for a scapegoat. Prince Andrew was unjustly blamed for insisting on the advance of 40,000 men on a march across a waterless desert. Relations between Prince Andrew and General Papoulas came to such a state that the Prince asked repeatedly to be relieved of his command. Refused permission twice, as the General was reluctant to lose his services and his experience, he asked for leave of absence and this was granted. He returned to Athens in the autumn.

King Constantine had already come back to his homeland. The desert was no place for a man of his indifferent health, and long drives over rough roads through thick clouds of dust took their toll. Often tired, he never gave way to fatigue and nothing exasperated him more than being treated like an invalid. By September he was in a state of chronic exhaustion. The officers took him to convalesce at Broussa, on the Sea of Marmara, hoping that he might recover sufficiently to return to the army, but the doctors insisted that he would probably die if he did not go back to Greece as soon as he was well enough to travel.

Much capital was made of this by Venizelist elements in the army, working in league with exiles in Constantinople. They spread the story among troops that their King had abandoned them.

The shivering Greek army continued their heroic but almost hopeless struggle that winter, through the near-Arctic storms of Asia Minor. In Athens the government, led by Gounaris, was desperately aware that without foreign troops or financial aid, matters would grow worse by the week.

They had a fervent, but hardly influential, champion in the shape of King Constantine's aunt, the ageing widow Queen Alexandra, full of indignation on behalf of 'poor excellent *honest* Tino who has been so infamously treated by the world & France'. Her endless letters to her son, King George V, begging him to do all he could for his beleaguered cousin whose father had been put on the Greek throne largely by a British government, had little effect. While Lloyd George admitted that King Constantine's personality was a positive factor in raising the morale of his forces, he still refused to recognize him officially, on the grounds that it was a matter to be settled by the Allies collectively. King George explained sorrowfully to his mother (9 October) that there was nothing his government could do in the face of French hostility:

A short time ago we sounded France as to whether she would be inclined to recognise Tino, but Briand refused absolutely so there the matter stands. The only way to help Tino in his difficult position would be to recognise him, but that at the present moment is impossible. I am not prepared now, on account of the strong feeling (which may be quite unjust) which certainly exists in this country against him to do anything, in fact no one would even listen to me if I did.[11]

At length, the Powers started to become apprehensive that a terrible Greek débâcle might cause them grave embarrassment. Discussions began between Whitehall and the Quai d'Orsay and Rome, but were interrupted by the fall of the French government, causing talks to be started a second time. In February 1922 Gounaris, who had succeeded Ralli, appealed to Britain. His statement, published in the British press, stated bluntly that Greece was penniless and at the end of her tether, and she must either receive aid at once or else abandon Asia Minor, leaving the Christian populations to a bloody fate.

Lord Curzon, Secretary of State for Foreign Affairs, felt Gounaris was exaggerating. Until the Powers could arrive at some conclusion, it was vital for Greece not to abandon her ground in Asia Minor. Lloyd George was equally firm; though still professing sympathy for Greece, he insisted that she must hang on if she wanted any aid.

Matters went from bad to worse. Prince Andrew returned to Smyrna after working with the Supreme Army Council, where he tried to persuade General Papoulas to put an end to the disloyal plotting which was rife among the forces under his command, but without success. Making it clear that the continuance of the existing command could only end with disastrous results, he applied for and was given command of the Fifth Army Corps of Epirus and the Ionian Islands, with headquarters at Janina in Greece.

In March Greece declared willingness to accept a British proposal for a compromise peace based on the withdrawal of their forces and the establishment of a League of Nations protectorate over the Greeks of Asia Minor. But the Turks, fully aware that the military tide had turned in their favour, mounted a massive offensive against Smyrna in August. It ended in complete victory within less than a fortnight. Smyrna was sacked, looted and burnt, and several thousand Greek troops and civilians were burned alive, drowned or massacred. Some Greeks took to the sea, but many were drowned in a desperate effort to escape. An estimated 30,000 Greek and Armenian Christians perished. 'Infidel Izmir', as the Turks had called Smyrna on account of its huge non-Muslim population, was consumed in the holocaust as panic-stricken refugees sought to escape to the neighbouring Greek islands.

For such a disaster the Allied Powers were largely to blame, first for emboldening, and indeed committing, the Greeks to such an adventure, and secondly for withholding military support which had been virtually promised at one stage.

The effect on Greece and her public morale was shattering. Inspired mainly by anti-monarchists in Constantinople, and led by Colonel Nicholas Plastiras, a party of defeated troops demanded King Constantine's abdication, the dissolution of parliament, and the appointment of a new emergency government, backing their demand with a threat to advance against Athens.

Had he been in better health, King Constantine could have stood firm. He still had a strong following in Greece. But the thought of civil war appalled him and he had no desire to fight any more, either militarily or politically. On 27 September, after consulting his trusted friend Metaxas, he issued a proclamation declaring that 'In order that my presence on the throne may not interfere with the sacred unity of the Hellenes and the assistance of our friends, and in all order to avoid all misconception on the subject, I have abdicated.'[12]

In London there was undisguised relief. 'A paltry personage vanishes from the Near Eastern stage', began a leader in *The Times* next day, recalling that the King, who had served in the Prussian army as a young man and 'imbibed the Potsdam traditions of militarist monarchy', had done what he could during the war to curry favour with Germany and Bulgaria, 'while assuring us of his affection for England'.[13]

In such unpropitious circumstances, at the nadir of his family's fortunes, did King George II of the Hellenes ascend the throne.

CHAPTER ELEVEN

'Too sincere and upright a man'

On 30 September King George II received members of the Revolutionary Committee, headed by Plastiras, and assured them solemnly that his father's abdication was 'sincere'. He would not try to regain the throne.

At the time of his accession, Princess Elisabeth – now Queen – was in Bucharest, recovering from a severe bout of typhoid followed by pleurisy. She had to cut her hair because it was falling out, and, with a sense of the theatrical which outdid that of her mother, she dyed what was left red, stained her eyebrows pitch black, powdered her face white, and applied dark make-up to accentuate the circles below her eyes. This cultivation of her 'tragic, ghostlike appearance' found no favour with the family. Even worse than her appearance was her state of mind, which as both her husband and her mother recognized, was not becoming for a queen. Queen Marie complained that she was 'in every way utterly unprepared for such an event'. She showed no interest nor love for Greece, 'she has studiously refused to have a child, she knows no one, she cares for no one, she trusts no one.'[1]

After Queen Elisabeth's miscarriage at Smyrna and subsequent ill-health, her mother's strictures were unnecessarily harsh. Yet in the circumstances it would have been some consolation for King George II to have a devoted wife prepared to stand by him, as his mother and grandmother had stood by his kinsmen and predecessors. But Queen Elisabeth's self-absorption alienated everyone, and Queen Marie's pious hope that the difficult situation in Greece might be the making of her went unfulfilled. She went to Athens once she was well enough, but with great reluctance. Much of her time was spent bewailing her fate and sending frantic cables to Prince Paul of Serbia and Prince Barbo Stirbey, one of her mother's favourite ministers in Roumania, to come and rescue her.

Immediately after King George's accession, Prince and Princess Christopher returned to Athens. They had learnt of King Constantine's abdication while in Paris, and the Princess wisely advised her husband to go home, get possession of all his stocks and bonds and take them out of the country, otherwise it would 'only be a question of time now before George is turned out too, and then everything will be taken from you'.[2] When he sent his passport to the Greek minister in Paris for a visa, he was informed that he could only remain in Greece for eight days.

Going first to Corfu to stay with Prince and Princess Andrew at Mon Repos, he was shocked to find the house under police surveillance, with reports being made on every visitor. Princess Andrew informed him nervously that her husband had been summoned to Athens to give evidence in the trial of ministers who were accused of having instigated the Asia Minor campaign.

In Athens the tension was immediately apparent, with people in the streets apprehensive or sullenly indifferent. When Prince Christopher went to Tatoi he found King George II almost a prisoner. Dreading a revolt of his own subjects, he looked worn out and had hardly slept for several nights. Spies surrounded him day and night and reported all his movements. He could not even drive from Tatoi to Athens with his uncle, but had to go alone in an inconspicuous car from which the royal pennant had been removed, driven by a chauffeur in plain clothes.

The few weeks between the abdication of King Constantine and his final departure from Greece were not merely uncomfortable, but also fraught with danger. Most of the ministries in Athens were in a state of confusion and seven former ministers were arrested. Some staunch republicans were so set on vengeance that they advocated seizing the former King instantly and executing him. A senior French diplomat in the capital warned that it was essential to get him away if he was to avoid assassination. The tragic fate of Tsar Nicholas II and his family overshadowed the minds of Greek royalists, who intended to make certain that history would not repeat itself in Athens.

Prince Nicholas sent a message to the head of the British Naval Mission, asking if a British man-of-war could take the whole family away from Greece as they were in imminent danger. A Foreign Office dispatch from London blandly remarked that 'It is certainly to be hoped that we shall not become involved in the misfortunes of the Greek Royal Family. On the other hand we would, of course, intervene to avoid actual bloodshed.'

King Constantine, Queen Sophie, their daughters Princesses Irene and Katherine, left just before midnight on 30 October in an insanitary steamer, SS *Patris*, en route for Palermo in Sicily. Military honours were paid, and a number of the former King's friends were on the pier to say goodbye, with men and women crying as they saw him leave for the last time.

At first there was no accommodation ready for the family and they spent a week in a bug-infested ship before moving into a hotel in Palermo. A British naval officer who accompanied them reported with approval on their bearing throughout this time. Though obviously very tired and under tremendous strain, they showed great dignity and control and made light of the inconveniences which they had to put up with.

Meanwhile Queen Olga, now aged seventy-one, was staying in England; her eyesight was deteriorating and she had been in Paris for treatment. Queen Alexandra invited her to Sandringham, where she was entertaining her more sprightly younger sister, the Dowager Tsarina. The three widows, two in failing health, could reminisce about older, happier times.

Queen Olga also paid a visit to King George V and Queen Mary at Windsor Castle, where she was wheeled around the passages in a bathchair. Noticing an equestrian bronze statue one day, she peered at it and told her attendant that the figure was evidently Queen Victoria. 'Oh no, Your Majesty,' he replied solemnly, 'that is Lady Godiva!'[3] King George roared with laughter when she told him, and to the end of his life he never tired of telling family and friends.

Back in Athens, the news of Prince Andrew was black indeed. He had been brought to Athens on a false pretext and arrested immediately on his arrival. He was now in solitary confinement in the house of a friend, awaiting trial. Nobody except his valet was allowed to go near him. Guards kept strict watch and all letters and parcels that came to the house were confiscated. General Pangalos, newly appointed Minister of War, asked him how many children he had, and when the Prince told him, he remarked, 'Poor things, what a pity they will soon be orphans!'[4]

The rest of the family outside Greece spared no effort to save Prince Andrew. Queen Olga appealed to King George V in England, King Alfonso XIII in Spain, and President Poincaré in France, all of whom promised to do what little they could. Concerted protests were the result, which even Venizelos could hardly ignore. Guessing what would happen, he speeded up the trial of the prisoners – including Gounaris and two other former Prime Ministers, two former ministers, and a previous Commander-in-Chief – by telegraphing to his subordinates, 'Whatever you have to do, do it quickly. Tomorrow may be too late.'[5] They took him at his word. The men were taken out to the prison courtyard, lined up against the wall and shot. Britain immediately severed diplomatic relations with Greece and the minister left Athens that same night.

On 2 December, after seven weeks of imprisonment, Prince Andrew was tried in the Chamber of Deputies by a jury of officers, who had previously decided that he must be shot. Representatives of King Alfonso and the Pope left Madrid and Rome for Athens, and, at the request of King George V, Captain Gerald Talbot, a former naval attaché in Greece, came out as well. It was due to his intervention that the court reconvened and commuted the sentence from execution to banishment for life. The Prince was reunited with his wife, who had almost given up all hope of ever seeing him again, and their five children. An orange box was converted into a cot for eighteen-month-old Prince Philip, as the family travelled to Rome, Paris and London in time for Christmas.

Meanwhile, Prince and Princess Nicholas and their daughters were spending the festive season at the Villa Hygeia, Palermo, with King Constantine, Queen Sophie and their younger children. Prince Christopher had stayed with them shortly before Christmas, and found the people of Palermo 'kindness itself'. It was 'very different from those miserable years in Switzerland with the whole of Europe against us'. Yet the change in the former King was shocking. 'He seemed to have aged many years in the last few months. He had not lost his sense of humour, laughed and took part in everything going on around him, yet he was like a ghost among the living. His heart was broken.'[6] As the brothers bid each other goodbye, the youngest had a premonition that he would never see the eldest again.

King Constantine had grown lean and hunched. Suffering from a form of arteriosclerosis, he spoke little and on occasion paced restlessly around indoors. When depression struck, he sat for hours in silence, looking into space. During his first exile, he had been sustained by the plans he could make for the future, but now there was no future to look forward to. Of one thing he was convinced, that he had done his duty to the last.

On the afternoon of 10 January 1923 he gave a tea party at the Villa Hygeia for some of the local nobility who had befriended him and his family, and in the evening he attended a party in the hotel ballroom. He seemed in better spirits than usual and was looking forward to starting for Naples in two days' time with the family to stay at Palazzo Capodimonte, at the invitation of the Duke of Aosta. Afterwards, they planned to take up residence in Florence.

But that evening was his last. After taking his bath the next morning, he was dressing for breakfast when a maid called the family urgently. He had collapsed on the bed and lost consciousness. A doctor at the hotel was summoned, and called two specialists at once. Yet there was nothing they could do. By 1.30 that afternoon the King was dead. In his hand was a leather pouch containing a handful of Greek soil. The official cause of death was given as haemorrhage of the brain, but the family were convinced that he had died of a broken heart.

'He strove always to do his duty,' Prince Nicholas wrote in tribute to his eldest brother five years later, 'but he was too sincere and upright a man to stem the tide of politics with all its duplicity, craftiness and venomous dealings.'[7]

In his former capital even in death he was not forgiven. When the news broke, a correspondent for *The Times* in Athens reported that 'it has been intimated that tomorrow morning newspapers must limit themselves to a bald announcement of King Constantine's death and refrain from publishing biographical notices or leading articles.'[8]

King George and Queen Elisabeth announced that they would not attend the customary New Year service in the Cathedral at Athens on 14 January, owing to mourning. The King had received a telegraph from his mother: 'Father died suddenly heart failure. All my thoughts with you – Mother.'

According to contemporary reports, Queen Sophie also notified the Revolutionary Committee by telegraph, asking at the same time for permission to have him buried in the family vault at Tatoi. When this wish was rejected by the Council of Ministers, Metaxas wrote to the Prime Minister, pointing out that the late King's body should be brought home, if not as the former monarch, then on the grounds that he was the father of the present King, but his letter went unanswered. It was believed that the government thought that the conveyance of his body to Athens would be made the excuse for an overwhelming show of public veneration and loyalty, and 'would give rise to a recrudescence of bitter partisan feeling on both sides and undo the work of reconciliation which has been begun between the opposing camps'.[9]

Later sources said that Metaxas wrote to General Gonatas, on hearing of the King's death, demanding that his body should be brought back to Greece and given a state funeral. The government telegraphed Venizelos for advice and he suggested that permission should be granted, on condition that the body was brought ashore at Oropos and taken direct to Tatoi for private interment. The proposal was put to King George, who angrily rejected it on the grounds that if his father was not going to be buried in Greece with full honours as befitted a King, then he would not be buried in Greece at all for the time being.[10]

The family in exile then decided that he should have a private funeral in Naples, but the Italian government ordered that full military honours should be paid; his last journey should be worthy of a King. The Duchess of Aosta and her family immediately came to call on the widowed Queen Sophie, and with the greatest kindness and sympathy took charge of everything. The coffin was first drawn through the streets of the city on a gun carriage, escorted by Municipal Guards and detachments of infantry, followed by Queen Sophie, Princess Irene and the Duchess of Aosta, together with local dignitaries, to the church where a funeral service was held before it was taken on board a steamer to Florence and transferred to its resting place in the crypt of the Russian Church. Although they were not his soldiers, as a military funeral it was almost everything the exiled King and former military leader could have wished for on his last journey.

A book for expressions of condolence was opened at the palace. The British consul, Charles Bentinck, and members of the diplomatic corps, were among the first to inscribe their names. One wonders whether they felt a sense of shame at the part their governments had played, albeit passively, in hounding a popular and much-loved sovereign from his throne to exile and a premature death.

Meanwhile, like his late younger brother, King George II was King in name only. He had been greatly embittered by the shabby treatment meted out to his father and the death sentences carried out by the revolutionary committee, headed by General Plastiras. He found it difficult to maintain even formally polite relationships with those responsible. His initial intention was to go into voluntary exile as a gesture of protest aginst the executions. Metaxas counselled patience, advising him to bide his time until the revolutionaries fell out among themselves.

A period of rule by nominees of the committee followed. Efforts to form a government including royalists and Venizelists failed. In October, to end the stalemate, a military, pro-royalist counter-revolution broke out under the leadership of three of the army officers, but was quickly suppressed by the Athens government. Metaxas had been told the details of this move in advance and was so appalled by its amateur planning that he had tried to dissuade its organizers from going through with it, but without success. Reluctantly he threw in his lot with them, and after the collapse of the coup he managed to escape to Italy on board a Norwegian ship which happened to be sailing that day from Patras.

King George was accused of complicity in the plot. Metaxas's links with the palace were no secret. Extremist republican elements in the army, led by Major-General Pangalos, brought pressure on the government to depose the King on the grounds that he no longer enjoyed the confidence of the armed forces. They demanded that the monarchy should be abolished and a republic be installed in its place immediately after the elections of 16 December 1923. General Gonatas duly wrote to the King saying that as the newly elected National Assembly was about to examine the question of the regime, it was considered desirable that during this time 'Your Majesty should be graciously pleased to absent yourself abroad on leave', to prevent disorder while the committee decided on the form of government they wanted.

Faced with a similar problem to that of his father fifteen months before, King George concluded that the interests of his country demanded the avoidance of further strife at all costs. He declined to abdicate, but agreed to leave the country, ostensibly on a visit to his wife's parents in Roumania. On 19 December he, Queen Elisabeth and Crown Prince Paul were escorted to a waiting warship. They were seen off by the loyal Prime Minister and Madame Gonatas, the latter weeping profusely as she presented the Queen with a large bouquet of flowers.

On 25 March 1924 the Assembly passed a resolution, proposed by the new government under the republican Alexander Papanastiou, abolishing the monarchy, declaring Greece a republic, and depriving all members of the dynasty of their Greek nationality as well as of any rights to the throne. The resolution also provided for the compulsory expropriation of property belonging to members of the deposed dynasty, and stipulated that property which had come into the possession of the royal family in the form of gifts from the state, local municipalities, and the like, should revert automatically to the previous owners without compensation. Included was the estate of Tatoi, which King George I had purchased from his private funds and stipulated in his will should always belong to the reigning King. Members of the dynasty were forbidden from residing in Greece. The decision was ratified by plebiscite, controlled by the police, the following year.

Taking pity on his stateless exiled relations, who were still nominally Princes or Princesses of Greece and Denmark, King Christian X of Denmark issued them all with Danish passports.

CHAPTER TWELVE

'The well-tried system of constitutional monarchy'

On their departure from Greece in December 1923, King George and Queen Elisabeth were offered a wing of the Cotroceni Palace in Bucharest by King Ferdinand and Queen Marie. They were there when they received news from Athens of the abolition of the monarchy.

The signs of strain in their marriage were becoming ever more evident. Elisabeth, confessed her mother, was 'one of the griefs of my life'. She had never really cared for George, and found the humiliation of exile and lack of material possessions deeply galling. Embittered by her misfortune, she sought revenge on her younger, happily married sister, Queen Marie of Serbia, by taking advantage of her illness while on a visit to Belgrade to flirt with King Alexander, a faithful albeit unimaginative husband, who was too naïve to realize he was being used as a pawn by his sister-in-law. She idled most of her time away at gaming tables or gorging rich cakes – she cared nothing about her figure – and gloating over a magnificent collection of pearls which the sympathetic Queen Sophie, always ready to see the best in everybody wherever possible, had given her.

After a few months of exile in Bucharest, at Cotroceni and later at a rented house on the Calea Vitoriei, King George was frustrated by this life of emptiness. The show and ceremony of the Roumanian court grated on him, as it had on his mother. He had a ready ally in Queen Marie, who felt guilty about the effect her daughter's behaviour was having on him. Years later, he told her: 'You were the only one who made my life supportable.'[1]

His journeys abroad, particularly to Florence to visit his mother, and to Britain, became longer and more frequent. For some time he followed the routine of staying with his wife in Bucharest for six months of the year, but under duress. In 1932 he decided to live entirely in England, accompanied by his devoted friend and equerry, Major Dimitri Levidis, and faithful manservant 'Mitso' Panteleos. Though he had little reason to love the country which had played a shameful role in undermining the position of his family, a love for the English way of life was engrained in him. Like his exiled uncle, the former German Emperor William, he gave the impression that all he ever wanted was to live the peaceful life of an English country gentleman. He was certainly the most Anglicized of his family.

While making many friends, he took care to avoid any political or other activity that would embarrass the British court or government, particularly as he was a regular visitor to the British royal family.

During these years of exile, with his lack of steady income, he could enjoy only the simpler pleasures of life in London. He knew and liked Chelsea and Whitechapel, and quiet old-fashioned pubs in secluded squares, equally as well as the smarter haunts of Mayfair. Browsing around shops on his own was a similar source of delight. He also liked to join close friends in unpretentious little parties where he felt free to talk without somebody placing political implications on every word he said. In company he could pass easily as an Englishman among those who did not know him, and it was only because his command of spoken English was generally more correct and formal than the average Englishman that he revealed himself as a foreigner.

Although naturally serious by disposition, he was a clever mimic and was always ready to make lighthearted jokes at his own expense. One evening in London he was leaving a rather large formal dinner party. His hostess joined him and the other guests at the door as they waited for their cars. When the footman announced, 'The King of Greece's taxi', she whispered firmly in his ear, 'Not taxi, Herbert. The King of Greece's car.' 'Oh no,' King George added cheerfully, 'the King of Greece's taxi. I can't possibly afford a car of my own.'[2]

When not in London he spent much of his time in the country, visiting friends. He was fond of shooting, particularly in Scotland. Outside sport, his main interests were old English furniture and silver, on which he soon became an expert. During a stay at Balmoral with the Duke and Duchess of York, he made friends with their elder daughter, four-year-old Princess Elizabeth. He entered so readily into the spirit of her games that she was soon addressing him as 'Georgie', despite the Duchess' scolding. 'But I like him', the Princess answered with determination, 'and I'm going to call him Georgie.' It would doubtless have given him great satisfaction to know that some seventeen years later she was destined to become the bride of his cousin Philip; their engagement was announced a mere three weeks after his death.

Most of the other members of the family in exile settled in England or Paris. Prince and Princess Nicholas and their family spent the summer of 1924 in England. After a while they moved to Paris, where Prince Nicholas became a prolific painter, finding a ready market for his work, signed 'Nicholas le Prince', while his wife opened and supervised the running of a children's home for orphaned Russians.

Prince and Princess Andrew lived near St Cloud, but they were beginning to drift apart. Andrew's temperament had suffered from his experiences, and Alice was slipping deeper into a world of religious reflection and self-questioning. They were perhaps not the best parents for Prince Philip, a young boy with four much older sisters, all of an age to start thinking about husbands. He was educated at Cheam, Berkshire, and spent school holidays with his maternal grandmother Victoria, Dowager Marchioness of Milford Haven.

Dowager Queen Olga was staying in London with her youngest son, Prince Christopher. His wife died suddenly on 29 August 1923 from cancer, and the Dowager Queen then stayed for a while with her daughter Princess Marie, also living in London in a rented house overlooking Regent's Park. Prince Christopher decided to make a permanent home for his mother in Rome, where the climate would suit her better, and she joined him there after he bought a house which he named Villa Anastasia in memory of his wife.

Her health was failing and she died in Rome on 18 June 1926, at the age of seventy-five. Her body was taken to lie beside that of her son King Constantine, in the crypt of the Russian Orthodox Church in Florence. In republican Greece it was rumoured that she had left a fortune of some twelve million francs, to be divided among her surviving children. The assertion hurt them deeply, for she had lost all her private fortune in Russia as a result of the revolution. All she had to live on was a modest pension paid by the Greek government, and she herself paid pensions to so many people who had faithfully served her that she only had about £20 a month left for her own use.

Prince Christopher stayed on in Rome, and on 11 February 1929 he married Princess Françoise, daughter of the Duc de Guise, pretender to the throne of France.

Prince Paul had gone to Bucharest with his brother in 1923 and was staying with his sister Helen, the wife of Crown Prince Carol of Roumania, when the republic was proclaimed in Greece. Like his brother, he found the opulence of the court at Bucharest not to his liking. After a while he went to Florence to stay with their mother, who had made her home there with her two youngest daughters, Princesses Irene and Katherine. He missed his naval career and deplored the inactivity of his new existence. Returning to London, he contacted old friends, looking for employment, preferably in connection with cars or aircraft. One of these was Henry Drummond Wolff, who had been to Greece in 1922 in connection with an order for aircraft for the Greek Air Force. Wolff helped him to obtain employment as a factory hand, if he did not mind such a humble post, in the Armstrong-Siddeley works at Coventry. Prince Paul immediately accepted, on condition that his identity should not be disclosed; he wished to be known simply as Mr Paul Beck. He found rooms in a house in Leamington and drove to Coventry every day in a second-hand Morris Cowley. He enjoyed his work as an apprentice, and though some of his colleagues soon discovered his identity it did not affect their relationship with him. Sometimes he would drive to London to visit relatives, but he was always back at Leamington by first thing on Monday morning.

After about a year he resigned his job and returned to London, taking a small flat near Victoria. He found relaxation in the social round, and the tall prince with the booming laugh and the rimless monocle was to be seen at fashionable parties in London and at country weekends. He joined the Royal Air Force Club, Piccadilly, and when in London he would drop in regularly for a meal or a drink. He was a gregarious young man and made friends easily. None the less, he found it a lonely existence, and before long he developed a great emotional attachment for a young Englishwoman.

Marriage crossed his mind, but word about the liaison reached Queen Sophie in Florence, and without any warning she arrived in London to find out for herself what was going on. She made it plain to her son that she was firmly opposed to a second morganatic marriage in the family. For him to make one would be a tacit acceptance of the unlikelihood of the restoration of the monarchy in the near future; it would be a great blow to their supporters, and above all to King George himself. For their sake, and also for the sake of his mother who was visibly ageing beyond her years, Prince Paul agreed to postpone any plans for marriage indefinitely. The affair ran its course and died a natural death.

In the spring of 1930, at a dinner party in a London club, Prince Paul met Captain Frederick Wessel, an old contact who mentioned that he was going on a cruise to the Greek islands in his motor yacht later that summer. Paul begged to be allowed to accompany him, but Wessel feared that he risked being thrown into prison for bringing a 'prohibited person' onto Greek territory. With misgivings, he agreed, on condition that Paul concealed his identity and abstained from any political activity while in Greece. Paul eagerly consented and subsequently presented himself at Villefranche on the first day of the cruise, having grown a beard, left his monocle behind, and introducing himself as the Captain's cousin Peter Wessel whom he had hired as a deck-hand for the cruise.

Subsequent exploits appealed greatly to their sense of adventure. While in Greece, they went to see Tatoi, where the garden was open to the public and the rooms inside covered with dust sheets. A few people recognized the *Diadoch*, or thought they did, but they agreed to be sworn to secrecy. When a taxi driver commented that Wessel's cousin looked very like the Crown Prince, everyone roared with laughter, including the taxi-driver himself, who sportingly said no more about it. During a dinner party at a hotel in Athens, Oliver Harvey, First Secretary at the British Legation, recognized him immediately and discreetly advised Captain Wessel to 'get the hell out of here', as there was nothing anyone could do if they got into trouble for bringing a 'prohibited person' into the country. The rest of their cruise passed without incident, and after two months they docked at Palermo, where Paul shed his assumed identity and left by train for Florence to visit his mother.

Only Queen Sophie's knowledge of the capriciousness of the Greeks, who might recall their royalty as suddenly as they had expelled them, prevented her from buying a permanent home at Florence. Yet she had her eye on a suitable property. Near Fiesole, on the wooded hill of San Domenico overlooking the city, lay a charming fifteenth-century villa. She told her daughter Helen that, if they had to stay there permanently, that was where she would like to live.

Having her family around her provided some comfort. She doted on her granddaughter, Princess Alexandra. The girl went to boarding school in Sussex, as her aunts had done, and was utterly miserable there. Only visits from her mother, who went to stay in England wherever she could, made her existence bearable. Queen Sophie also had the companionship of her daughters. Princess Helen's marriage had fallen apart after the flagrant infidelities and bullying of her husband, Crown Prince Carol, and they were divorced in 1928. Carol had renounced his place in the succession, and as a result King Ferdinand had been succeeded on the

Roumanian throne on his death in 1927 by Carol's and Helen's only child, five-year-old Michael. Three years later Carol returned to Roumania, asserted his rights and claimed the throne, reigning until driven into exile in 1940.

Queen Sophie was to be seen at some of the royal gatherings in Europe during the decade, which proved a welcome diversion. In October 1923 she attended the christening of Crown Prince Peter of Serbia at Belgrade, and the wedding of her niece Princess Olga to Prince Paul of Serbia the following day. Her second cousin Albert, Duke of York, noted that she had 'aged a great deal, poor lady, after all she has been through'.

Yet like her eldest son, Queen Sophie seemed to bear no grudge against one of the countries which had, if not connived at the downfall and premature death of her husband, was far from guiltless. 'I am so homesick and dying to see dear England again', she wrote from Florence to King George V (15 March 1928), when broaching the subject of coming to stay for a while after putting Princess Katherine into school for the summer term at Broadstairs. 'I have absolutely nothing to do with politics . . . so hope I can give no offence by living quietly – and out of the world in a small place if my means permit. I am too old and sad and tired to go out in society. Journeys are so expensive and life in England especially so, I could only afford a very simple lodging.'[3]

She followed events in the life of her cousins at Windsor with unfailing interest, and when King George V recovered from a serious illness during the winter of 1928–9, she sent a message to express her delight; it was 'the greatest joy' to see his picture in the papers again.

As forgiving as ever, on the occasion of his seventieth birthday in January 1929 she made a special journey to see her eldest brother, the former German Emperor William, now a comfortable exile in Doorn, in the Netherlands. She could have spared herself the trouble. Though he had mellowed in the ten years since his abdication, he greeted her politely yet distantly, and during their conversation he never once mentioned her past sorrows or asked about her plans for the future. They were like two strangers meeting for the first time, and she returned to Frankfurt hurt and embittered.

It was a year of sorrows for Queen Sophie. In April she lost her only other surviving brother, the more affable Prince Henry, and in November her sister Victoria, the widowed Princess Adolf of Schaumburg-Lippe, passed away. Victoria had disgraced the family by marrying a Russian vagrant, Alexander Zoubkov, who had disappeared with her fortune. After opening divorce proceedings against him, she became seriously ill and died in November. It was rumoured that she had committed or attempted suicide.

In 1931 Queen Sophie herself became ill. Entering hospital at Frankfurt for an operation, it was discovered that she had cancer. Her children were told that it was too late to arrest the disease, and they gathered round her, to be with her as she slipped quietly away on 13 January 1932. Her body lay in state in the great hall at Friedrichshof, the home which had been bequeathed to her sole surviving sister, Princess Frederick Charles of Hesse. She was then taken to Florence, to lie beside the remains of King Constantine and Queen Olga, in the crypt of the Orthodox Church.

The villa which she had loved so much was bought by Helen. Renamed the Villa Sparta, it became a family home for her exiled sons and daughters.

That same year King George separated completely from his wife, who made it evident that she was happier on her own in Bucharest. For both, the marriage had been a hollow one ever since they left Greece. Three years later Queen Elisabeth was advised to bring a divorce action against him on the grounds of desertion, as he had been absent from the country for so long. At a special court session in Bucharest on 6 July 1935, the marriage was dissolved. The Queen, who thenceforth resumed her Roumanian nationality, was represented by an advocate, while nobody represented the King. The first he knew of it, allegedly, was when he read the news in a London paper.

At the time he was living in a small two-room suite in Brown's, a modest hotel in Mayfair, scrupulously abstaining from any involvement in politics while observing with detachment and interest the workings of parliamentary democracy at Westminster.

To emissaries from Greece, who came to his little sitting-room, he made it quite clear that only if the Greek people showed their desire for the restoration of the monarchy by plebiscite would he return home. He was not prepared to go back at the behest of any single political party, but only as King of all the Hellenes, and this was the reply he also gave to the Greek minister in London when the latter formally called to announce to him the resolution passed by the National Assembly restoring the monarchy; he would only return if invited by the people.

Queen Sophie had once said that she would like all her daughters to marry Englishmen. Her youngest daughter eventually did so; but it would have given her almost as great pleasure to know that one of her nieces was to marry an English Prince. In 1934 Princess Marina, the 27-year-old daughter of Prince and Princess Nicholas, became betrothed to King George V's youngest surviving son Prince George, who was shortly to be created Duke of Kent. They were married at Westminster Abbey on 29 November 1934. Among the bridesmaids were the bride's cousins from Florence, Princesses Irene and Katherine, and a niece of the groom, Princess Elizabeth of York. It was probably during the wedding festivities that the latter first met thirteen-year-old Prince Philip of Greece and Denmark, whom she was later to marry.

King George II of the Hellenes attended the wedding as a guest. It was the first time he had been seen in exile in England attired in Greek military uniform, which strictly speaking he was not entitled to wear. Such a move might have sparked off protests from the Greek Legation in London, but no comment was made.

Preparations for the wedding had been overshadowed by the assassination of another Balkan king, Alexander of Yugoslavia, while on a visit to Marseilles in October. To King George II had fallen the melancholy task in London of attempting to console the dazed schoolboy of eleven, who as a result had suddenly found himself King Peter II of Yugoslavia.

Soon after the wedding, King George II left for India, as a guest of the Viceroy and the Indian Princes, on a tour which was to last for several months. It was a trip taken purely for pleasure by a man with wide interests, during which he was to be the guest of a number of high officials in India. He was a good shot and fond of shooting, especially in Scotland. The Indian princes received him with the formal respect due to a monarch, a striking change from the lukewarm attitude sometimes adopted towards him by certain members of London society. As the first spell of banishment had lengthened, and Greece appeared to be settling down to a permanent condition of republicanism, so some of the 'smart set' were less ready to welcome him than formerly. Though not a vindictive man, King George would have hardly been human if he had not remembered and been deeply hurt by such fickleness. He found no such treatment in India.

Meanwhile, the Greek republic lurched from one crisis to another. Between 1924 and 1935 the country underwent twenty-three changes of government, one dictatorship, and thirteen coups of varying degrees. From a perpetual state of financial chaos and virtual anarchy, order was restored by the Minister of War, General Kondylis. Emerging as the 'strong man' after his role in suppressing a major insurrection in the spring of 1935, he became Deputy Prime Minister. Formerly a staunch republican, by now he could appreciate the merits of a constitutional monarchy. Speaking to the Greek parliament in July 1935, he declared that, despite his fight for a republic in the previous decade, he saw that eleven years of such a regime, instead of internal peace, had brought them 'civil war, the undermining of respect for the State, spiritual anarchy'. The only solution, he was convinced, was 'to bring back the well-tried system of constitutional monarchy'.[4]

To an extent he was preaching to the converted. It was apparent that there was an ever-growing tide of opinion in favour of restoring the monarchy, and even electing a new king if the last occupant of the throne showed scant enthusiasm for reclaiming his inheritance. Earlier that year the British minister in Athens, Sir Sidney Waterlow, had observed the name of George, Duke of Kent – recently married to a granddaughter of King George I – being spoken of as a possible monarch. Mindful of the way in which an earlier generation of Hellenes had 'chosen' Prince Alfred some seventy years earlier, he was quick to dismiss the possibility.

Kondylis' unbridled enthusiasm for restoring the monarchy led him into conflict with the Prime Minister, Tsaldaris, who resigned in October 1935. Under Kondylis, the National Assembly passed a resolution in favour of the restoration of the monarchy, and he was promptly nominated Regent in the interim.

When the Greek minister in London called upon King George at Brown's Hotel with a formal announcement of the resolution, the King was adamant. He would only return if invited to do so by the people. A plebiscite was accordingly held on 3 November, producing a vote of 1,491,992 in favour of restoration and 32,454 for the republic, and the hotel loyally hoisted the Greek Royal Standard over its porch. A delegation from Athens met King George II and Crown Prince Paul at the Hellenic Legation in London and begged them to return to their country. With little illusions as to the task which awaited him in Athens, the King assented.

CHAPTER THIRTEEN

'Learn to trust no one'

On 14 November 1935 King George and Crown Prince Paul left London for Greece. The Prince of Wales and other members of the British royal family came to Victoria Station to see them depart. In Paris the following day they were received with full honours and entertained at an official banquet by the President of the Republic. At Florence their sisters and other relatives, including Prince Christopher, awaited them on the platform and they all attended a memorial service for King Constantine and Queen Sophie in the Russian Orthodox Church. They spent the night at Villa Sparta, now the property of Helen, Queen Mother of Roumania,* and then continued their journey to Rome, where King Victor Emmanuel of Italy invested them both with the Order of the Annunziata. At Brindisi they embarked on the Greek cruiser *Elli*, and on 25 November they were back in Greece after almost twelve years of exile. As they disembarked at Phaleron, to be welcomed by crowds waving flags and banners, cheering wildly, they must have wondered how long it would last this time.

In at least one sense, nothing had changed. During King George's exile, the palace at Athens had been used for state banquets and receptions. Most of the building was unfurnished and he had to sit on his luggage in a corridor, while a bedroom was hastily prepared for him.

The King's first political act was to confirm General Kondylis, who had ceased to be Regent the moment he stepped on Greek soil, as Prime Minister. He invested Kondylis with the Grand Cross of the Order of George I, and instructed him to prepare for signature a Royal Decree granting a general amnesty. Kondylis demurred, arguing that the political and military leaders of the revolt of March 1935 should be excluded from

---

* Her son Prince Michael had become King of Roumania in 1927 at the age of five, on the death of his grandfather, King Ferdinand, as Helen's husband King Carol had renounced the succession. Though the latter returned to reign as King of Roumania from 1930 to 1940, his divorced wife retained the title Queen Mother throughout his reign.

the amnesty, but the King resolved to make it unconditional. Unable to accept so broad a pardon, the Prime Minister again offered his resignation, which was accepted. In his place Dr Constantine Demerdzis, a Professor of Civil Law at Athens, was appointed.

In his proclamation King George had announced his intention to 'consign the past to oblivion'. For twelve years he had observed the mother of parliaments at Westminster, and looked to reigning in a country of democracy where the crown was above politics. In seeking a clean break with the past, he wanted a fresh mandate for the government. Parliament was dissolved and new elections held on 26 January 1936. The two main parties won a roughly equal number of seats, while the Communist Party held the balance of power with fifteen members. Members of the latter party, who made no secret of their hostility to the restoration of the monarchy, were ready to use their parliamentary strength to hinder legislation. The sudden deaths from natural causes of Demerdzis, Kondylis and other major leaders of the past during the first few weeks of the year, led to a period of confusion in which the parties all intrigued and manoeuvred for their own political ends.

The Deputy Prime Minister, Ioannis Metaxas, who had always been consistent in his support for the monarchy, was appointed Prime Minister. When factional obstructionism threatened to paralyze the parliament, and the Communists tried to exploit disaffection throughout the country via links with other underground organizations active in the Balkans, the King and government were faced with an awkward situation. Metaxas was authorized by parliament to govern by decree, subject to a small parliamentary committee reflecting the numerical strength of the various parties in the chamber, excluding the Communists. The latter proceeded to stir up unrest, fomenting disorder and strikes.

In Spain Communist agitation had plunged the country into civil war. Unrest was spreading throughout Europe. Hitler had occupied the Rhineland, Italy was celebrating her conquest of Ethiopia and consolidating her position in Albania, and King George came reluctantly to the conclusion that Greece could not afford to be distracted by civil war or political chaos. Democracy was a luxury which the country could yet ill afford.

On 4 August Metaxas summoned his ministers to a Cabinet meeting and informed them that he was going to seek the King's consent to the dissolution of parliament without new elections, and the suspension of certain articles of the constitution. In other words, he was requesting royal approval for dictatorship. Three ministers resigned immediately in protest, but Metaxas had forestalled them by posting guards outside with orders not to let anyone leave the building without his permission. Metaxas obtained the King's consent and issued a proclamation announcing that martial law was now in force throughout the country. Any opposition to the government would be crushed at once.

In future years King George's approval of Metaxas assuming the dictatorship brought him much criticism. However, he had no alternative. Constitutional action would have been impossible to prevent the Communists from threatening to create anarchy and civil war as they had in Spain. A general strike might bring the country to its knees, and foreign interference would surely follow for Italy and Bulgaria would not have hesitated to intervene in a civil war brought about by the Communists.

Moreover, Metaxas had the army behind him, and although he had always been a devoted servant of the Greek monarchy he might have demanded the King's abdication, which would have split the country as it did when King Constantine's abdication was demanded; similar consequences would have doubtless followed Metaxas's resignation. During the rest of his life, the honest Metaxas proved beyond doubt that he was no Venizelos, but King George knew better than to take chances. As he told the Duchess of Brunswick a couple of years later, with some bitterness, 'It's lamentable that we should learn so much from life, and learn to trust no one.'[1] He saw the dictatorship – henceforth known as the 'Fourth of August' – as an interim emergency, but nothing more.

In November 1936 Crown Prince Paul went to Florence to arrange for the coffins of his parents and grandmother to be brought home. They were conveyed from the crypt of the Orthodox Church, placed on a special train and taken to Brindisi, where they were transferred to the Greek battle-cruiser *Averoff*. On 17 November they were disembarked at the Piraeus and brought to Athens. Drawn by sailors and escorted by kilted Evzones of the Royal Guard with arms reversed, the three catafalques passed through silent crowds to the Cathedral. For six days they lay in state while the people filed past to pay homage. On the seventh day they were taken to Tatoi and laid to rest among other members of their family.

King George and Crown Prince Paul lived together at the palace for the first few months of the former's reign. By royal standards they had little money to spare, and could often be seen shopping in Athens, buying curtains and other necessities for the palace, at bargain sale prices wherever possible.

Yet though living under the same roof, they found it difficult to establish a close relationship with each other. King George was undoubtedly soured by his experiences, particularly with regard to the regular humiliation of his family and the failure of his marriage. As a result, he had withdrawn into himself and become increasingly aloof. The brothers had never been together very long in the same place as adults, though their paths had regularly crossed.

While in India King George had made the acquaintance of a married English lady, referred to by the US minister in Greece as 'Miss Brown', and others, including Lady Diana Cooper, as 'Mrs Jones', with whom he conducted a discreet liaison. In order to avoid scandal they went to great lengths to keep the affair as private as possible. King George found it difficult to unburden himself to other people in general, and his reticence on all matters, from the government of Greece to Miss Brown, dismayed Prince Paul, who sympathized with his brother but felt hurt at not being taken into his confidence.

A further bone of contention was Metaxas, whom the Crown Prince did not trust. Moreover, he had joined the Boy Scouts at an early age, and on coming of age he had been appointed Chief Scout of Greece. Metaxas was particularly proud of his National Youth Organization (EON), modelled to some extent on the Hitler Youth Movement. Crown Prince Paul was angered by official pressures put on the Scouts to join the EON. Metaxas was aware of the heir to the throne's attitude, which he suspected was shared by the King.

In August 1936, while cruising on board his yacht *Nahlin*, King Edward VIII of Great Britain visited Greece. On meeting King George II at Corfu, he was struck by the contrast between the apparently contented man he had seen at Brown's Hotel the year before, and the disillusioned sovereign back in his own land. Embittered by finding the loyalties of his people divided between innumerable factions and cliques, and Metaxas's proclamation of martial law, King George bitterly declared that he was a King in name only and 'might just as well be back at Brown's Hotel'. As King Edward took his leave, King George gripped his hand, saying, 'I hope you have better luck.'[2]

It was ironic that King Edward's days on his throne were numbered, owing to his personal life which was not so far removed from the position in which his Hellenic second cousin found himself. During their Mediterranean cruise, the party on board the *Nahlin*, including the King's future wife, Mrs Wallis Simpson, were discussing King George II's relationship with his mistress. Mrs Simpson innocently asked why the King did not marry her. With remarkable lack of tact under the circumstances, one of the guests replied that it was impossible for the King to marry a woman who was both a commoner and already married. King Edward VIII's willingness to make public his relationship with Mrs Simpson, which distressed his immediate family and government, was in marked contrast to the discretion of King George II, who perhaps saw from the behaviour of his cousin in Britain the effect such a liaison could cause, and was determined not to provoke similar offence.

The King still made an annual visit abroad each autumn and early winter, spending much of his time in Britain. His motives were partly diplomatic, for a few days in London provided him with an opportunity to see British ministers and service chiefs to discuss supplies of arms and equipment for Greece's armed forces, and partly to stay with his British cousins at Buckingham Palace. At the same time he had a chance to stay at Brown's Hotel again, where he could visit old friends on a purely social basis, and browse unhindered in his favourite London antique shops. In view of his weariness at the apparently insoluble state of affairs in Greece, and the recognition that he was probably as much a puppet of the well-intentioned Metaxas as his brother had been of the unforgiving Venizelos, it was hardly surprising that he looked forward to these vacations, perhaps the only times when he could really relax.

On his return to England in September 1936, King Edward VIII had reported to Queen Mary that King George had 'seemed thin and homesick for London'. 'I don't envy the rulers of those Balkan countries',[3] was her comment.

Prince Paul had rejoined the navy, with the rank of Lieutenant-Commander. He was attached to the Chief of Staff on special duties involving regular spells at sea, but his functions and duties as heir to the throne precluded his being put on full-time service.

As it was unlikely that the divorced, childless King George II would marry again, it was important that the Crown Prince should marry and ensure the succession. No pressure was put on him to do so, but he had already met the princess who was to become his consort.

Like him, she was a descendant of Emperor Frederick III and the former Princess Royal of Great Britain. She was Princess Frederica, daughter of the Duke and Duchess of Brunswick, the latter being the only daughter of the former Emperor William II. Aged twenty, she was fifteen years younger than Paul, but very mature for her age and the difference did not trouble them. They were engaged in September 1937. As Frederica was in line of succession to the throne of Great Britain, although a long way down at thirty-fourth, she came within the provisions of the Royal Marriage Act. The prior consent of King George VI was required and duly given at a meeting of the Privy Council at Buckingham Palace on Boxing Day.

Crown Prince Paul and Princess Frederica were married in the Cathedral at Athens on 9 January 1938. Two ceremonies were held, one according to the Greek Orthodox Church and the other the Protestant Church, to which the bride still belonged. Their honeymoon took them to Switzerland, to the groom's sisters at the Villa Sparta in Florence, to Doorn to visit the bride's grandfather, the former Emperor William, and to England for a few days. On their return to Athens in March, they took up residence at Psychiko in Athens.

The wedding was soon followed by sadness, for Prince Nicholas was seriously ill. He died in February, pleased to have come home to Athens after the vicissitudes of the last two decades.

By this time the shadows were falling over Europe. Greece particularly distrusted the actions of fascist Italy, which had in previous years proved a good friend to the family, particularly at the death of King Constantine. In April 1939 Italian forces landed in Albania, on the border of Greece. At this the Greek exiles in Paris, headed by General Plastiras, who had withdrawn from their country in protest at Metaxas's dictatorship in August 1936, declared that in view of the perils facing their country, they withdrew their opposition to him.

Tension was rising as the engagement of King George's sister Princess Irene, still living at the Villa Sparta, to Aimone, Duke of Spoleto, cousin of King Victor Emmanuel, was announced. The marriage took place in the Cathedral at Florence on 1 July 1939, but the Italians demonstrated their hostility towards Greece by forbidding the flying of any Greek flags. King George was so angry when he heard of this effrontery that he threatened to boycott the wedding and return to Athens at once. He was persuaded by Metaxas to stay and not precipitate a crisis with Italy which, as Prime Minister, Metaxas was anxious to avoid.

Two months later Europe was at war. The 'phoney war' that lulled the neutral countries into a false sense of security erupted into full-scale conflict the following spring. In April 1940 Denmark and Norway were invaded by Germany; in May, on the same day that Winston Churchill was appointed Prime Minister of Great Britain, Belgium and the Low Countries were attacked; and with the seemingly inexorable advance of Nazi Germany, Italy entered the conflict in June on the German side. Although Mussolini declared that same day that Italy 'had no intention of dragging into the conflict other nations who are her neighbours by land or sea', including Greece, Yugoslavia, Turkey, Switzerland and Egypt, almost at once the Italian government launched a propaganda campaign against Greece, coupled with a policy of intimidation based on accusations that Greece was tolerating and conniving at violations of her neutrality by allowing British warships to use Greek waters in their operations against the Italian navy.

Earlier in the year Prince Christopher had died in Rome, leaving a widow and a son by his second marriage, Prince Michael, less than a year old. As a young man, Prince Christopher had been offered, and refused, no less than three different crowns in Europe: those of Portugal (where his friend, King Manuel, had been deposed only two years previously), Lithuania and Albania.

In his memoirs he left what might serve as a fitting epitaph for his brothers and nephews. 'Nothing under the sun would induce me to accept a kingdom', he wrote. 'A crown is too heavy a thing to be put on lightly. It has to be worn by those born to that destiny, but that any man should take on the responsibility in these troubled times, not being constrained by duty to do so, passes my comprehension.'[4]

In the midst of these uncertain events, the Greek succession was assured. Crown Princess Frederica had already given birth to a daughter, Princess Sophia, in November 1938; on 2 June 1940, a salute of 101 guns in the capital announced the birth of a prince. King George, who was at Psychiko with the rest of the family when the child was born, was much moved by the event. In a rare display of emotion, he warmly embraced his brother. The baby prince, second in succession to the throne, was baptized in July and given the name Constantine.

It was but a momentary distraction from the clouds gathering above Greece and her throne. The previous year, Joachim von Ribbentrop, German foreign minister, had suggested to Mussolini that Italian pressure on Greece would be facilitated if King George II, who was known to regard the Axis powers with distaste, could be ousted from his throne. With Italy's entry into the war, it was only a matter of time before pressure was intensified. A senior Nazi party official approached the Counsellor of the Greek Legation in Berlin, M. Tziracopoulos, and asked him to inform King George II and Metaxas in person that Germany was prepared to use her good offices to dissuade Italy from attacking Greece, and perhaps even at the end of the war to give support in respect of certain Greek territorial aspirations, should Greece discard British influence and observe benevolent neutrality towards the Axis for the remainder of the war. As British influence was exercised through King George, so the German argument continued, he should abdicate in favour of Crown Prince Paul, whose abstention from any political activity made him an unknown quantity so far as his sentiments were concerned, and whom the Germans assumed to be less biased against them because of his marriage to a German princess.

Tziracopoulos returned to Athens at once and told King George, who replied furiously that he was to go back and tell them that 'so far as the throne is concerned I don't give a damn, but they had better not stick their noses into this country's business if they know what's good for them.'[5]

On 28 October Metaxas angrily rejected an ultimatum from the Italian government demanding the right to occupy various unspecified strategic points in Greece for the duration of the war against Britain, and announcing that Italian forces would begin their advance into Greek territory within three hours. King George supported his Prime Minister as the nation went to war. He assumed supreme command of all the armed forces, a role which involved presiding at day-to-day meetings with the War Council, conferring constantly with Metaxas and the services chiefs, maintaining contact with the Allies, and above all providing the spiritual and moral leadership required by the nation.

Meanwhile, Crown Prince Paul stayed in Athens, inspecting the work of service personnel and keeping the King closely informed. As he was a captain in the Greek navy, he took a particular interest in inspecting the naval base. While in Athens the brothers regularly attended meetings of the War Council in the Grande Bretagne Hotel, Constitution Square, where it had established its headquarters and where they had rooms when late business prevented them from returning at night to Tatoi, where the rest of the family had settled. Crown Princess Frederica, who had already begun to take an interest in hospital and welfare work in accordance with family traditions, helped by launching an organization for collecting and distributing warm clothing and other comforts for the troops. She had recruited only women volunteers, mostly members of Athenian society who were glad to prove that they too could play an active part in promoting the war effort. Princess Katherine, the King's youngest sister, Princess Alexander and her daughter Princess Alexandra all dedicated themselves tirelessly to voluntary welfare work for the Greek troops.

Italy's invasion of Greece was a bitter pill for Irene, Duchess of Spoleto, to swallow. Loyalty to her husband prevented her from speaking out openly in sympathy for the country of her birth, and she busied herself in Red Cross work in Italy. Yet before the war was over, division of loyalties would make her fate almost as harsh as that suffered by her father.*

Metaxas died in January 1941. The dictator of 1936 was now regarded in a much more benevolent light than formerly. Harold Nicolson, broadcasting on the BBC, paid tribute to the man who had found Greece torn by internal strife and doubtful of her own future, yet galvanized her to a sense of her own traditions and power; 'we here in England must salute with respect the passing of so great a man.'[6] Meanwhile *The Times* echoed his words the next day, remarking that it was Greece's good fortune that Metaxas had been recalled by King George II 'to restore the political structure'. Flags in England flew at half-mast, a rare instance of such a tribute being paid to a foreign statesman who was not a head of state.

Between October 1940 and April 1941 Greece put up a heroic struggle against the Axis powers, wresting almost half the kingdom of Albania from Fascist Italy. On 6 April 1941 the German army struck from across the Bulgarian frontier and met with little opposition. The Greek and

---

* On the death of her brother-in-law, Amadeus, Duke of Aosta, a prisoner of the British in Africa, she and her husband succeeded to the title. They were nominated by Mussolini as King and Queen of the puppet state of Croatia, an 'honour' which they refused, much to the dictator's anger. After an armistice was signed with the Italians in 1943, she and her widowed sister-in-law were 'warned not to escape', and with her baby son they were taken to Bavaria the following summer by SS officers as diplomatic internees. After being held captive in ever-worsening conditions, they were rescued at the end of the war just before fleeing German troops could carry out orders to execute them. They escaped to Italy, but the Duchess's period of married happiness was brief, for in 1948 her husband died on a visit to South America.

Allied forces were driven further back. Anxious at reports of weakening morale among the forces, the King issued a statement that 'the honour and interest of Greece and the Greek race preclude all thoughts of capitulation, the moral calamity of which would be incomparably greater than any other disaster.'[7] Alexander Koryzis, who had succeeded Metaxas as Prime Minister, believing the situation to be helpless, told the King that they had no choice but to surrender. The King rounded furiously on him, and he took his leave in silence, went back to his house and shot himself in despair.

The King and his government decided that to stay on the Greek mainland would only make him a helpless tool in Nazi hands. They accordingly chose to establish a national government in Crete and continue to defy the German demand for submission from there. The result was a number of vital battles that depleted Germany's airborne forces, and additionally a diversion which postponed Hitler's attack on Russia. Its significance went largely unnoticed at the time, although the *Daily Telegraph* suggested, with remarkable foresight, that only when the war was won 'and the time-table of Hitler's aggressions is dragged into the full light of day shall we be able to assess the true measure of the debt which the cause of civilisation and liberty owes to the Greek King and his nation.'[8]

CHAPTER FOURTEEN

'The ancient ties between Crown and people'

When King George decided to leave his kingdom for Crete, the rest of the royal family came with him. On 22 April 1941 Crown Princess Frederica was evacuated by flying-boat with her two young children. Princesses Katherine and Alexander, the latter with her daughter Alexandra, were also in the plane, but Crown Prince Paul remained behind with the King. As the passengers were ferried to the shore by launch after arriving in Suda Bay, German planes suddenly appeared and divebombed the anchorage and town itself. They escaped unhurt, and the King, the Crown Prince and Emmanuel Tsouderos, who had just been appointed Prime Minister, were evacuated the following day.

In May Hitler proclaimed during a speech in Berlin that King George II was Germany's chief enemy in Greece. A quisling government was set up by the Germans in Athens, 'abolishing' King George and the monarchy, and making the 'kingdom of Greece' the 'Greek state'. That same month a German airborne attack on Crete was launched, and Major-General Bernard Freyburg, the Allied Commander in Crete, insisted that the King should be evacuated to a safer place; 'If he is killed it can't be helped; what we have to avoid at all costs is his being taken prisoner.' He was taken to Egypt and stayed in the Greek Legation at Cairo.

King Farouk of Egypt and his Italophil government soon made it clear that the indefinite presence of the Greek King and government on their territory was unwelcome. British and South African governments both extended an invitation to them, and after consultation it was decided that the King and the Crown Prince should move to London, where other Allied governments-in-exile were already established; Crown Princess Frederica and the rest of the family should go to South Africa.

On 21 September the Greek royal party, including Prime Minister Tsouderos and the King's equerry Levidis, arrived on board *Durban Castle* at Liverpool, where they were welcomed by the Duke of Gloucester on behalf of King George VI. The latter, Queen Elizabeth and Winston Churchill were at Euston Station to greet them as the train brought them to London. The King took up residence at Claridge's Hotel, which would be his home on and off for the next five years. The Crown Prince occupied two rooms next to him, while the Greek government-in-exile were accommodated in a block of flats overlooking Hyde Park. At the end of the year the King was awarded the Distinguished Service Order for courage under enemy fire, the only reigning sovereign ever to receive this decoration.

In July 1942 his niece Princess Marina, Duchess of Kent, gave birth to a second son, named Michael. King George of the Hellenes, King Haakon VII of Norway and his son Crown Prince Olav – who had also been driven out of their kingdom by the Axis Powers – were among guests at the baby's christening at Windsor Castle on 4 August. It was the last time most of them ever saw his proud father, the Duke of Kent. Three weeks later, to the day, he left for Iceland on a Royal Air Force welfare mission, and his plane crashed into a hillside in Scotland. The Duke and all but one of the other fourteen men on board were killed.

In the spring of 1943 King George, Crown Prince Paul and the Royal Hellenic government of the moment returned to Cairo to prepare for an invasion of Greece, occupied by the Germans and their Allies. During the months of frustration which followed, they became miserably aware that they were further than ever from the hearts of the Greeks on the mainland. Not only had Tsouderos found himself forced to accept sweeping changes in the government, which made it strongly republican in character, but the Communists were almost ready to seize power.

The most highly organized and disciplined political party in Greece, the Communists had been driven underground during Metaxas's rule. Working clandestinely, they developed their organization during the resistance against the Axis occupation. Profiting from the knowledge that undiluted Communism had little electoral appeal in Greece, they set up their own National Liberation Front (EAM), ostensibly a coalition of several left-wing groups under the leadership of veteran Communists. In 1942 they established a guerrilla movement, the National Popular Liberation Army (ELAS), which like its parent body worked alongside and in concert with the British military presence in Greece. So effectively did the EAM and ELAS do their work, that the British authorities failed to realize that they were controlled by leaders who were more interested in taking over Greece after liberation than in carrying out effective military occupations against the Axis powers.

On 4 July 1943 King George II broadcast to the Greek people, promising that general elections would be held within six months of the liberation of Greece, and that the Constitution of 1911 would be in force until the Greek nation expressed its sovereign will. This was tantamount to a repudiation of the Metaxas regime, and also an affirmation that the King intended to return to Greece in due course with his government and army. It met with no approval from the EAM, which demanded the following month that the King should issue a proclamation announcing that he would not return to Greece unless specifically invited by plebiscite.

Alarmed at this confirmation that the Communists were apparently strengthening their hold on Greece, the King referred this new development to Churchill and Franklin D. Roosevelt, President of the United States of America, asking their advice. Churchill agreed that if substantial Greek forces were to take part in the liberation of Greece, the King should return with the Anglo-Greek army; and it would be 'a great mistake to agree in any way' to remain outside Greece while fighting for the liberation continued, and while conditions precluded the holding of a peaceful plebiscite. From South Africa, General Smuts, who while acting as host to several members of the family had developed considerable respect and affection for them, endorsed the King's intentions even more firmly, insisting that 'King George has always been strongly pro-Ally and sacrificed much for the Allied cause and we have every reason to stand by him in this crisis.'[1]

Churchill and Roosevelt cabled to the King, assuring him that he could count on the support of their governments, whatever his decision. Matters would probably have remained thus, had it not been for the collapse of Italy in September 1943. Most of the arms and equipment of the surrendering Italian units in Greece fell into the hands of the ELAS, making them less dependent on Allied aid and less amenable to Allied persuasion.

Pressure continued on the King to reconsider his attitude, and in November he wrote to Prime Minister Tsouderos, saying that when the time came, 'I shall examine anew the question of the date of my return to Greece in agreement with the Government.' The text was released for publication, but in the process of translation from the original Greek, the three crucial words 'the date of' were omitted. The impression thus given, either by accident or by design, was that the King was ready to reconsider not merely the date of his return, but the matter of whether he should return at all. At his insistence a correction was hastily issued, but it was too late to alter the initial impression, which was seized on as an admission that the King was contemplating abdication.

Churchill and Anthony Eden, his Foreign Secretary, accordingly shifted their ground. The Italian surrender had changed things, in that the likelihood of a German withdrawal rendered a major Allied military operation in that area superfluous, and thus giving way to the Communist guerrilla forces. Eden presented a draft proclamation to King George, recommending that he announce he would not return to Greece after the liberation, but would appoint a Regent, and remain abroad until the result of a plebiscite was known.

While in Cairo for an Allied conference in December 1943, Eden proposed to King George that Archbishop Damaskenos of Athens should be appointed Regent. His political sympathies, however, were highly suspect, as he had been ready to endorse the behaviour of the quisling government. King George sternly rejected the proposal. He had led the nation against the enemy when Greece was invaded in 1941, and he felt it was only right that he should return to his country with his government and troops when the day of liberation came. To accept the idea of the appointment of a Regent for an unspecified period immediately following the liberation was to accept his own exclusion from participation in the liberation, and this he was not prepared to do. He was supported by Roosevelt, so the Regency proposal was shelved – but not for long.

King George returned to London in February 1944. Princess Alexander and Princess Alexandra were already there. The latter had met and fallen in love with the exiled King Peter of Yugoslavia, and her mother, who had never forgotten the slights to which she had been exposed during her brief period of marriage, gave her full approval to their blossoming romance. Despite the bitter opposition of the King's mother, Queen Marie, and his ministers, they were married in March 1944 at the Yugoslav Embassy in London. Among the guests were the two Kings George, of the Hellenes and Great Britain.

One evening in London at about this time, King George was dining quietly with a couple of friends in the intimacy of a small West End restaurant. A rather drunken but amicable American sailor, who had no idea of the King's identity, insisted on shaking him by the hand and asking him his name and where he came from. 'Oh, my name's George,' the

King smiled. 'I'm from Greece.' The sailor introduced himself as Steve from Texas. 'Well, I'll be seeing you, George.' Rather unsteadily, he returned to his table, where the startled waiters informed him of his new acquaintance's identity. A few minutes later he returned, accompanied by a similarly tipsy sailor whom he introduced as his buddy, Sam. 'He's from Texas too. Shake hands with George, Sammy; he's a King, and he comes from Greece, and he's a good guy.' Following more handshakes, the Americans were led back to their table by an embarrassed member of staff, leaving the King and his companions almost prostrate with laughter.[2]

There was little laughter or good cheer for him elsewhere. In March 1944 Tsouderos cabled from Cairo to the King to say that a secret emissary from occupied Greece had brought with him messages to the effect that various political leaders in Greece demanded the immediate appointment of Archbishop Damaskenos as Regent, and urged him to accept. The King refused, replying that he considered himself mandated by the Greek people to continue the struggle against the enemy and to safeguard the rights of the nation while under foreign occupation and unable to express its free will.

Nevertheless, later that month the formation of a 'Political Committee of National Liberation' in occupied Greece was announced, evidently a rival authority to the Tsouderos government-in-exile in Cairo. King George warned him against entering into any obligations with the committee, but it was too late. Intensive Communist propaganda had bitten deep, and the Committee, which made no secret of its Communist control, was represented by a group of officers demanding to see Tsouderos and handing him a memorandum signed by several army and air force officers. It was the signal for open mutiny in some units of the Greek navy and army, demanding the dismissal of Tsouderos and his government. Tsouderos accordingly cabled his resignation to the King in London. The King refused to accept it and cabled back to Tsouderos, asking him to stay on for the time being. He was supported by Churchill, who cabled to speak of his shock at hearing of the resignation and exhorting him to remain at his post at least until the King's return to Cairo in a few days.

On 7 April the British ambassador accredited to King George II in exile, Sir Reginald Leeper, cabled the Foreign Office in London, insisting that the King's return to Cairo would be unwelcome; 'he would find himself isolated and unable to do anything and would be a grave embarrassment to us.' Churchill replied with a retort that 'our relations are definitely established with the lawfully constituted Greek Government headed by the King, who is the ally of Britain and cannot be discarded to suit a momentary surge of appetite among ambitious emigré nonentities.'[3] King George returned to Cairo the following day, and received Tsouderos and all the other Greek politicians in Cairo at the time. He accepted Tsouderos's resignation as Prime Minister and on his recommendation appointed Sophocles Venizelos to follow in his father's footsteps. Thanks to British military assistance, the mutineers were surrounded. Most of them had been misled by Communist propaganda and never appreciated that their action would result in facing British troops, and within a fortnight the mutiny was over.

The day after the mutiny was suppressed, Venizelos submitted his resignation, having held the post a mere eleven days, and was succeeded by George Papandreou. In May a three-day conference was held in the Lebanon on the future of Greece after the liberation. In order to satisfy the republican elements in his Cabinet, Papandreou issued a statement in June to the effect that it was the view of the government that the King should await a popular vote before returning to Greece. Reluctantly, King George assented. He had no choice but to do so.

Later he told Levidis that the most miserable day of his life – and there had been many before – was when he watched everybody, except for himself, his brother and other members of the Greek royal family, returning to their homeland. It was a damning testament to the extent to which the Allies had allowed republicans in the Greek government to dictate to them, despite Churchill's assurances of standing firmly beside the King.

Yet it did nothing to weaken his high personal regard for England and the English way of life. It speaks volumes for his magnanimity that he could understand the views of those officials who stood in his way during the war years, and he had little patience with people who asked him how he could love a country that treated him so badly. It also testifies to his personal courage that he lived in London throughout the bombings and the V1 and V2 raids that constituted Nazi Germany's last desperate attempt to force the English civilian population into submission.

After his return to Greece, Papandreou found himself confronted by demands from the EAM that he should resign and make way for somebody more republican and more amenable to the Communists. He was prepared to stand down, but Churchill insisted he should not give way. Increasingly alarmed at the threat of Communist domination of the Balkans and Eastern Europe, he arranged to meet Papandreou, who agreed that there was no need for King George to make any new declaration regarding his future intentions.

By November the last of the German forces had left Greek soil, and the country was free again after three and a half years of enemy occupation. It had, however, left the Communists equally free to seize complete power. Athens was the only part of the country not under Communist control. Under Lieutenant-General Sir Ronald Scobie, nominated by the Allied command as Commander of Allied forces in Greece, British troops intervened. It was evident that the ELAS held sway. Pressure was placed on Churchill to persuade him to get King George to agree to the appointment of Archbishop Damaskenos as Regent. Churchill was reluctant to 'throw over a constitutional King acting on the true advice of his Ministers' in order to bring to power 'a dictator who may very likely become the champion of the extreme left'.

Torn between all sides and conflicting opinions, Churchill and Eden went out to Athens to see the situation for themselves on Christmas Day 1944. They were convinced that there was no alternative to a Regency. On 29 December they were back in London, and that evening summoned King George to 10 Downing Street.

What followed was not so much a discussion as an ultimatum. Voices were raised as the two British ministers entreated and bullied the King at length, telling him bluntly that he had until 2 a.m. to appoint the Archbishop as Regent. If he refused, the British government would recognize the Archbishop anyway, withdraw all recognition from King George, and allow him to remain in Britain only as a private individual. He flung open the door and walked out, his face white and taut, as he returned to his hotel. On recovering his composure some minutes later, he went back to Downing Street and informed Churchill and Eden that he had no choice but to acquiesce to their demands. At the same time he extracted from them an assurance that the insurrection would be suppressed at all costs, and that the Greek people would not be abandoned to the tyranny of an armed Communist minority.

On 3 January 1945 Damaskenos, newly appointed Regent, accepted the resignation of the Papandreou government in Athens, and appointed General Plastiras as Prime Minister. Plastiras, a staunch republican, had not altered his political complexion since leading the revolution which had forced the abdication of King Constantine in 1922. Brought back to Greece from his exile in France by the British in December 1944, at the height of the fighting in Athens, his government consisted almost exclusively of republicans. A few days later ELAS, fighting a losing battle against the British troops, began to withdraw from Athens, taking hostages with them, most of whom died of exposure in the winter weather or were shot. A truce was followed in February by an amnesty which provided for the demobilization of ELAS, and the holding of a plebiscite and elections under Allied supervision. Communist activity in Greece continued, with the full protection of the law, and large quantities of arms were carefully secreted for future occasions.

By the time the war ended in Europe in May 1945, King George was seen as a dubious rallying-point for the monarchists, partly because of his support for Metaxas, and partly as his disingenuously translated letter on his return to Greece was used as a propaganda tool by the Communists. Damaskenos enjoyed the role of Regent and was reluctant to relinquish his power. In the autumn he announced that the plebiscite on the King's return would not be held until 1948. King George protested angrily at this delay, and Churchill – Leader of the Opposition in Britain since the election of a Labour government at Westminster in July – added his protests.

Humiliated, virtually abandoned and even insulted by Allied officialdom, King George was regularly tempted to contemplate abdicating in weary disgust, nominating Crown Prince Paul as King *in absentia*. The only reason he did not do so was because he felt he could not abandon the majority of his people to the mercies of an extreme left minority. Nevertheless, by now he was seriously considering abdication. Dedication to duty would not permit him to do so while the status of the crown was in abeyance, but once the monarchy was sufficiently re-established in Greece for such an action not to place the throne in jeopardy, he intended to lay his burden down. His grandfather had announced his intention to do so on the occasion of his Golden Jubilee, and had only been prevented from doing so by the bullets of an assassin.

Now, some three decades later, King George II was embittered and exhausted by the machinations of the last few years. Shortly after the end of war in Europe, he bought the lease of a house in Chester Square, Belgravia, London, where he and Miss Brown could consider settling down to lead the quiet, dignified life of an English gentleman and his wife. They spent several months furnishing and decorating it, attending public auctions to buy old silver and pictures, and laying down a modest wine cellar. Her health was beginning to fail, for she was suffering from persistent bouts of migraine, the first symptoms of Parkinson's Disease. She likewise looked forward to a life of retirement.

Elections were held on 31 March 1946, in the presence of British, American and French observers, and the result was a clear victory for the Populist (royalist) party and its allies, who won 231 of the 354 seats in parliament. At the opening session the Populist leader, Constantine Tsaldaris, announced that a plebiscite on the future of the monarchy would be held on 1 September. During the interval between the elections and plebiscite, the electoral registers were checked and revised under British and American supervision.

King George stayed quietly at Claridges in London, refusing to anticipate the result of the vote. He appreciated that rural Greece was predominantly royalist, while urban areas were divided between royalist and republican sentiment. He was careful to say and do nothing that might directly or indirectly influence the nation in favour of his return. Other members of the family were more openly optimistic, having heard from various sources that there was a growing feeling among people of all shades of political opinion for the return of the unifying influence of the crown.

When the count was held after the polling stations closed, the King's aides and secretaries waited impatiently in their room at Claridges by the tape machine for the early results to be announced. As the first figures came through, the King walked into the room and read the first result. The village of Spata, a few miles from Athens, had an electorate of 303, and 301 votes were cast for his return. He stood motionless for a minute, then walked away without a word to anyone, to the restaurant where he generally ate alone. Tears were in his eyes.

By the time the results had come through, it was seen that in an exceptionally high poll, 90 per cent of the registered electors, 69 per cent voted in favour of King George's return, 20 per cent against his return (though not against the monarchy, as such), and 11 per cent in favour of a republic.*

---

* As Arthur Gould Lee remarked,[4] it was ironic that King George was not allowed to return when Greece was liberated from the Germans, despite his undertaking to abide by the result of a plebiscite on the future of the monarchy, in the light of events in Italy. Despite its record of Fascist collaboration, the house of Savoy was permitted to stay in Italy until the result of a similar vote was announced. Held in June 1946, some ten weeks before that in Greece, it resulted in a verdict in favour of a republic.

Four days later the Prime Minister arrived in London and formally announced the result to the King. He issued a proclamation to his people acknowledging that they had 'confirmed the ancient ties between Crown and people', and that the verdict 'should be interpreted as a solemn injunction to put a final end to a long-standing division which has weakened our nation and presented us abroad in a false light.'[5]

Before leaving London for the last time, the King made discreet inquiries about the personal interests of those to whom he wished to give presents. On being told that one of the British police officers guarding him was fascinated by old English inn signs, he searched throughout several bookshops for a book on the subject, until he found exactly the right one to give him.

On 26 September 1946 the Greek destroyer *Themistocles* sailed from Alexandria with the Crown Prince and Princess on board. The next day King George flew out from Heathrow Airport to Athens. He had planned to meet his brother and sister-in-law in Eleusis Bay so they could enter Athens together the following morning.

At Phaleron Bay they disembarked to a salute of 101 guns, and the royal party squeezed into a rather decrepit open car, the only motor vehicle that could be found at short notice with a rear seat wide enough to accommodate three people. Driving straight to Athens, they attended a Thanksgiving Service at the Cathedral, conducted by Archbishop Damaskenos, who had surrendered his powers as Regent and now reverted to his ecclesiastical duties. At Constitution Square afterwards, where the King received congratulations from the civic and military authorities and the Diplomatic Corps, crowds cheered enthusiastically and called for him to come out onto the balcony.

On their return to the palace, which had been used as temporary headquarters by one of the revolutionary political organizations, the brothers were shocked at the chaos which met their eyes. Furniture and possessions had been looted or destroyed, lamp and bathroom fittings had been wrenched off the walls and smashed. The woods at Tatoi, which had not fully recovered from the arson attack of 1916, had been despoiled to provide fuel for the people of Athens during the German occupation. Corpses of victims of the revolutionary court of 'justice' lay in shallow graves outside.

As there was no hope of occupying his old home for many months, the King sadly took up residence at the palace built as a residence for the Crown Prince during the reign of King George I. For a while he lived alone, until Princess Katherine joined him, while the Crown Prince and Princess returned to their villa at Psychiko.

Greece was still a land divided. In the north, civil war was breaking out with the Communists, who were aided by Soviet satellites beyond the frontiers. British troops were in firm control in the centre of Greece, and the Greek army was being reformed and re-equipped with foreign aid to deal with the Communists. The country had paid a high price for her loyalty to Britain and the Allies since 1941. Over half a million members of the armed forces, merchant marine fleet and civilian population had been killed by enemy action, guerrilla warfare, or died from starvation; 78 per cent of her shipping had been sunk; 95 per cent of all railway engines and rolling stock had been destroyed; three hundred villages had been razed to the ground; and hyper-inflation had brought financial ruin to many individuals who had survived the hardships of the war. The multi-party governments provided little hope of political stability, and the unhappy King found himself in the role of a chairman of feeble and unruly Cabinets.

His personal daily routine changed but little. Highly disciplined by nature, he had been accustomed to have so little useful work to do during his long periods of exile that he contrived to make every trifling act count for something in what would otherwise have been an empty day. Systematic and precise in his affairs, he opened all letters addressed to him, even when obviously trade circulars. His equerry Levidis and the secretaries had to refer all engagements to him for approval – no decisions could ever be taken for granted.

Never extravagant by nature, he threw nothing away. After opening parcels, he folded the paper for later use and kept the string. He used economy labels in his office long before the idea was introduced in Britain, and opened envelopes carefully with a paper knife so they could be used again.

The King's insistence on opening all post himself once almost led to a scene. A rather dishevelled-looking package from Germany, addressed to 'S.M. Koenig, Athens', was placed on his desk as usual. As he wrestled with the knots, Levidis produced a pocket knife and held it out without a word. The King looked at him coldly without speaking, and went on untying the string. At length he removed the paper and found a small wooden box with the lid nailed down. Alarmed, Levidis suggested he send for somebody else to open it. Shaking his head, the King opened a drawer in his desk and took out a packet of tools, removed the lid and the packing, and with horror Levidis saw a clockwork device of springs and wheels. Convinced that it was a bomb and that there was no time to lose, Levidis seized it from under the nose of his master, took it out of the room and ordered a servant to place it in a bucket of water until the police arrived. Far from being pleased, the King was annoyed. He glanced at Levidis coldly, and without a word began opening his letters.

The device was examined by explosive experts, who realized at once that 'S.M. Koenig' did not mean 'Seine Majestat Koenig', but was the name of a clockmaker in Athens. The well-meaning Levidis was the butt of much laughter at the palace that afternoon, not least from the King himself.

The strain of the last few years soon told on the King's health. Early in the new year of 1947, he was complaining to friends of heaviness, giddiness and pain in his chest. To Miss Brown he wrote (11 March) that he had had 'a mild sort of breakdown, which I tried my best to keep to myself'. The royal physician examined him and decided that nothing was wrong beyond nerves, brought on by overwork. 'Of course my existence is not one to improve all this. I hardly get out at all, irregular meals and maddening worries.'[6]

On the evening of 31 March he attended a charity film performance of *Henry V* at the British Embassy. The following day he was at work in his office quarters as usual. A servant went up to his study at lunchtime and the King told him that he had no appetite, but would attempt a light meal in his room if his aide Colonel Pallis would join him. The Colonel arrived a few minutes later to discover him lying unconscious on the settee. Princess Katherine was summoned, but to her distress found that her brother was beyond help.

The flag on the palace was lowered to half-mast, and the Premier and other ministers were informed. At four o'clock it was announced on Athens radio that the King had died at 1.55 p.m. of arteriosclerosis. His passing was so sudden and unexpected that at first some people thought it was a tasteless April Fool's joke.

Newspapers in Athens vied with each other to pay their tributes the following day. Even those which had often criticized him in the past recognized and respected the sovereign whose devotion to duty had brought about his early demise. Perhaps the most moving was that of the *Kathimerini*, which wrote that 'Last night was surely the first through which King George slept peacefully.'

CHAPTER FIFTEEN

'The people of Greece are monarchist in sentiment'

The accession to the throne on 1 April 1947 of Prince Paul, the third son of King Constantine and the third to wear the crown, seemed to symbolize a fresh start to the monarchy of the Hellenes. King George's reign, broken by two long periods of exile, had been a troubled one. If one accepts that he never formally abdicated, only seven of his twenty-five years as King were actually spent in Greece; and though the mild dictatorship of Metaxas was not to be compared with those of Hitler and Mussolini, his period of rule was still held against the reputation of the sovereign who had endorsed his actions, albeit with misgivings.

Now the crown passed to a man with a young, vivacious wife and a family of three children, all aged under ten. King Paul had suffered least of the family from the tribulations of politics and exile that had dogged his parents and elder brothers since the Great War. He looked to the future with optimism, unfounded though it may have been.

Optimism was certainly an important qualification for any sovereign or political leader in post-war Europe. In Greece the internal situation was as acute as any of her fellow-European nations, for the communist insurrection which had led to fighting in northern Greece the previous year escalated into full-scale civil war soon after his accession. A new method of terrorizing Greek families into unwilling support for the Communists was the threat of abducting children, who would be raised as 'ideologically sound' Marxists across the frontiers in the Communist states of Bulgaria, Albania or Yugoslavia.

When the King and Queen visited the north during the first summer of their reign, they travelled in heavily protected convoys, through a destitute countryside where the villages were menaced by guerrillas as threatening as any brigands in previous eras. In July Queen Frederica broadcast from Athens, appealing for support for a Northern Provinces Welfare Fund, a charity for which she worked unstintingly throughout her husband's reign. The main beneficiaries were orphans and families threatened with abduction. By the end of the year over fifty children's communities were set up under the auspices of her fund.

The year 1947 was to see two more marriages uniting the house of Glucksburg with Great Britain. While sailing from Egypt for England to join King George the previous year, his youngest sister Princess Katherine was introduced to Major Richard Brandram, who was attached to the British Mission in Iraq. During the summer they became engaged, but they were requested to keep the news secret until the unsettled situation in Greece had been resolved. It was officially announced in February 1947.

When Major Brandram arrived in Athens for the wedding, the court was in deep mourning for King George II, but the ceremony went ahead as planned on 21 April. Two services were held in the ballroom of the palace, one Anglican, and one Greek Orthodox. Among the wedding presents received was a marriage dowry of £10,000 subscribed by all ranks of the army, navy and air force, a fitting gift to the Princess who was their godchild. As she had married a commoner, the question of her married title gave rise to difficulties, solved in July when King George VI issued a Royal Warrant which ordained that HRH Princess Katherine of Greece and Denmark should henceforth hold the style, title and precedence of the daughter of a duke in the British Peerage, thus becoming Lady Katherine Brandram.

That same month the engagement was announced of King George VI's elder daughter and heir to the throne, Princess Elizabeth, to Prince Philip of Greece and Denmark, the son of Prince Andrew, who had died in December 1944 in France. The wedding at Westminster Abbey on 20 November was attended by a grand gathering of European royalty. Unhappily, King Paul was seriously ill with typhoid fever and unable to travel to England. He was represented by Queen Frederica.

While in London she met Winston Churchill, who was then Leader of the Opposition. He asked her with an air of reproach, 'Wasn't the Kaiser your grandfather?' To this she retorted that indeed he was, but Queen Victoria was her great-great-grandmother, and 'If you had the Salic Law in England, my father would be your King today.'[1]

Another royal guest at the wedding was King Michael of Roumania, whose absence in Britain was seized by the Communist-controlled government in Bucharest as an opportunity to depose him and declare a republic. He was already engaged to Princess Anne of Bourbon-Parma, but as he was forbidden to return to Bucharest the wedding took place in Athens in June 1948. The King's mother, Queen Helen, came back to her homeland from exile for the festivities, as did the elderly Prince George, now the only survivor of King George I's children. He still came with his wife to winter each year at Athens.*

While King Paul was unwell during the winter of 1947–8, Queen Frederica deputized for him, visiting the war zone, braving the danger of mortar attacks and land mines. One journey early in 1948 was ostensibly a normal welfare visit to the provinces, but her real purpose was to go to Konitsa, a mountain town near the Albanian frontier, and the scene of major military action between the troops and Communists. The road was heavily mined and under constant fire from Communist batteries, and the Corps Commander tried to dissuade her from such a hazardous sortie, but she would not be deflected. The troops were enormously grateful for her courage in coming to see them, and after she had gone, the High Command persuaded King Paul to confer on her the Greek Military Cross, awarded expressly for bravery under enemy fire. The people of Konitsa endorsed this honour by erecting a life-size statue of the Queen in the middle of the town.

Like Queen Sophie, Queen Frederica had a heavy cross to bear in Greece – her German nationality. Left-wing politicians found her ancestry as a granddaughter of Emperor William II a perfect propaganda weapon, and taunted her with having had brothers in the SS. Energetic, informal and intelligent, her no-nonsense manner won admiration from some but was enough to make others criticize her as 'very Prussian'. When interviewed by reporter Charles Fenyvesi during the 1970s, a 'soft-spoken middle-class Greek in her fifties' remarked categorically that the Queen 'was a Nazi' and had been 'a terrible influence' on her son's life, while King Paul was 'nice but weak; the only strong thing he did was to drive his sports car like an absolute maniac.'[2]

---

* As the oldest member of royalty present at the Coronation of his nephew's wife as Queen Elizabeth II of Britain in June 1953, Prince George represented a special link with Europe's past which seemed a world away to most of the spectators. Alone among the family, he enjoyed a serene old age. Whereas none of his brothers or sisters had attained the age of seventy, he exceeded the longevity of his paternal grandfather and lived to the age of eighty-eight, surviving until November 1957.

Those who saw the King and Queen at closer range formed a very different impression. A leader of the Greek Liberal Party, Themistocles Sophoulis, told biographer Arthur Gould Lee that 'King Constantine was loved by the Greek people because he went out among them and showed them that he loved them. The present King and Queen are doing the same and earning the same response. And the Queen is especially loved for her untiring work for those who have suffered so much in the country's troubles from 1941 to the present day.' These were not the views of a fervent monarchist, but from a man who had been a republican since his youth, and declared for a republic at every election up to and including the plebiscite on the return of King George II in 1946. Though he remained a republican, he could still approve of a constitutional monarchy, 'for when the King firmly observes the principles of democracy, the gap between a republic with an elected leader and a republic with an hereditary one becomes of no practical consequence.'[3]

In October 1949 the Communist 'Provisional Government of Free Greece' publicly admitted defeat with a face-saving announcement that the guerrilla forces had 'ceased operations to avoid the complete annihilation of Greece'. Though the defeated remnants were kept on a token war footing for some years in their east European and Russian exile, the civil war was effectively over. Yet the conflict had wrought perhaps as much havoc as the Second World War itself. One-tenth of the Greek population had been left homeless, and the King broadcast an appeal for help in the reconstruction of 7,000 villages destroyed in the fighting.

There was little respite for Greece in the years ahead. In August 1953 the first of a series of earthquakes wrecked Zakinthos. At each disaster the King and Queen travelled personally to the devastated areas, comforting the shocked victims, and helping cut bureaucratic red tape to speed the task of reconstruction. Their far-sightedness and courage did much to maintain the popularity of the royal family in Greece.

A perpetual problem throughout much of King Paul's reign was that of Cyprus. The island had been under Turkish sovereignty since the sixteenth century, but by the Congress of Berlin in 1878 the British had acquired the right to station troops there in return for guaranteeing protection for Asiatic Turkey from Russian attack. In 1914 the British formally annexed the island when the Turks declared war, and an offer to cede it to Greece on condition the latter joined the Allies against Germany was rejected. Becoming a British Crown Colony in 1925, it had been subject to riots by the majority Greek-speaking population, who demanded union with Greece.

In 1948 King Paul had declared in an interview with the *New York Times* that they looked forward to the union of Cyprus with the rest of Greece. A vigorous campaign for union under Archbishop Makarios, and escalating acts of terrorism, led eventually to the compromise solution of the declaration of an independent republic of Cyprus in 1960. During the intervening twelve years, the King's regular speeches on the question, referring to the demands of Greek Cypriots for freedom and the right of self-determination were unfairly seized on by more sensationalist elements in the British press, trying to assert that King Paul and Queen Frederica were anti-British. Such comments wounded them deeply. Like most other members of his family, King Paul loved Britain next only to his own country, had many close British friends as well as close ties with the British royal family, and had spent some of the happiest years of his life on British soil. As a Greek he deplored official British policy towards Cyprus, but it pained him that he should be regarded as anti-British.

There were frequent journeys abroad. In 1952 King Paul paid a state visit to Turkey, the first occasion upon which any head of a Turkish state entertained a Greek sovereign, and the King dutifully laid a wreath on the tomb of the father of modern Turkey, Kemal Ataturk, whose military campaign had set the seal on the doom of his father in 1922. Other visits stressed the need for tact and diplomacy. They went to Belgrade as guests of Marshal Tito, and to Rome as guests of the Italian President; to West Germany where the Queen's parents, the Duke and Duchess of Brunswick, still lived; to the Lebanon, Ethiopia, India, Thailand, and to the United States, where they were not the first crowned heads to encounter egalitarian republican democrats unimpressed by royalty. Even so, American support under the Truman Doctrine and the Marshall Plan had helped to strengthen links between the United States and Greece. The King and Queen regarded General Eisenhower and General Marshall as personal friends.

In October 1955 King Paul appointed Constantine Karamanlis, the former Minister of Public Works, as Prime Minister. For the next few years Greece enjoyed unprecedented stability of government, industrial development flourished, and the tourist trade improved. In October 1956 the parliamentary opposition had voted against an increase in the King's personal revenue because of alleged anti-democratic activities of certain courtiers, but Karamanlis rose to the support of his sovereign, and in

October 1959, after further parliamentary attacks, defended him from a smear campaign by a number of opposition deputies and journalists who were deliberately seeking to 'undermine the foundations of the state'.

On 2 June 1958 Crown Prince Constantine attained his majority. King Paul had felt handicapped by the fact that, while heir to the throne, he himself had been permitted to take virtually no part in affairs of state, owing to the reticent King George II's reluctance to share responsibility. He was determined that his son and successor would labour under no such disadvantage. For the last few years he had encouraged Crown Prince Constantine to be present in the audience room while he himself was conducting business of state or in conference with his ministers. The Prince sat quietly behind his father, listening to everything but saying nothing. As he became older, the King would occasionally interrupt proceedings to explain some point in further detail, and often elaborate after the audience was over. Now the Crown Prince had come of age, he was encouraged to comment and join in the discussion when present at audiences. From time to time he would be asked by his father to deputize for him in official duties, and would often accompany his parents on tours of the provinces.

In December 1959 Duke Albrecht of Bavaria, head of the house of Wittelsbach, sent his son Prince Maximilian to Athens to present the coronation regalia to King Paul. On his deposition in 1862 the Duke's great-great-uncle, King Otho, had taken the crown, orb and sceptre back to Bavaria with him. As a Roman Catholic in an Orthodox kingdom, he had never been formally invested with the regalia of kingship. Neither King George I nor his successors had had a coronation, a ritual which forms no part of the Greek Orthodox Church. On receiving these gifts, King Paul spoke of the debt of modern Greece, and in particular the city of Athens, to the Bavarians, praising King Otho as a Hellene who had laid the foundations of the Greek state.

As a youth, Crown Prince Constantine was an enthusiastic sportsman, showing a particular penchant for yacht racing. In 1960 he was helmsman for the seven contests of the sailing Olympics at Naples, putting up a performance which made him the first Greek since before the First World War to win an Olympic gold medal.

Nine months later he and his elder sister, Princess Sophia, were in England for the Duke of Kent's wedding at York Minster. Princess Sophia met Prince Juan Carlos of Spain, who had the unique position of being a

Crown Prince to a throne-in-waiting. Shortly afterwards, their engagement was announced and the wedding was celebrated in Athens in May 1962. More than a hundred royal guests came to Athens, among them the bride's grandmother, at whose own wedding in Berlin in May 1913 many of the members of Europe's royal and imperial families had been united for the last time before Armageddon. During the festivities, it was observed that Crown Prince Constantine would dance only with Princess Anne-Marie of Denmark, daughter of King Frederick IX. At an official banquet, held during a state visit to Greece by King Frederick and Queen Ingrid some months later, King Paul announced the young couple's engagement.

Nevertheless, the Greek monarchy's popularity seemed to be evaporating. When parliament met to approve a dowry for a royal princess, the Opposition fiercely contested the amount involved, and their tactics included a boycott of royal occasions. Also bringing disapproval was a speech in which King Paul declared to army officers at Salonika, 'God has united us! I belong to you and you belong to me.' Although intended merely as affirming traditional bonds linking a Commander-in-Chief and his officer corps in common service, it evoked a protest from Opposition leader George Papandreou, who appeared to detect a hint of dictatorship in the words.

With some anxiety, Karamanlis wrote to the King in October 1962, after fresh proposals to increase the royal revenue led to bitter parliamentary debate, emphasizing King Paul's popularity, but listing several points which could be damaging. They concerned the complaints of ostentatious living, too frequent visits abroad, royal speeches (the contents of which were unknown to the government), royal expenditure requiring additional revenue, absence of a government spokesman at the palace, and failure to have the Queen's Northern Provinces Welfare Fund constituted on a regular basis.

The King sent a reasoned reply pointing out the flaws of many of the arguments. For example, the Greek monarchy was less ostentatious than any other still extant in the world; journeys abroad were shorter than they had been in earlier reigns, and modern transport made it possible to return far sooner in the event of emergency; expenditure requiring extra taxation should naturally be avoided, but he economized by travelling around the country by jeep, and using a converted minesweeper as a substitute royal yacht; and although he agreed that the Queen's fund should be reconstituted, he resented the campaign of vilification aimed 'not only against my person but also against my wife, my children, and my late parents'. He reproached Karamanlis for not having explained to Greek public opinion the need for increased royal revenue, for failing to protect the royal family by forestalling unjustified attacks in parliament and the press, and for not giving publicity to royal gestures of goodwill, such as his recent donation to the state of his private estate at Polidhendri for development as an agricultural training college.

Yet the attacks continued. King Paul had long intended to pay a state visit to Britain. In April 1963 Queen Frederica and their youngest daughter, Princess Irene, visited Britain privately, principally to attend the wedding of Princess Alexandra. Outside Claridge's Hotel they were confronted by angry demonstrators seeking a political amnesty, and in particular a woman seeking to petition the Queen on behalf of her husband, a communist imprisoned since the civil war. The Queen and her daughter were pursued into a cul-de-sac where they had to take refuge in a private house. Some British papers became so hostile to Queen Frederica that Karamanlis urged cancellation of the forthcoming state visit.

Throughout most of his life King Paul had enjoyed good health. Like his brothers and most of his uncles, he had suffered from short-sightedness, probably inherited from his grandmother Queen Olga. He had worn contact lenses for many years, and in 1959 he underwent a successful operation for cataract. From early youth he had smoked heavily, using a cigarette holder to keep the smoke away from his eyes. Queen Frederica had also smoked as a young woman, but gave up shortly after they married. 'Who is stronger, you or that piece of dried cabbage?' she asked him in exasperation, in what proved to be the last of several attempts to persuade him to follow her example. Inserting a new cigarette in the holder and lighting it, he replied: 'That piece of dried cabbage is stronger, and you had better get used to the idea.'[4]

In June 1963 he was taken ill and rushed to hospital for an immediate operation for appendicitis. Although he suspected that his health was not good, he was determined to make the state visit to Britain, at which Karamanlis resigned in protest. The visit went ahead, lasting for three days. It was dominated by demonstrations, mainly by nuclear disarmers who were angered by Greek commitment to NATO, but some cheers; and Queen Elizabeth II created King Paul a Knight of the Garter.

Yet King Paul's health was visibly declining. Towards the end of the year, he complained of pains in his leg. A general election in February

1964 brought George Papandreou and his Centre Union of leftish liberals into power. King Paul signed a decree confirming the regency of Crown Prince Constantine, and the next day he underwent an operation for stomach cancer. For a week his chances of recovery seemed fair, but the disease was too far advanced. He died on 6 March 1964.

King Constantine II inherited much goodwill when he came to the throne. It lasted beyond his wedding on 18 September to Princess Anne-Marie. Yet the period of tranquillity was destined to be brief. A fresh crisis over Cyprus brought Greece to the brink of war with Turkey, and a series of recurrent political crises led to instability. Elections were due in May 1967, but forestalled by a 'Colonels' Coup', carried out by relatively junior army officers who claimed they were saving their country from communism. Taken by surprise, King Constantine was anxious to avoid bloodshed and he followed a line of passive resistance. He insisted that any new regime must have a civilian Prime Minister if it was to be treated as a government, and a highly respected lawyer, Constantine Kollias, accepted this invidious post. However, the King refused to endorse publicly any of the measures which the Colonels proposed, hoping that the folly of their actions would soon discredit them. An attempt at a counter-coup in December misfired and, declaring that 'my throne is not worth the price of Greek blood', he, the Queen and their two young children flew into exile in Rome.

The military triumvirate which now governed Greece was fearful of international ostracism, and it invited him back a few weeks later on its own terms. He answered that he would not return unless he could exercise the sovereign powers vested in him by the constitution; it was not in his nature to serve as a puppet. Queen Frederica and Princess Irene later settled in Spain, while the King and Queen went to England.

On 1 June 1973 the military regime in Athens formally deposed King Constantine and set up a republic, with George Papadopoulos as President. Eight weeks later, a plebiscite confirmed the passing of the monarchy. Bloodshed in the streets of Athens, where tanks were used against a protest by students, emphasized the moral bankruptcy of the new regime. In November the President was arrested by his own security chief, Brigadier Ioannidis, who thereafter ruled Greece with an iron hand while using the honest, well-intentioned General Phaidon Gizikis as nominal President.

In July 1974 Ioannidis encouraged a Greek insurrection against Archbishop Makarios in Cyprus, and yet again the threat of war between

Greece and Turkey loomed large. Ioannidis's nominees were in no position to carry out effective mobilization, and Gizikis invited Karamanlis to return from Paris and form a civilian government. The military dictatorship was over. King Constantine expected to be recalled as well, but was advised that a plebiscite would be held; until then, Greece would remain a republic, and he was advised not to come back and provoke disturbances during a delicate period of political transition.

On 17 November Karamanlis won a landslide victory in a general election. On 8 December the plebiscite returned a verdict showing voters in favour of the republic by two to one. The Greek monarchy was over.

'My predecessors were sent into exile by revolutions, never by the people', King Constantine remarked a few years later. 'The people of Greece are monarchist in sentiment.'[5] When his mother, Queen Frederica, died of a heart attack while on a visit to Madrid on 6 February 1981, President Karamanlis gave permission for her to be buried at Tatoi beside her husband. Although the exiled royal family were allowed to attend the funeral, King Constantine was not permitted to spend even a single night on Greek soil, as the government feared that 'monarchist manifestations could provoke counter-demonstrations and riots'.

Controversy broke out twelve years later, in August 1993, when he returned to Greece for a private family holiday, or in his own words 'a very emotional pilgrimage to our homeland'. Within two days of their arrival, two parliamentary deputies and a bishop were threatened with a charge of treason by the government for publicly greeting their former King at Salonika airport, not far from where his grandfather and namesake liberated the city from the Ottoman Turks in 1912, and where King George I was assassinated the following year. After visits to Greek troops stationed on the border, and to the former Yugoslav region of Macedonia, the government sent two torpedo boats to shadow the King's yacht around the coast, and heavy bombers from the Greek Air Force practised low runs over the deck. The 'escort' was only withdrawn when he promised to keep away from areas where crowds of royalist sympathizers were waiting to welcome him.

'When people are so fed up with the politicians and all their lies and preposterous behaviour,' a Greek journalist commented, 'there will be many who will look at that calm, royal figure on TV, speaking Greek so well after all these years, and wonder if he might be better for their lives.'[6]

The history of the royal house in Greece has been a turbulent one, but there is still support and enthusiasm for the monarchy, as in other European countries where Kings and Emperors ruled and reigned at the dawn of the twentieth century. With the unsettled state of affairs in eastern Europe across the Balkans and Russia from the late 1980s onwards, it would be impossible to predict the future. To quote Alan Palmer, one of the family's most recent biographers, 'a resilient dynasty, led by a sovereign of personality and vigour, will never slip silently off the margin of history so long as there remains a challenge to which it may yet provide an answer.'[7]

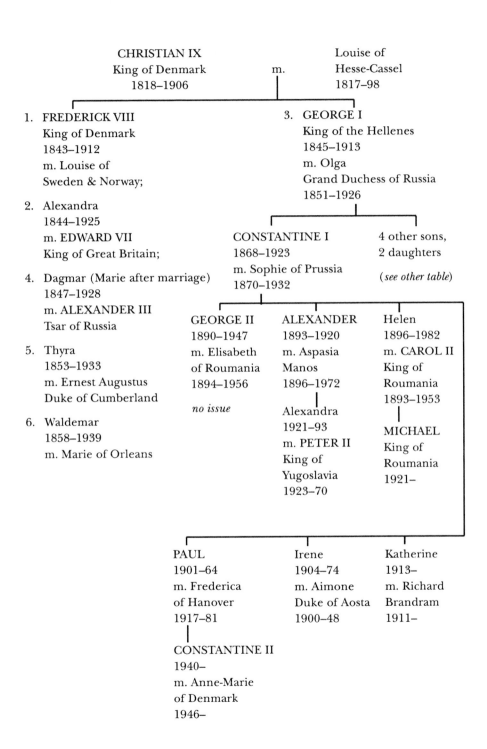

CHRISTIAN IX
King of Denmark
1818–1906

m.

Louise of
Hesse-Cassel
1817–98

1. FREDERICK VIII
King of Denmark
1843–1912
m. Louise of
Sweden & Norway;

2. Alexandra
1844–1925
m. EDWARD VII
King of Great Britain;

4. Dagmar (Marie after marriage)
1847–1928
m. ALEXANDER III
Tsar of Russia

5. Thyra
1853–1933
m. Ernest Augustus
Duke of Cumberland

6. Waldemar
1858–1939
m. Marie of Orleans

3. GEORGE I
King of the Hellenes
1845–1913
m. Olga
Grand Duchess of Russia
1851–1926

CONSTANTINE I
1868–1923
m. Sophie of Prussia
1870–1932

4 other sons,
2 daughters

(*see other table*)

GEORGE II
1890–1947
m. Elisabeth
of Roumania
1894–1956

no issue

ALEXANDER
1893–1920
m. Aspasia
Manos
1896–1972

Alexandra
1921–93
m. PETER II
King of
Yugoslavia
1923–70

Helen
1896–1982
m. CAROL II
King of
Roumania
1893–1953

MICHAEL
King of
Roumania
1921–

PAUL
1901–64
m. Frederica
of Hanover
1917–81

CONSTANTINE II
1940–
m. Anne-Marie
of Denmark
1946–

Irene
1904–74
m. Aimone
Duke of Aosta
1900–48

Katherine
1913–
m. Richard
Brandram
1911–

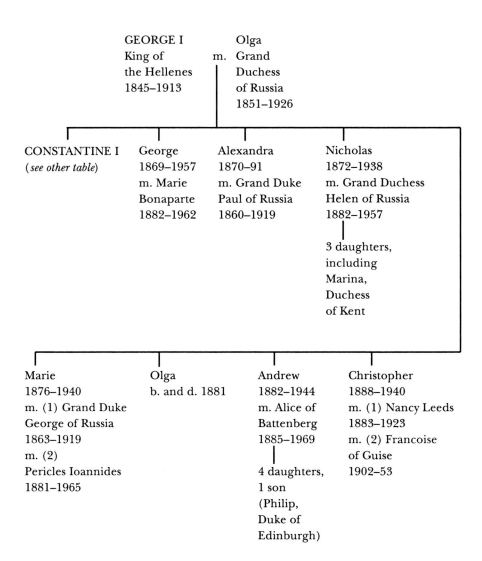

GEORGE I
King of
the Hellenes
1845–1913

m.

Olga
Grand
Duchess
of Russia
1851–1926

CONSTANTINE I
(*see other table*)

George
1869–1957
m. Marie
Bonaparte
1882–1962

Alexandra
1870–91
m. Grand Duke
Paul of Russia
1860–1919

Nicholas
1872–1938
m. Grand Duchess
Helen of Russia
1882–1957

3 daughters,
including
Marina,
Duchess
of Kent

Marie
1876–1940
m. (1) Grand Duke
George of Russia
1863–1919
m. (2)
Pericles Ioannides
1881–1965

Olga
b. and d. 1881

Andrew
1882–1944
m. Alice of
Battenberg
1885–1969

4 daughters,
1 son
(Philip,
Duke of
Edinburgh)

Christopher
1888–1940
m. (1) Nancy Leeds
1883–1923
m. (2) Francoise
of Guise
1902–53

Reference Notes

PROLOGUE (pp. 1–13)

1. Minet, 'King-making . . .' (*Royalty Digest*)
2. ibid.
3. *The Times* 26.1.1863; Van der Kiste & Jordaan 45
4. Bell 119
5. Madol 138
6. ibid. 140–1
7. ibid. 142
8. ibid. 143
9. ibid. 144
10. ibid. 145
11. ibid. 146
12. Christopher 30
13. Christmas 54
14. ibid. 56

CHAPTER 1 (pp. 14–26)

1. *Illustrated London News* 10.10.1863
2. Battiscombe 60
3. *Punch* 24.10.1863
4. *The Times* 12.11.1863
5. ibid. 19.11.1863
6. Rumbold II 125
7. Christopher 16
8. ibid. 17
9. Rumbold II 137
10. Christopher 31
11. Rumbold II 152–3
12. Nicholas, *My fifty years* 59
13. *The Times* 26.3.1869

14. RA.T4/59
15. as 14
16. Lee I 264
17. RA.T4/106
18. Lee 265
19. *Letters of Queen Victoria* II i 570–1
20. Rumbold II 138
21. as 17
22. Grand Duchess George 2

CHAPTER 2 (pp. 27–35)

1. Benson 162
2. Wolf I 289
3. *Letters of Queen Victoria* II ii 17–8
4. *Your dear letter* 277
5. Lee I 266–7
6. ibid. 267
7. *Darling child* 219
8. Lee I 437
9. RA.T7/37
10. Lee 489
11. Blake 696
12. RA.T7/89
13. Van der Kiste & Jordaan 125
14. *Letters of Queen Victoria* III i 139

CHAPTER 3 (pp. 36–46)

1. Marie, Queen of Roumania I 216
2. Christopher 46
3. Nicholas, *My fifty years* 35
4. Benson 157–8

5. Anon, 'Balkan rulers' (*Royalty Digest*)
6. Christopher 34
7. ibid. 41
8. Nicholas, *My fifty years* 17
9. ibid. 21
10. Christopher 43–4
11. *Letters of Queen Victoria* III i 321
12. Nicolson 39
13. ibid. 30

9. Christmas 176
10. Gould Lee, *Helen* 19
11. Battiscombe 281
12. Christmas 400
13. *The Times* 20.3.1913
14. Christopher 118
15. Gore 276
16. Pope-Hennessy 478
17. Battiscombe 281
18. *The Times* 19.3.1913

CHAPTER 4 (pp. 47–62)

1. Corti 313
2. *Beloved and darling child* 77
3. *Letters of the Empress Frederick* 392
4. ibid. 393
5. Corti 338
6. *The Empress Frederick writes to Sophie* 76
7. ibid. 86
8. Corti 339
9. Pope-Hennessy 256–7
10. Nicholas, *My fifty years* 27
11. *The Empress Frederick writes to Sophie* 245
12. *Beloved and darling child* 202; *Letters of Queen Victoria* III iii 150
13. *Letters of Queen Victoria* III iii 159
14. Mallet 103
15. Victoria Louise 19

CHAPTER 6 (pp. 78–88)

1. *The Times* 12.9.1913
2. ibid. 15.9.1913
3. ibid. 23.9.1913
4. ibid. 25.9.1913
5. Christopher 122
6. Nicholas, *My fifty years* 253
7. Gould Lee, *Helen* 34

CHAPTER 7 (pp. 89–101)

1. Nicholas, *My fifty years* 259–60
2. Woodhouse 198
3. Christopher 110
4. Fisher 1154
5. Nicolson 282
6. Van der Kiste 123

CHAPTER 5 (pp. 63–77)

1. RA.W43/3a
2. Ponsonby 223
3. as 2
4. *The Times* 16.11.1905
5. Nicholas, *My fifty years* 211
6. Lee II 517
7. Christopher 112
8. ibid. 47

CHAPTER 8 (pp. 102–11)

1. Nicolson 283–4
2. Gould Lee, *Helen* 54
3. Nicholas, *Political memoirs* 152
4. Lloyd George I 550
5. Nicholas, *Political memoirs* 264
6. Gould Lee, *Helen* 56
7. Nicholas, *Political memoirs* 295
8. Christopher 142

9. Nicholas, *My fifty years* 272–3;
    Political memoirs 287

9. ibid. 15.1.1923
10. Hourmouzios 51

CHAPTER 9 (pp. 112–24)

1. Gould Lee, *Helen* 26
2. *The Times* 26.10.1920
3. Christopher 145
4. Gould Lee, *Helen* 64
5. ibid. 66
6. Christopher 153
7. *The Times* 16.10.1920

CHAPTER 12 (pp. 145–53)

1. Pakula 327
2. Gould Lee, *Royal house* 212
3. Van der Kiste 173
4. Hourmouzios 72

CHAPTER 13 (pp. 154–63)

1. Victoria Louise 194
2. Windsor, Duke of 307–8
3. Pope-Hennessy 569
4. Christopher 116
5. Hourmouzios 113
6. Gould Lee, *Royal house* 70
7. ibid. 85
8. *Daily Telegraph* 31.10.1941

CHAPTER 10 (pp. 125–37)

1. *The Times* 18.10.1920
2. Hourmouzios 43
3. *The Times* 2.12.1920
4. ibid. 3.12.1920
5. ibid. 8.12.1920
6. Christopher 172
7. Nicholas, *Political memoirs* 33
8. Gould Lee, *Helen* 74
9. Nichols 100
10. ibid. 105
11. Van der Kiste 152
12. *Illustrated London News* 7.10.1922
13. *The Times* 28.9.1922

CHAPTER 14 (pp. 164–75)

1. Hourmouzios 146
2. Gould Lee, *Royal house* 209
3. Hourmouzios 152
4. Gould Lee, *Royal house* 154
5. ibid. 172
6. ibid. 184

CHAPTER 11 (pp. 138–44)

1. Pakula 317
2. Christopher 171
3. Nicholas, *My fifty years* 315–6
4. Christopher 173
5. ibid. 176
6. ibid. 180
7. Nicholas, *Political memoirs* 308
8. *The Times* 13.1.1923

CHAPTER 15 (pp. 176–86)

1. Victoria Louise 217
2. Fenyvesi 183
3. Gould Lee, *Royal house* 237–8
4. Hourmouzios 285
5. Fenyvesi 173
6. *Royalty Digest* September 1993
7. Palmer 119

Bibliography

I MANUSCRIPTS

Royal Archives, Windsor

II BOOKS

Andrew of Greece, Prince, *Towards disaster: the Greek army in Asia Minor in 1921.* John Murray, 1930

Aronson, Theo, *A family of Kings: the descendants of Christian IX of Denmark.* Cassell, 1976

— *Grandmama of Europe: the crowned descendants of Queen Victoria.* Cassell, 1973

Battiscombe, Georgina, *Queen Alexandra.* Constable, 1969

Bell, George, *Randall Davidson.* Oxford University Press, 1935

Benson, E.F., *As we were: a Victorian peep-show.* Longmans, 1930

Blake, Robert, *Disraeli.* Eyre & Spottiswoode, 1966

Christmas, Walter, *King George of Greece.* Eveleigh, Nash, 1914

Christopher of Greece, Prince, *Memoirs.* Right Book Club, 1938

Corti, Egon Caesar Conte, *The English Empress: a study in the relations between Queen Victoria and her eldest daughter, Empress Frederick of Germany.* Cassell, 1957

Donaldson, Frances, *Edward VIII.* Weidenfeld & Nicolson, 1974

Duff, David, *Hessian tapestry.* Frederick Muller, 1967

Fenyvesi, Charles, *Royalty in exile.* Robson, 1981

Fisher, H.A.L., *A history of Europe.* Edward Arnold, 1936

Frederica, Queen, *A measure of understanding.* Macmillan, 1971

George, Grand Duchess, *A Romanov diary.* Atlantic International, 1988

Gore, John, *King George V: a personal memoir.* John Murray, 1941

Gould Lee, Arthur S., *Helen, Queen Mother of Rumania.* Faber, 1956

— *The royal house of Greece.* Ward Lock, 1948

Grenville, J.A.S., *Lord Salisbury and foreign policy: the close of the nineteenth century.* Athlone, 1970

Hibben, Paxton, *Constantine I and the Greek people.* Century, NY, 1920

Hourmouzios, Stelio, *No ordinary crown: a biography of King Paul of the Hellenes.* Weidenfeld & Nicolson, 1972

King, Stella, *Princess Marina, her life and times.* Cassell, 1969

Lee, Sir Sidney, *King Edward VII*, 2 vols. Macmillan, 1925–7

Lloyd George, David, *War memoirs*, 2 vols. Odhams, 1938

Madol, Hans Roger, *Christian IX*. Collins, 1939

Magnus, Philip, *King Edward the Seventh*. John Murray, 1964

Mallet, Victor (ed.), *Life with Queen Victoria: Marie Mallet's letters from Court 1887–1901*. John Murray, 1968

Marie, Queen of Roumania, *The story of my life*, 3 vols. Cassell, 1934–5

Mélas, George M., *Ex-King Constantine and the war*. Hutchinson, n.d., *c*. 1918

Nicholas of Greece, Prince, *My fifty years*. Hutchinson, 1926

— *Political memoirs, 1914–1917: pages from my diary*. Hutchinson, 1928

Nichols, Beverley, *25: being a young man's candid recollection of his elders and betters*. Jonathan Cape, 1926

Nicolson, Harold, *King George V: his life and reign*. Constable, 1952

Pakula, Hannah, *The last Romantic: a biography of Queen Marie of Roumania*. Weidenfeld & Nicolson, 1984

Palmer, Alan, & Michael of Greece, Prince, *The royal house of Greece*. Weidenfeld & Nicolson, 1990

Paoli, Xavier, *My royal clients*. Hodder & Stoughton, n.d.

Ponsonby, Sir Frederick, *Recollections of three reigns*. Eyre & Spottiswoode, 1951

Pope-Hennessy, James, *Queen Mary 1867–1953*. Allen & Unwin, 1959

Rumbold, Sir Horace, *Recollections of a diplomatist*, 2 vols. Edward Arnold, 1902

Tisdall, E.E.P., *Royal destiny: the royal Hellenic cousins*. Stanley Paul, 1955

Vaka, Demetra, *Constantine, King & traitor*. Bodley Head, 1918

Van der Kiste, John, *Crowns in a changing world: the British and European monarchies, 1901–36*. Alan Sutton, 1993

Van der Kiste, John, & Jordaan, Bee, *Dearest Affie: Alfred, Duke of Edinburgh, Queen Victoria's second son*. Alan Sutton, 1984

Victoria, Queen, *Letters of Queen Victoria, second series: a selection from Her Majesty's correspondence and journals between the years 1862 and 1885*, (ed.) G.E. Buckle, 3 vols. John Murray, 1926–8

— *Letters of Queen Victoria, third series: a selection from Her Majesty's correspondence and journals between the years 1886 and 1901*, (ed.) G.E. Buckle, 3 vols. John Murray, 1930–2

Victoria, Queen, and Victoria, Consort of Frederick III, *Your dear letter: private correspondence between Queen Victoria and the Crown Princess of Prussia, 1865–71*, (ed.) Roger Fulford. Evans Bros, 1971

— *Darling child: private correspondence between Queen Victoria and the Crown Princess of Prussia, 1871–78*, (ed.) Roger Fulford. Evans Bros, 1976

— *Beloved and darling child: last letters between Queen Victoria and her eldest daughter, 1886–1901*, (ed.) Agatha Ramm. Alan Sutton, 1990

Victoria, Consort of Frederick III, *Letters of the Empress Frederick*, (ed.) Sir Frederick Ponsonby. Macmillan, 1928

— *The Empress Frederick writes to Sophie, her daughter, Crown Princess and later Queen of the Hellenes; letters 1889–1901*, (ed.) Arthur Gould Lee. Faber, 1955

Victoria Louise, Princess of Prussia, *The Kaiser's daughter: Memoirs of H.R.H. Viktoria Luise, Duchess of Brunswick and Luneburg, Princess of Prussia*, (trans. and ed.) Robert Vacha. W.H. Allen, 1977

Windsor, Duke of, formerly King Edward VIII, *A King's story: memoirs of HRH the Duke of Windsor*. Cassell, 1951

Wolf, Lucien, *Life of the First Marquis of Ripon*, 2 vols. John Murray, 1921

Woodhouse, C.M., *Modern Greece: a short history*, 5th ed. Faber, 1991

III PERIODICAL ARTICLES

Anon., 'The Balkan rulers'. Originally in *Temple Bar*, 1886, reprinted in *Royalty Digest*, February 1992

Minet, Paul, 'King-making in nineteenth century Greece'. In *Royalty Digest*, October 1991

Zeepvat, Charlotte, 'To belong to the family: the Constantinovitchi'. In *Royalty Digest*, May 1993

IV PERIODICALS AND NEWSPAPERS

Daily Telegraph
Illustrated London News
Punch
Royalty Digest
The Times

Index

Index